ON THE SIDE OF THE
OF THE
ANGELS

ON THE SIDE OF THE ANGELS

Kristen D. Randle

Bookcraft
Salt Lake City, Utah

Library of Congress Catalog Card Number:
88–63691

ISBN 0-88494-690-8

First Printing, 1989

Printed in the United States of America

For Ginna

Is man an ape or an angel? . . .
I am on the side of the angels.

— Benjamin Disraeli

1

It was hot on the street. The sunlight fell straight down onto the broken asphalt and shattered into a million tiny flames; it flowed down the walls of the old brownstone buildings, washed across scorched sidewalks, and made bright, sweltering pools of the concrete porches. That's where the people sat, or up on the fire escapes, or they leaned out of windows, looking for some relief, for a breath of a stir in the hot, heavy air.

The sun glared off every metal thing; even childrens' jacks, left out on the sidewalk, got too hot to touch.

"September, soon. Summer almost over." The black man stretched his legs out, settling back against the steps, out on the porch of his building. The two white boys sitting with him scowled at him for saying it, remembering school, and not wanting to have to think about it. "Evening soon, then," the man said, unwilling to be sour in spite of the heat and the sweat.

Down at the end of the block, somebody had gotten the cap off a hydrant. A glittering arc of water gushed out of it onto the street, harsh and bright in the afternoon sun. The man looked down there, watching the children play in it, remembering how sweet and cool those gutter rivers could get to be, wishing he were young enough to want to go down there and play in it himself.

"Here come some more," said the one boy, the big one, Eddie, up on his knees, peering over the concrete balustrade of the porch. He slid down again so that he was sitting flat on the top step, looking pleased and very satisfied.

The other boy, bored and hot, didn't say a word.

"Oh, my, my, my," Eddie murmured, craning his neck so he could still see a way up the sidewalk. "Ain't that *fine*?"

The man stretched a little more and groaned to himself.

Three girls, coming down the sidewalk, eased themselves along; that's what Eddie was watching—the girls as they came, young and pretty in the glare of the afternoon.

They coasted along, even with the stairs, dressed for the heat, their faces cool and careful. And as they passed, they glanced up—oh, so casually—eyes set for what they'd come down here hoping to see, hoping to catch, maybe—the silent boy, the bored one, Cody McClellan. The tallest girl smiled up guardedly, her shoulder raised just slightly, as if maybe she meant something by it, or maybe she didn't—but that boy wasn't seeing a thing.

She swallowed her smile like it had been a simple mistake, and glided on past with her friends.

"Hey," Cody said suddenly, his voice low, looking like maybe he was a little surprised at himself for speaking up. The girls stopped dead and turned, the one girl smiling again, and you could see through her face as if it were an open window— how pleased she was, how satisfied.

But Cody wasn't saying any more than that. The girls waited for a moment, and him sitting there with that icy face of his, looking at them as though he wondered what they were do- ing there.

"Well," the girl said, shifting around uneasily, caught out and feeling awkward. "See you."

A little nod. He gave her nothing more.

The girl led the way off down the sidewalk again, making herself some dignity, her two friends catching up, looking back over their shoulders with enigmatic faces.

"They never see *no*body but you," Eddie whined, pouting as he slouched down on the hot step up behind.

"*Well*," the man said, turning his face full on Cody so he'd know he was being looked at.

Cody shook his head, leaning back against the stairs. "Some things are too easy," he grumbled.

The man shook his head.

"Well, what do you want?" Cody asked nobody in particu- lar. "They come down here off uptown like they're going to the zoo."

"They're *looking* for you, man," Eddie said, making it a complaint. "All that money they got, they could buy just about anybody. And they come looking for *you*." Then he chuckled to himself at the thought of it.

"Shut up, Eddie," Cody said absently, running his fingers through his hair as if he was trying to get some air in there.

The man smiled to himself, lifting his face to the sun. Then he looked down to where the water was still arcing into the street. There was a stickball game starting, just between here and there. It wouldn't last long, not in this heat.

Oh, he could see why those girls would come on down here, never mind what their daddies would say — hot and bored on an afternoon like this, and Cody sitting out on this porch with that face of his, pretty as a girl's. Parker chuckled to himself, just like Eddie had, shaking his head. Those girls wanting Cody.

And what would they do with him, if once they got hold of him? More than they'd ever want to try to handle, that boy. Mean, for one thing. And complicated, caught between hot and cold the way he was. Parker smiled.

"So," he said. "You boys not wanting to think about school?"

"Not really," Cody said, watching the tiny kids across the street, playing in a sliver of shadow.

"Cody hates that school," Eddie said. "I do, too. Stupid place. All they give you's trouble down there. Someday, they gonna give that boy Cody too much, and he's gonna take the place right down. Burn it to ashes, heh, man? Burn it down to ashes." He poked Cody in the shoulder. "Almost did it, last night, heh?"

Cody frowned, puzzled.

"Not a teacher in that school want to be caught out in the hall with that Cody. Not alone. Not—"

Cody turned around sharply. "Knock it off," he said. "What are you saying—'last night'? What happened last night?"

"Don't get mad at *me*," Eddie pouted. "*You* know it's true. Every last one of them—those teachers good and scared of you."

Cody glared over his shoulder at Eddie. "I don't know where you get this stuff," he murmured, cross now—leaning back against the stairs again. "You don't listen to him, Parker. He's a jerk." And then, frowning, "I want to know what you're saying about last night."

"It's *all* true," Eddie said, and he hauled himself up again so he could keep a lookout over the railing. "They're plenty scared of you, all the time, and you know it. And you know what about last night. Don't be telling me you don't know."

"Know *what?*" Cody was getting tired of the game, you could see that. But Eddie never knew when to quit.

"That fire last night down by school. Big fire, man. Whole dumpster. Practically took the side of the school off. And you didn't know about it. *Right.*" Eddie pushed at him again. "Maybe school's not going to start so early this year, heh?"

Cody's eyes narrowed, tipped his head a little. "You telling people I did that?" Cody asked, his face tight.

"Why not? Everybody knows 'bout you and fires," Eddie said, a little bit of pride in it.

"Then everybody knows a lie. And I think I know where it comes from," Cody said, turning around and glaring at him. "Who you been telling?"

"Just some guys. Don't get hot about it."

" 'Don't get hot about it,' he says. I don't have enough trouble already? You just . . . " Cody shook his head, letting the breath out from between his teeth. "Great," he said, jamming himself back against the steps. "That's just great. I suppose they're going to be coming around here, asking me questions again." He sighed. And then he turned around to take a piece out of Eddie with his eyes. "You just keep your mouth shut about me from now on, okay? I got enough trouble without your help. You understand me? You push me too far, Eddie."

"*Okay,*" Eddie said, saying with his hands, *calm down, calm down.* "Don't worry about it."

"Hmmph," Cody snorted, and he sat there, his elbows on his knees, staring out into the street, his face hard and cross.

Parker smiled to himself. He'd known these boys a long time, a *long* time — since before they either of them could crawl. There never had been much to Eddie but his size. Nothing much in his head, and nothing much in his heart, either.

But Cody, now — Parker smiled again, taking a slantwise glance at the other boy. There was a terrible kind of beauty about him, for anybody with the eyes to see it.

He was mean all right, when he wanted to be. But he was responsible, paying the bills for his mama since he was old enough to lift a broom — bright and quick, too, smart as they come. Life had made him hard on the outside, but it was something he had a right to; he'd been through enough.

And Parker was remembering when that boy was just little, the many's-the-time that child needed somebody so bad. Parker held a picture in his mind, a reflection of that tiny boy buried in Parker's own arms, nobody else to turn to. It had been a pain in

4

the man's heart—more than once—watching that child try to do what he had to do.

And as time went on, Parker kept on watching.

It was as if the things that child had been through all piled up behind him—hard cases off ugly bits of life, like cold stones, dropping behind him as he went—piling up, piece by piece, till there was a wall of it ringing him all around, a frigid wall made out of fear and weariness and absolute self-control. He'd built it into a safehold, all of ice—tough, and dense, and all smooth along the outside. You couldn't see through it. And it wasn't the kind of thing a person could follow him through, once Cody decided to retreat behind it—unless that person should understand exactly what that wall had been built out of—or how sanctuary and prison could be so much the same thing.

And should you ever get through that wall at last—somehow keep yourself from getting frozen out on the way—what you would find inside was *heat*: something seething, violent, ready to spill over and burn. The center of that boy was scarlet and sore with desire and pain and anger—too much hope, always making him turn on himself; too much loyalty, even when he caught hell for it. And what he *wanted*—he was scorched inside with it, his heart at the center, hot and liquid and ready.

And all the time, ringed around outside with cold, held in by that wall of ice.

The child was a contradiction, standing in his own way.

He shouldn't have been alone in it. Heaven knew, there were others like him—Parker too, in his day, when he was younger, when he was still wanting things. And the boy's mother, but there was no sanctuary left there, not for years gone past. So many walled in, everybody sitting in the center, nobody seeing out. It was enough to make you old, watching. It was enough to make you fear for people.

Now, there were some ways Cody knew well enough how to take care of himself. Parker had seen that, like the other night; the two of them had been walking home together from the warehouse, late—late enough to run into trouble down in the Ukraine's neighborhood, uptown gang and the local boys facing it off in the dark of the midnight street. Not the thing you want to walk into, not alone and out of your own territory.

And Cody had pulled that knife out, silky and smooth as a cat in the shadow, turning the blade so the streetlight flickered along the edge of it. They gave him room, knowing him enough to do that. And with their pressing business, they let him pass, him and Parker, Cody covering his back as cool as you please, arrogant and cold, but very, very careful—competent. He was good company on the streets so late, as long as you were *with* him.

Not that they hadn't been scared, both of them. Out of trouble, Cody stopped and sat a moment, Parker looking down at him.

"You do real well with that," Parker had said dryly, looking at the knife. "Something you like doing? Maybe you like a little trouble. Make you proud to be able to do that. You feel tough, now?" Parker could remember that feeling, himself.

Cody shook his head. "Last thing I want is a fight," he'd said, closing up the knife. "You just do what you have to do." Then he'd run his hand over the blade handle, pearly and pale in the streetlight. "Such a beautiful thing," he'd said, holding it in his lap. "Too bad it wants to be so mean."

Parker sighed, now, putting the memory away, squinting up at the sun—thankful for it, but willing it to go down. He took out his handkerchief and mopped at the back of his neck. "You going to graduate this year?" he asked the boys, flicking a touch of sweat out away from his eye.

Cody shrugged.

"Depends on what you mean, 'graduate,'" Eddie said. "You think they're going to keep us around down there after they don't *have* to?"

"What does it matter?" Cody asked, not looking for any answer.

"You don't think education matters?" Parker asked him.

"Depends on what business you go into," Eddie said. "I know a lot of guys, they're making the money, and they never did graduate. Old Cody, here—he's going to do for himself. You'll see. You can tell. He's the type, you know? Talks so *good.* Acts so smart. Women love it, don't they?" He shoved Cody again, from behind. "Money come to guys like that. They just know how to do it. I bet you Cody has money, right now. Lotsa money. Did a little early profit-sharing on old man Guicci, hey?"

Parker was only a little surprised how fast Cody turned around on Eddie. He took Eddie by the front of the shirt and gave him a good shake. "You shut up," he hissed, and he shook him again. Then he pushed him back sharply, two-handed, letting go of the shirt. "I have *had* it with you," he said, voice edged as bright and sharp as that pearly knife of his. "Get out of here."

6

"Come on—" Eddie said weakly, picking himself up, pulling his shirt back into shape.

"Go on," Cody said. "Before I hand you your face."

And then there was silence. Parker looked up, back over his shoulder. Eddie was standing up slowly.

"I don't know who you think you are, man," he said to Cody. But Cody didn't say anything more. He glared one more time, and then he turned his back on Eddie, leaning back against his elbows, but listening, Parker knew, just in case.

Eddie stood there a minute, trying to get the stuff together to stay. But he wouldn't be able to do it, and Parker knew it, and so did Eddie. He swore softly, just quiet enough not to get Cody on him again, then he turned around and went into the house. A few minutes later, they could hear him upstairs, swearing at his mother.

Parker sighed, letting some time slide by, listening to the sounds on the street. The stickball game had long ago been given up. The sun slanted slightly, and now there were slim shadows crouched in the creases and the corners.

"You push him pretty hard," Parker said, finally. "I thought he was supposed to be your friend."

"He's not my friend," Cody said, sharp and quick, "just because he lives upstairs."

"You been friends since you were babies," Parker said, all the time, knowing better.

"Not *friends*," Cody said again, carefully, so there would be no mistake.

"Then why you be hanging around with him?"

"I don't hang around *him*. He hangs around *me*. All the time, following me around, making a fool out of himself." He shook his head, angry now. "He does a job on me, you know . . ." holding up one hand, but giving it up, almost too much to explain. "He keeps trying to make me into some kind of—I don't know. Whatever it is he wishes *he* was. Some kind of tough guy. Half the trouble I'm in, I'm in because of him, the stories he goes around telling people."

"Hmm?" Parker said, meaning, and you're so innocent?

Cody scowled at him. "Just like that fire last night," he said, angry to the bone. "Telling everybody it was me. I was at *work* last night. But they're going to be coming around here, asking me questions about it, just like always." He shook his head again and swore, sharply; then he pulled himself back in, settling his face. "Anyway," he said, cooler now. "I wouldn't call us friends."

7

Parker nodded slowly. "You got a friend?" he asked, knowing the answer to that.

"Not one," Cody said, satisfied.

"You walk alone," Parker intoned, smiling a little to himself.

"Am I funny?" Cody asked, but without any anger.

"Everybody's funny," Parker said.

Somebody had come along and shut down the hydrant. And that's the way it went for everybody, most of the time. The children came scooting up the street, yelling and slapping each other with wet shirts.

"How come you never picked up with a gang?" Parker asked.

"Now, what would I want with a gang?" Cody asked him.

"Somebody to talk to," Parker suggested, not meaning it much.

"That's not what gangs do," Cody said, putting his hand flat, palm down, on the hot step, and taking it up again slowly.

Parker watched him.

"That stuff," he said. "What Eddie was saying about you and that school. Any truth in that?"

"No," Cody said. He stood up and leaned against the balustrade.

"None at all, now?"

Cody shrugged. "Not enough to count."

"Just a couple of broken windows and some spray paint on the walls," Parker said. Cody grinned out into the air.

"You think that's funny?" Parker asked him.

"I think it's appropriate," Cody said, and he sat back down again.

"You're going to get yourself in trouble," Parker said to him.

Cody pouted out his lip and shook his head, unconcerned.

Parker remembered that feeling, too, being young and thinking nothing bad could ever really happen. Cody should have known better than that. It made Parker feel ornery, made him contrary, and he looked at Cody out of the corners of his eyes.

"I been to jail once," he said. "I ever tell you about that? I did. Got caught up being disorderly one night with a bunch of guys. They have these handcuffs they put on you—little round rings, barely fit over your wrists, like *that*—" he held one wrist

8

up and circled it with his fingers—"hardly no chain between them at all, and they take you and they put you in this little room with bars all around, about a dozen of us, packed in there like so many fish, packed up against those bars, and them locking that door so we couldn't get out, not if we broke ourselves against it. We could hardly move in there, it was so close, hardly move for breath—and for the longest time . . ."

Cody stood straight up, put his hand out for the railing, short of breath, like he'd been under water too long.

"That's what it was like," Parker said.

Cody blinked in the sunlight, looking for something to focus his eyes on. Parker could see it, Cody trying hard to clean his mind out of the image Parker had put in there.

Then Cody glared down at him. "You don't do that to me, Parker," he warned after a minute, when he had his breath. "You take advantage." He sighed and then he swallowed, and he sat down again, a little pasty faced and crosser than ever.

"You still have that little problem," Parker observed.

"Yeah, I still have it. And you knew it." He took one long, slow breath.

"You wouldn't last five minutes in a jail cell," Parker said.

"You think I don't know that?" Cody said. "Sometimes I wake up at night, dreaming about it." He started breathing fast again. He shook his head, warding off the thoughts. "It's an old dream."

"It's easy to get yourself in there. One mistake, you be a dead man in five minutes in there," Parker said.

"When did I ever get in that kind of trouble?" Cody asked him, angry, wishing he'd drop the subject.

"You got more time on your hands, these days," Parker reminded him.

Cody shook his head, his mouth disgusted.

"Working in that warehouse, you might as well be locked up," Parker said, changing directions.

"We going to start that again?" Cody asked him. "Because I've got better things to do than sit around here and talk to you about that."

"It's the truth," Parker said. "That what you going to do the rest of your life? Work in that warehouse?"

"I do all right," Cody said, sullen.

But he didn't do all right. He hated it there. Parker had seen enough, seen it in Cody's face, in the way he made the supervisors treat him. He could have had office work, the way he had with numbers, but he put people off too hard, not wanting it. That place was hell for him.

"It's good enough for *you*," Cody said. "You've been there a *long* time."

"Why you always make things so hard for yourself?" Parker asked him.

Cody laughed, running his hand through his hair. He leaned back against the stair, pulling his shirt away from the sweat under it. "Just the way my mama taught me," he said.

"Well, there's truth there," Parker said. "But she taught you more than that—enough so you don't belong here, and you never will—not with the way you talk, not with how smart you are. You do not belong here. What you doing out on the streets at night, working in that warehouse? You belong in college, that's what. Your mama went to college, you can bet on that. And you're just like her."

"I'm not like her," Cody said, his voice turned stiff and his face shut down tight.

"Enough. You use words the way she does; when you want to, you sound just like her. And she went to college."

"And it did her so much good," Cody said flatly.

"She made her own choices. She going to make yours, too? How many times Mr. Guicci tell you, 'Go to college,' heh? 'Go to college—be a mathematician. An accountant, at least. *Do* something with your gifts.' How many times? A thousand times. I heard the man. You don't listen to anybody?" He sniffed. "There's nothing for you in this place."

"I'm doing okay," Cody said, stubborn and cross.

More people came creeping out now that there was some shadow coming. Sitting out and talking to each other, all up and down the street. Women, and some of the men coming home.

"This place going to kill you, Cody. You going to make it so." Parker was speaking quietly, now. "You make yourself look so tough, your clothes, your hair. You shut your face down, hard. You want everybody so they stay clear, and sure enough, you look so bad, everybody stays clear. You think those chickens won't be coming home to roost? What's the point?"

"It's a good disguise," Cody said, playing.

"Well, *that's* fine. That's just fine. Put on your disguise. Stay alone. Then you got nobody knows who you are, or what you are, or what you care about, what you want. And nobody cares. You push everybody till they want to beat your head in.

And somebody going to do that someday. You going to make them. That's what you want?"

"That's what I want."

Parker looked at him. "You want to be alone?"

Cody smiled, and he glanced at Parker. "I got you," he said.

Parker let the air out between his teeth. "You crazy," he said. But it was true. As long as there was air to breathe, Cody knew Parker would be there if he needed him. Just the way it always had been.

"This what you want—you go to college first, and then see if you want to come back here," Parker grumbled.

"Now, how am I ever going to get to a college?" Cody asked him, making it sound reasonable. "Assuming I ever *wanted* to go. They don't just let you in off the street."

"You been in tighter spots than that," Parker said. "There's always a way. And you the boy who can find it." He blew, mopping at his forehead. "It's hot."

Cody sighed. "You mess with me too much," he said.

"Somebody got to mess with you."

Old Mrs. Corietta came up from downstairs, banging her garbage can on the railing. Parker jumped up and went down to help her.

"Hot enough for you?" she sang out to the two of them. "It'll be cold enough soon enough." Parker took the can from her and set it out on the curb. "Thank you, Mr. DuBois." Her hand fluttered up by her forehead. "It's not so bad downstairs," she said cheerfully. "Maybe you two would like to come down and have some lemonade? You could cool off a little."

Parker put his hand on the stair. "You want to come?" he asked, squinting up. That boy, sitting there like his face was carved in stone.

"No, thank you. That's nice, Mrs. Corietta," Cody said, making a smile for her.

"Raspberry ice?" the old lady coaxed.

But Cody shook his head, smiling again for her. "Thanks anyway."

Bothered. Parker could see it in his eyes. That kid was thinking now.

"You go drown yourself," Cody told him. "Leave me alone . . . looking at me that way."

He was bothered for sure. And Parker went away down the stairs into the cool, altogether pleased with himself for it.

11

And Cody *was* bothered.

He was tired of the heat, tired of sitting on the steps. Out of patience with it. More tired than anybody could have known. It was all he could do these days, putting one foot in front of the other without tearing his hair out. And he didn't need people talking at him, making it worse.

Whatever it was he wanted, he already knew this wasn't it.

He stood up, stretching himself a little the way a cat will, but thinking all the time, and irritated with Parker for putting ideas in his head about things he wasn't going to get.

He could hear Parker laughing downstairs. He shook his head. Classical music from the second floor. Eddie's music, upstairs. Cody grimaced, sweat running down inside his T-shirt and down the back of his neck.

He shoved himself away from the steps, hands in his pockets, moving down the sidewalk. Not a lot of time before work. Enough to go down to Elaina's. Just for a while. Just long enough, he could get Parker and those words of his out of his mind.

He shoved his hands deep into his pockets. The knife pressed against his knuckles, clean and cool. Not much else in there, a few dollars, some coin, a key.

He fixed his mind on Elaina. She was his medicine, these last days, these last six months. She kept him sane. Her hands, that sweet face of hers, her family—she gave him a place, something to hold in his mind when things got too bad. Her quiet, his need.

No matter that there wasn't much between them besides that. At least she never messed with him like Parker did, pushing. She was satisfied with the way things were, as her mother was. Not worrying about what might be. Satisfied with him.

He was afraid, now. Afraid of going to work with Parker's talk still going around in his mind. Afraid he wouldn't be able to take it tonight. Afraid he wouldn't be able to stand it anymore—as if he had a choice.

You work with what you've got. That was what he'd learned. *And you'd darn well better learn to be satisfied with it, or you'll make yourself crazy wanting what you can't have.*

He looked up as he passed the deli down towards the corner, next block down. "Zino's," they had painted across the window —new paint, the name arched like a rainbow. Zino's oldest son, Big Lonzo, stood in the doorway like a block of wood, arms folded, watching Cody come down the sidewalk, not saying a word.

Cody shrugged to himself, moving on. But the new paint and the look on Lonzo had made him flinch. *Nothing stays the same; the good goes, the bad gets worse.*

He wondered sometimes if he was going to end up married to Elaina. It was what her mother wanted. And her father. He was part of the family, now, kids crawling all over him the moment he walked through the door. He wondered if that would keep him, the food and the fondness and the warmth. Married to her soon, then making lots of little Catholic babies, working at the warehouse the rest of his life so they could keep a tiny box of an apartment of their own.

He scared himself, thinking about it. *Probably,* he told himself unhappily. *For the rest of my life.* If he hadn't needed her so much, he would've quit long ago, given it up. But that was the way things were. And for now, it was going to have to do.

"Hey! Cody!" somebody was calling. Cody threw his head up, looking around before he stepped off another curb into the street. A boy was coming toward him across the intersection, walking quickly, lightly, the oldest of Elaina's little brothers, coming along as if he was something made of air.

Cody stepped back up on the curb and waited. Berto, dark and slender, flashed a smile and jumped up on the curb just as a taxi cut the corner behind him, making it close.

"Hooo—" Berto said, looking back over his shoulder. "Who takes a cab down here?" He was nervous. Anybody could have seen it, the way he was bouncing around. And Cody stepped back inside of himself, right away wary.

"So," Berto said. "I been looking for you for a couple of days."

"Yeah?" Cody said.

"Yeah." The boy smiled again. Something was up, and he didn't know how to talk about it.

"You going down to see my sister?" he asked, slipping his hands in his back pockets, squinting at Cody against the low sun.

"I was thinking I might," Cody said.

Berto nodded to himself, balancing half off the curb on the balls of his feet. "Well—" he said, and then he shrugged, looked up at Cody, still squinting.

"You know Louis Almonde?"

Cody moved one shoulder slightly. He knew Louis very well.

"Two days ago, they pull his brother in off the street. They got him with drugs, too fast for him to dump them." Berto shrugged again. "It's good they got him. He was a bad one."

"So?" Cody asked, keeping his voice quiet, and his face, but getting impatient.

"So, isn't it a good thing?" Berto asked, looking back over his shoulder down the street the way he had come.

"It's a wonderful thing, Berto. It has some significance?"

Berto did a little moonwalk on the curb and grinned at Cody. Still nervous. "So, now it's Louis bosses *Los Angeles del Noches.*"

And now, they were getting somewhere.

"He's been wanting you a long time," Berto said, looking at Cody out of the corners of his eyes. "Now he's boss, and he's got to talk, and then he's got to do what he says. He never could get you going. Now, he's going to. Everybody's watching."

"Yeah?" Cody said.

"He told my sister, day before yesterday, she sees you again, somebody going to get hurt down there. He says it like he means it. He got my mother scared. Everybody's waiting to see if he's as good as his brother. If he gets you, he is."

"Ah," Cody said—angry now, hard faced.

"He's been hanging around down there, down by our place. Sit around on the porch with all his guys, like a big party, waiting for you. We were afraid you might be coming down pretty soon. They'd make you a lot of trouble. So my mother and Elaina, I told them I would come down and find you first. I been waiting on this corner two days."

"Two days?" Cody said to him, amused. "You know where I am. You need to find me, you can come down."

Berto grinned. "They might be asking me where I been. Now, I say to them, 'Down on the corner.' "

Then Cody was looking off down the street, weighing it in his mind. Berto must not have liked it, what he was seeing in Cody's face. He edged closer, keeping up the talk.

"You don't have to go down there, man. You don't have anything to prove. Nobody's going to think you're scared of Louis—"

Cody laughed. "Why not?" he said. "They think I'm stupid?" He snorted.

"They know what you can do," Berto said, still talking, persuading. "Nobody with any brain want to get in your way."

"You scared of Louis?" Cody asked him.

"Me?" Berto said, puffing out his chest. Cody grinned at him, and Berto let the air out. "Maybe," he said and he laughed.

But it really wasn't very funny. And Berto started up again, trying to build a wall out of words—

"He says he's going to mess her up good if he finds out you been down there again. You know, it's something he'll do. She doesn't care so much about that. She's scared what they would do to you. And she's right. No matter how good you are, there's twelve of them. And they hungry. It's just the way things are. You can't come down there. Not until it changes. Nothing anybody can do about it, except get hurt."

Cody spat a word and came down off the curb, took a step past Berto. Berto reached out and put a hand on his arm. Cody stopped, looking at him.

"You my brother, man." Berto caught him by the eyes, quiet now, speaking plainly. "You don't go down there. She doesn't *want* you." Berto meant this, no laughter in it. "You want to die? It's *over*. There's more to life than my sister. You got plenty of places you got to go." Then, lighter. "And if you get lonely, you can always go see Bernice Alteiri—" He grinned again, his teeth very white in the evening shadow, but his eyes still had no laughter in them.

Cody stood there, permitting the hand on his arm, looking hard at Berto. Berto gave it back to him. The family didn't want him down there. So, it was the truth. And there was no arguing that. "It's the way things are," Berto had said. "She doesn't want you."

Cody shook the hand off and sat down on the curb, suddenly very, very tired. All that anger, and nothing to do with it. Nothing but sit on it. He heard Berto sigh. *They were afraid I would come anyway,* Cody was thinking. *What do they think I am?* Then Berto dropped down beside him, feet in the street.

"It's not like they won't miss you," he said, worried that maybe he'd made it sound too hard. "Everybody's crying. Louis's mother thinks it's a good thing. She says Elaina shouldn't be hanging around with an Anglo punk like you. My mother says to her—'I guess, if anybody knows about punks, *you* do.' Louis's mother, she took offense. 'At least she should be marrying in the church,' she says, like church got something

15

to do with it." He laughed, gave Cody a punch, stood up again. "Hey," he said, stepping out into the street. And then he stopped.

"You better keep your knife on you when school starts," Berto said. "He told them he's going to get you, he don't care where. And you know him; it's your back he's going to be watching."

"I know," Cody said. The thought made him very weary.

Berto trotted off across the street.

"Hey," Cody called.

Berto stopped, turned around.

"You tell your mother tonight, tell her I heard you. And tell Elaina." It was thank you. Berto grinned, walking backwards. He made the sign they had for *brother*, then he turned around and trotted off down the sidewalk towards his neighborhood.

Cody sat very quietly, his hands pressed together, palm to palm. Sometimes he wondered when it would finally get to be too much, what would happen when the anger got big enough, he couldn't hold it anymore—if, in the end, he would finally come apart. Maybe kill somebody sometime because of it. Get himself killed, maybe.

And now he was going to have go to the warehouse.

All night at that place, and only this and Parker's talk for comfort. It was going to be like walking into hell with a handful of matches.

He sighed and rubbed his forehead, got up slowly, and watched as Berto disappeared around the corner, back to the place he belonged.

2

He was hungry. In the midst of all the anger and the acid in his stomach, he knew he was empty. Elaina's mother would have taken care of that for him tonight. Now he was going to have to take care of it for himself. But that wasn't such a bad thing; hunger was something that could be dealt with easily enough.

The shadows had gotten broad and black — sharp lines and shapes on the street and across the faces of the buildings. Black and white abstract. No color. Only shades of heat. Cody closed his eyes against it, and sighed. He turned around and walked back down towards his own place.

He didn't want to have to go to Zino's, but there wasn't any food at home, and now there wasn't time to go anywhere else. *You would think a woman would get hungry sometimes, that she'd notice there was no food around and go buy something herself.* But his mother never did. Never did anything like it. For a moment, he was mad at her, but it wasn't something he allowed, and he put the feeling away from him.

He peered at the window of Zino's as he went past it; you could still see some of the old paint — the old name — on the window, just traces of it. He felt around in his pocket and came up with a five-dollar bill. Zino's Big Lonzo was still standing in the doorway, arms crossed, like there was nothing else in the world to do but stand there. Cody could hear an electric fan running somewhere back in the shop. Lonzo looked down over his beefy arms, glowering at Cody, taking up the whole doorway.

"I'd like to buy a loaf of bread, if that's all right," Cody said, letting the acid he was feeling in his stomach flow through the

17

words. It was going to take every little thing he had left—and that wasn't much—being humble with Lonzo.

Lonzo grunted, as if he had the right to consider. Then he stepped back into the shop, just enough to let Cody pass through. It was dark in there, like a cave. And they'd changed everything. Nothing was the same, everything in a different place, except for the case lots. It gave Cody the creeps, being in there and having it so different. Having Lonzo behind the counter.

He found the bread and picked up a loaf of wheat. Then he went over to the deli case and looked in. He wasn't believing the prices they had on the stuff.

"A pound," he said to Lonzo, pointing to a heavy round of waxy yellow cheese. Lonzo'd been hovering around like he was afraid Cody was going to take a sausage and shove it up his shirt or something.

"You got the money for this?" Lonzo asked now, his little, stupid eyes narrow.

Cody held up the five, afraid what he might say if he once opened his mouth to answer. Lonzo nodded and hauled out the cheese for cutting.

"You're getting yourself a nice profit on that," Cody said, just pointing it out.

"That's what we're in business for," Lonzo said, leering. He wrapped the sliced cheese up loosely and dropped it into a bag and then he punched the keys on the old cash register, flourishing his hands as if he was enjoying himself.

"With the money you're making," Cody said, "you could at least get somebody in here who knew how to sweep a floor."

Lonzo sneered, slapping the change down on the counter without counting it back. "And I suppose that'd be you," he said.

Cody looked back at him coldly, embarrassed that he should have left himself so open. "You couldn't afford me," he said. He picked up his bag of groceries with dignity and started towards the door.

"I bet," Lonzo said. "Besides, we're not *hiring.*" Even with his back turned, Cody could see Lonzo, leaning out over the counter, sneering and grinning. The anger came up inside of Cody, hot and painful, catching him off guard. It scared him, the way the feelings were getting out of hand, what he wanted to *do.*

"See you," he said, making it very pleasant, screwing down hard on himself, trying to shove his anger all back down where it had come from. He heard Lonzo say something behind him, but he blocked it out and stepped out in the last light of the afternoon. The back of his T-shirt was sticking to him. He carried the little sack on his hip, and he pulled at the front of his shirt, letting some air in.

He went on down the sidewalk worrying. If he'd been able to get to Elaina's, he could have stayed there till the clock sent him to work. He didn't want to go home, but his mother was going to be hungry, too. He was feeling wedged in between Zino's and his own place, like there was just a little space between them, getting smaller all the time, and his palms began to sweat against the brown paper of the bag.

He was wondering if his mother was maybe still asleep, hoping that she was. He didn't know what he was going to do if she was on a bad one. He wondered for the hundredth time if it could be normal for you to love somebody so much, and *hate* her at the same time. It didn't seem natural to him. It seemed crazy.

The trouble with her was that you never knew what you were going to get. True, sometimes she had good days. Not very often anymore, okay — but when it was good, she could be quiet, almost nice — wistful, kind of, with this deep thing in her eyes that made him ache for her. Those times, he almost wanted to touch her, except that wasn't the way things were between them.

Other days, it was not so easy. Sometimes, she was just private and angry. Or nervous. On the nervous days, she talked a lot, usually about something that made her mad, something that was unfair, like God or the government or society.

That wasn't so hard to handle.

But there were the other times. The very bad times; she drank a lot. She always had. But lately, it was way too much. When she drank, she could be very hard to live with. She was a very smart lady, smart enough to be able to do a lot of damage where she wanted to. And that was the thing: when she drank, she wanted to do damage. To everything, everybody. But there was usually only one person around she could hurt. And when she had her mind into it, she could be very scary.

And there were other things she did, other things she took — pills, maybe. He didn't know what. He didn't want to know. He didn't even know how she could get the money for anything like that; it wasn't as if she had a job anymore. Without his job, they wouldn't have had lights or water or anything, not for years. She did manage to pay the rent. He didn't ask about that, either.

Now he hitched the bag up into his arms and went up the steps of the porch. Eddie's music was still on upstairs, loud and ugly.

Cody stood at the top of the porch stairs a minute, thinking about Eddie, wondering how long it would be till Eddie got him into a kind of trouble he finally couldn't get himself out of, wishing there was something he could do about it before things got any worse — if things *could* get worse. Eddie, making everybody think Cody'd started that fire. Muddying the waters. Making it hotter for him.

Thinking about it frustrated him. So he put a stop to it, pushing the door open. He started up the creaking stairs, going slowly, shifting the bag so he could hold onto the railing. His stomach got tighter every step he went up, dreading what he was going to find once he got home.

He was hoping she would be alone up there, at least. Every second, breathing was getting harder for him, as if he was running up the stairs instead of walking, as if something was wrong inside of him. And there was. There was something wrong, something finally slipping out of control. He could feel the knife in his pocket, cool and heavy against his leg every time he stepped up a stair.

He was hoping nobody was with her, because if she had one of her friends up there, the way things were tonight, Cody was afraid he might just end up hurting somebody. For the first time in his life, he was scared of what he might do.

He came to the landing and stood outside the door, listening. The hall was quiet, except for down at the end, Salgados's baby was yelling. He put his hand on the doorknob and turned it. The door wasn't locked. He pushed it open and reached in for the light. The front room was empty.

He heaved a sigh. The place didn't look so bad, at least. A couple of days before, he'd spent two hours trying to get something off the walls after one of his mother's little "parties." She didn't care what the place looked like. So he did what he could; kept up with it the best he could. Sometimes, walking through the door like this, what he saw nearly wore him out.

"Cody?" she called. She was in the kitchen, and she was slurring. Cody closed his eyes and leaned back against the door-jamb. He felt a tremendous fear coming up inside of him.

"It's me," he said, finally, and he closed the door behind him, locking it. They had four little rooms up here. For all he knew, he'd been born in this place. He bumped the door with his hip to make sure it was closed.

He crossed the room and pushed the door open with his shoulder. She was leaning against the sink, wearing her old flowered wrapper. You could tell right away, looking at her, she'd been pretty once. And maybe that was the saddest thing, to be able to see what she might have been . . .

Now she was leaning back against the cabinet, one arm folded across her body, holding the wrapper closed; in the other hand, she held her glass.

Without saying anything, he dropped the bag on the table and pulled out the bread and the cheese.

"Nice of you to think of that," she said, with absolutely no sincerity. "There's never anything in this house to eat. I tell you," she said, putting the drink down and picking up her cigarette, "if I don't do it, nobody around here does anything." She looked at him meaningfully, taking a pull at the smoke. She stubbed it out in a saucer and picked up her drink.

"You want a sandwich?" he asked.

"Why, *thank* you," she said.

He unwrapped the cheese. Then he pulled his knife out of his pocket and flipped it open. "Ooo—what a mean boy you must be," she said, watching him slice the cheese with it. He went to the refrigerator for mayonnaise, but all there was was margarine. "It'll have to do," his mother said grimly. So he spread the bread with the margarine and put the slices of cheese carefully down on the bread. "And meticulous, too," she said.

"You want a drink?" she asked him. She had the bottle down off the shelf. "But you don't drink, do you?"

He put the top on each sandwich and used the knife to make neat diagonal halves. "Of course," she went on, "you've noticed that *I* do."

He stiffened.

"And you think I drink too much."

He put her sandwich down carefully on her side of the table.

"Don't you?" she asked, pursuing it.

"Mom," he said. "I am not going to get into this discussion with you." He went over to the sink and ran water over the blade of the knife, rubbing at it until it was clean again, drying it on his shirt. Trying to keep himself even. He put the knife down beside the sink.

"You think I have a problem," she said, narrowing her eyes at him.

In the end, she always did this to him, always made him answer her. He couldn't help it, she made him so frustrated.

"How do you know what I think?" he said, scared to death

21

of giving in, even a little, to the anger—scared he wasn't going to be able to pull it back in again, once it was out. Something inside his mind was slipping sideways. His heart was beating much too fast, and his palms were still wet.

"I *know*," she said, saying it as if it weren't so hard to see through him. "I know exactly what you think. I know *precisely* what you are. And I know *how* you think."

He put his hands down flat on the edge of the sink. And he said—without even knowing he was going to say it—"So, you know me so well. I must be just like my father." And then he could have bitten his tongue off.

He glanced up at her, keeping his face hard. She was staring at him. It was the first time he'd ever even mentioned his father to her, since he was little. He'd done it to hurt her. But all he'd done was give her a weapon.

She looked him up and down for a moment, doing this private little half-smile. Then she raised her eyebrows and laughed and shook her head.

"You never had a father," she said. "You were an immaculate conception." She thought it was very funny.

He clamped his teeth together and made no answer.

He made a move to pick up the sandwich, but then he left it where it was. He couldn't have eaten anything. He looked up at the clock over the sink. There wasn't much time left.

"No, seriously," she said, almost dreamily. "You want to know what you are? I'll tell you what you are." She hung a look at him, a half-flirty, half-smirk look. "You're nothing," she said simply. She took another drink.

Then she looked at him again, her eyebrows raised innocently. "That's it," she said. "Nothing at all."

It was like spitting in his face. Every time.

She picked up the bottle and emptied it into her glass.

"Of course, you're the kind of boy every mother *dreams* of. Bright. Capable. Well groomed." So ironic. "But someday—" she was gazing off over the rim of her glass, "someday you're going to slip up. Some girl's father is going to get you. Or some little gang you've messed with. And the people who clean up the street in the morning, they'll find little bits of you all over the place." She smiled at him sweetly. She was enjoying herself.

"Sooner or later, you're going to do something stupid," she sipped gently. "And that'll be the end. Juvenile hall, baby. It's going to happen—don't think it won't. It's what you were made for. And don't expect me to come and visit you." She shook her head as if it were just too bad, and then she laughed.

"I don't think so," he said quietly, wishing he could just keep his mouth shut.

"No?" she said, smiling to herself.

"No," he said.

"No," she said. "You're right. You're going to get a scholarship and graduate from Yale and win a Nobel prize, right?"

"Maybe," he said.

She laughed and took a long drink.

"It's not that funny," he said.

She looked at him, very amused. "Isn't it?" She laughed again. "You're serious. Look at that face." She chuckled into her glass. "You know, you're incredibly arrogant. Yale, huh? You'd make a perfect lawyer. I can just see you with a three-piece suit and a briefcase."

"Maybe." He couldn't take his eyes off of her face. He knew better than to listen, but his defenses didn't work with her.

"Don't be stupid," she said flatly. And then she snickered to herself. "But see," she said. "That *is* the whole problem, isn't it?" She took down another bottle and filled her glass again, lit another cigarette.

"I'm not," he said, quietly.

"Oh?" she said. "I suppose you're just incontro*vert*ibly attracted to failure." She took a long, thoughtful pull on her cigarette. "It would be interesting," she went on, "to see what they'd do if you ever handed in something halfway intelligent over at that school." She chuckled. And then she laughed, and she arched her eyebrows at him. "They'd think you were a little cheater, that's what they'd do." She wagged her finger at him. "They know you over there only too well, my friend."

It was only the truth, but Cody couldn't answer her. He stood there like a fool with his eyes wide open, caught in the middle of thinking, *Fine, then maybe it's time I show everybody just what I can do.* She'd answered it without his saying a word. Even drunk, her aim was so true. And he was damned— because she was right. If he suddenly started doing well, there wasn't a soul in that school who would believe it. There wasn't going to be a way out.

"No," she went on, following it up. "A pretty face and a flair for vandalism just aren't enough anymore, more's the pity." She smiled into her glass. "But even if you'd been a good little scholar right along, there just isn't any money, is there? Small detail. Too bad." She tipped the glass up.

He took a careful breath, fixed his eyes on a tiny hole in the wall.

"Disappointed?" she asked, giggling. She came over close, picked up his hand, turning his wrist up. Then she drew her finger across it, simply, almost gently, just below his hand. Very pointedly, she looked down at his knife then up at him raising her eyebrows—then that smile. He pulled his hand away, shocked at her.

"It's always an option," she said shrugging, watching him slip the knife back into his pocket.

He would have died before he let her see what she was doing to him. But he couldn't let it rest. He opened himself up to his anger, just enough to cover the hurt, and he kept the mask on his face. He spoke very quietly as she moved away again.

"I am going to go to college."

She smiled.

"If you could make it to college, I can." He said it simply.

She looked at him sharply, and then the hard look came. He knew he had just crossed the line with her; her life was very much her own business, and she'd never told him she'd been to college. "The difference is," he said, guessing, his hands shaking, stomach ice, "I'm going to make it through. I'm not going to quit."

The game was over.

"Oh, really," she said, the edge in her eyes and her voice was dangerous.

"Yeah," he said, making himself sound very cool. "Really."

She turned herself so that she was facing him. She swayed slightly, but she was holding herself upright.

He couldn't meet her eyes. So he sat down, turning his back on her, like he was bored with the whole thing.

She didn't say anything. He was scared of her now, but he couldn't shut himself up.

"I'm not scared of life, Mother," he said. "You just do your best with it. I don't have to prove anything to anybody." *Except to you, and to me, and to everybody else.*

"Is that so?" she whispered.

"Yeah. I'll pull my grades up," he went on, conversationally, his mouth dry and his blood beating in his temples.

"I doubt it," she said, dripping disdain.

Reaching. Reaching for anything. "And maybe get a scholarship. Or if I can't, I'll just drop a line to Uncle Erin—"

He heard her suck her breath in suddenly.

"And I'm going to tell him—" he said, too far into it to quit.

"What do you know about Erin?" she asked. The tone of her voice made his skin creep, but he still didn't turn around to face her.

" '. . . You don't know me but . . .' "

"What do you know about Erin?" she asked again, louder this time.

"He's my *uncle*," Cody said, and then he did face her. Her face was white and her eyes were burning.

"What did you expect? You think we live in a vacuum, here? You think I don't notice, people around us have families? You think I wouldn't wonder about my family? You must have noticed," Cody went on. "He sends Christmas cards every year."

"And what do you do? Dig them out of the trash?"

"Yes, ma'am," he said, matching her face. "That's just what I do."

She came up to him suddenly and hauled on his hair, jerking his head back so that all he could see was the ceiling. The violence of it shocked him again.

"How *dare* you?" she hissed, glaring down at him. He'd never seen her face like this before, violent, nakedly furious. "How dare you?" she said again, louder, pulling back harder, choking him, hurting him. "That is my personal business. Mine, you understand me?"

He wrenched himself away from her, knocking the chair over sideways.

He stood back against the wall, his chest heaving, and his whole body trembling. "I think it's my business, too," he said. "I mean, don't you? I mean, he *is* my uncle. A nice middle-class uncle with a nice little family. Nothing like the way we live. Not a thing like you. If I write to him—and I'll tell him, 'You don't know me, but I'm your nephew. And I need money, because my mother doesn't have any because at some point in her life, whatever it was she wanted, she didn't get, and now all she does with her whole life is sit around and blame everybody but herself—' "

She screamed. She balled up her fists and pressed them to her temples and screamed. He'd never heard anything like it, a terrible, terrible sound; her face twisted and she threw the glass at him, hatred and outrage making her fast and strong. He moved aside as it smashed against the wall, inches away from his head, pieces of it catching the side of his face. He could feel the sting of it through everything.

She screamed again.

He stood there, staring at her. He couldn't have moved. There was somebody yelling something upstairs.

Then it all got very quiet. She started to cry. She sank down on a chair and sobbed.

He still stood there, chilling and shaking all over, staring at her.

She put her arms on the table and dropped her face down on them. There was no sound in the whole place now but her crying, and the drip in the sink, and the muffled voices from the upstairs apartment.

He swallowed and put his arms around himself, trying to warm up, trying to breathe. And then he leaned over, pressing the butts of his palms against his eyes. A few minutes later, he could get his breath, and he stood up straight again.

He put his hand to his face, up by his eye. It came away bloody. He put his head back against the wall and took one long, slow, ragged breath. "I can't do this anymore," he whispered. "I just can't."

It was over now. Eventually, she'd stop crying and then she'd go to sleep right there where she was sitting. She'd sleep it off. Tomorrow, she wouldn't even remember this.

He swallowed, tasting bile, and then he pushed himself away from the wall.

He rubbed at his eyes, and then he made his way out through the door, down the little hallway to his tiny room. It was nearly dark now. He found his way to his bed by the dim light that came in through the alley window, and sat down on the mattress, his heart still pounding, almost making him dizzy.

And it was past time for him to be at work.

He sat on the bed, hugging himself, still trying to get warm. There was music coming through the wall, Latino stuff.

He was going to have to be at the warehouse.

He looked around at the window, and then all around the room.

There was no way he could go to that place another night. That warehouse. There was no way.

The walls of the hot little room started pressing in on him.

He stood up, suddenly breathing hard again, his hands clammy.

The space around him was drawing itself in.

He began to walk around the room, making tight, tiny circles.

He'd never had a problem in this room before, small as it was—not even in the dark. It had been his room, his only place, and now he felt betrayed. He couldn't hold his hands steady. He had to get out of this room. He had to get out of the apartment. And he thought about the street, and the streets beyond that, and he thought about Louis waiting for him, and he knew he didn't want to die.

He went over and switched on the light. The walls pulled back a little. He pulled a box out of his closet and dug through it, coming up finally with an envelope. He dropped it, picked it up, dropped it again, finally trying to steady it with both hands, while he worked the card out of it, a renaissance Madonna and child, blue on a field of white.

A picture fell out of the card, fluttering to the floor. He picked it up and looked at it, and there they were, the middle-class family in their best clothes, smiling for the camera, a nice-looking family from another planet. He stared hard at the picture for a moment, and then he put it back inside the card and tried to shove the card back into the envelope. He gave up finally, took the picture out of the card, and stuffed it in the envelope by itself, letting the card drop to the floor.

He turned the envelope over and looked at the return address. And that's when he understood that he was going to leave. It wasn't a rational decision. It was almost a reflex. It was the only alternative.

He stood up, pulling the cover off his pillow, and he went around and around the room, trying to think what things he should take with him. There were just a few things he had of his own, a couple of pair of shorts, his other pair of pants, two shirts, his book—an old copy of *Nicholas Nickelby* he'd gotten somewhere—the worn-out little stuffed dog Mrs. Guicci had given him to keep the dark off, and the envelope with the picture in it.

Then he pulled the mattress away from the wall and pried frantically at the baseboard. It had suddenly come to him that she might have found the place and taken all the rest of the money. He shoved his hand into the hole under the wall.

But no. The money was there, and he grabbed it and pulled it out.

He'd been saving this a long time. Every cent he had left after the bills, it was here—every cent he'd ever earned, except what he'd spent on the clothes and the knife.

He felt guilty, holding it. But this was all he had, and it was going to buy him a ticket out.

It was dark outside the window now. He was a little worried about carrying this kind of money around on the street in the dark. He wadded up the bills and stuck them in the pocket beside his knife. He stood up and tied a knot in the end of his pillowcase.

It was very dark in the apartment. He made his way back down the hallway to the kitchen. His mother hadn't moved. She was asleep, huddled up against the table.

He took a deep breath, standing over her. She looked so quiet, now.

He stood there looking at her a long time, his chest and his throat so tight he could hardly breathe. "I'm sorry, Mother," he said finally. "But I've got to go." If he was having to choose between her life and his, he was choosing his and he knew it, and he hated himself for it. "If I stay here anymore," he said to her, "I know it's going to kill me. And I don't think you really want that." It was a little joke he had with himself.

He left the kitchen, crossed the living room, and let himself out of the apartment without a sound, locking the door behind him. He hesitated then, standing in the hallway, and he dug in his pocket for some of the money. He stooped and pushed a ten dollar bill back under the door; then he checked everything once more, just to make sure it was locked. He stood there with his hand against the door for one more moment, and then he left that place—going silently down the dark stairs and out to the empty streets.

3

He'd been dreaming, something uncomfortable and strange. It resolved itself slowly into something like motion . . . swaying . . . rounded bumps. Cody didn't understand the motion at first; he didn't understand anything, only that his head hurt and he was very stiff—and very tired.

He groaned to himself and stretched a little, and then the chair he was sitting in seemed to slide over sideways, and he got a sharp smack on the forehead. He pried open his eyes, but for a moment the brightness was too much, and he had to screw his eyes closed again to clear them. He was remembering a little, now—at least he knew that he had left home and he didn't know where he was.

There was a wood—a confusion of tangled shade and brightness—passing along on the other side of the glass, fresh and wet with the early morning, a jungle of leaves like tiny translucent screens, brilliantly green, glowing with the morning, rimmed with silver. It was a place so exquisite, so unexpectedly lovely, he knew right away, wherever he was now, he'd lost himself, and he'd never want to find his way back home again.

He sat on his side of the window, forehead pressed against the cold glass, still swaying and bumping along, but understanding it now—something like music inside his chest making a song out of the silence. Looking down into that green world, he could believe in almost anything—except that he was doing what he was doing, and that it might actually work out.

And then, suddenly, the trees gave way to open, brilliant early morning air, and the ground fell away in a long, lazy roll to a wide valley, stretches of green fields and brown fields, dark ribbons of road between them, and tiny clusters of buildings and trees. The roundness of the land was like a huge cup, filled up and brimming with the first heavy golden air of morning.

The bus crested the hill and started down into the valley, leaving Cody's understanding behind, white knuckled and grabbing at everything he'd ever understood about reality. He was suspended in the air—the entire wide and open sweep of the earth rolled away under him, making him feel as if *he* were falling, as if there was nothing to hold on to. It made him light-headed, light-stomached.

He was floating at the edges of more sky than he'd ever in his life seen before—an unlimited, wide-domed blue clarity, ringed but not enclosed by clouds—an undefined expanse of air, a magnificence he could never have imagined on his own. The beauty of it was like a sudden pain in him and it immediately turned to fear, like the feeling that came with small places, but then again, not like it. It was because there were no limits here; he couldn't get himself oriented.

He must have gasped. A voice came from beside him. "It's beautiful, isn't it."

Cody glanced over his shoulder, embarrassed and feeling slightly naked. He forced his hands open, trying to let go of the arms of his seat. The bearded man in the next seat was looking out of the window past Cody's shoulder, and there was no mistaking the pleasure in his face.

Cody turned again to the window, his amazement and his fear mingled into something like awe. "Yes," he said, having to clear his throat of sleep before he could make it intelligible. "It's beautiful."

Through the clouds at the far edge of the sky, a single shaft of light shot out and down, its huge, translucent foot firmly settled on the floor of the valley below.

"You can travel the world around," the man said quietly, "but it doesn't get any better than this. Not anywhere."

Cody glanced at him again. The man had on a well-worn, brown leather jacket. He looked at Cody and smiled, his eyes turning to wrinkles at the corners. Then the man's eyes slid past him again, going to the window, as if he were reluctant to lose sight of what was out there.

"Where'd you come from?" the man asked.

Cody rested his forehead against the window again, braving the chill of the glass. "New York," he said.

The man laughed. "City? or state?"

"City," Cody said, maybe for the first time understanding that there was a difference.

"You've been out of the city before," the man said. It was a statement rather than a question. The man wasn't patronizing him.

"No," Cody said, too much out of his element to worry about dignity. "I never have."

"Ah," the man said. He chuckled. "Welcome to the open spaces."

Cody let his breath out, half laugh, half sigh.

"You'll get used to it," the man said, leaning down to adjust the big, beat-up leather bag he had at his feet. "Unfortunately, sooner or later, you lose that weightless feeling. You'll get used to this, and it'll be strange going back."

The bus was nearing the bottom of the hill.

"It's the color," Cody said, almost reverently, the loveliness of the leaves still whispering inside of him, and the buttered brilliance of the air. "The *light*."

"I know. Gets to you, doesn't it? It's an incredible thing. You can't touch it with your hand, but it's there all the same, like some kind of magic. Light is the essence of the universe, my friend—the definition and the shape and the discoverer of all things." He spoke as though he were amusing himself, but when Cody looked at the man's face, he saw just the pleasure and the sharp clearness of the man's eyes.

"Where are you from?" Cody asked.

"I live in the city now, too," the man said, and suddenly, Cody could see that he looked tired. The man tilted his chin towards the window. "But I was brought up out there," he said. "That's where my family is."

"What do you do?" Cody asked.

The man nudged the sloppy leather bag, as worn and comfortable-looking as the jacket. "I'm a photographer," he said.

"Oh, yeah?" Cody asked, pulling himself up straighter in his seat. There were little kinks in his back.

"Sleeping in a bus," the man said, agreeing with what Cody's face must have told him.

"It's gotta get easier," Cody said.

"It doesn't," the man grinned.

"You work for a magazine, or a newspaper, or what?" Cody asked.

"I'm freelance," the man said. "I do a little bit of every-thing."

31

"Oh, yeah?" Cody said. "You do a lot of traveling?"

The man smiled. "Some," he said. Cody got the impression it was supposed to be an understatement.

"Your pictures ever get published?" Cody asked him.

"Once in a while," the man said.

"Well, like where?"

The man shrugged. "If I told you *National Geographic*, would you leave me alone about it?" he asked, not unpleasantly.

"Maybe," Cody said.

"*National Geographic*," the man said. "I go where people are, and that's what I shoot. People. Just living their lives."

"Have you ever been to Africa?" Cody asked. He was feeling the stirrings of respect.

"A couple of times," the man said, smiling the way people do when they'd really rather not talk about themselves.

"Really," Cody said, impressed. "What are you doing riding a *bus*?"

The man smiled again. "What can you see from an airplane?" he asked.

Cody was comfortable with the answer. He turned to the window again. They were down on the valley floor now, and the sun was a little higher, the air settled in for the day.

"Here," the photographer said. He leaned over, then he straightened up and put a magazine on Cody's lap. *Photography*.

"What?" Cody asked, looking down at it blankly.

"It's not yours? I thought it was yours. You had it last night."

"I did?" Cody blinked hard, trying to remember. "Oh. Yeah, I did." He was remembering the cover. And the terminal, how weird it had seemed, sitting there. And everybody staring at him, like he was the quintessential character, the thing they'd expected to find tucked away in a weird, dark bus terminal in the middle of that city in the middle of the night.

He couldn't stand the waiting and the staring and the thinking—not so sure he wouldn't turn around and go back home after all—so he'd done something for himself; he'd wasted good money on a magazine—and he'd chosen this one because the cover had drawn him in. Only because of that. He put his hand on it now, touching the colors.

"You're interested in photography?" the man asked him.

"I don't think so," Cody said.

The man looked down at the magazine.

"I liked the cover," Cody explained.

The man nodded. Then he put his head back against the seat and closed his eyes.

Cody sighed.

It was not his world he was seeing outside this window. He was the stranger here — passing through a landscape empty of meaning for him, lost here. He couldn't shake the feeling that he was traveling through some other space, heading for an abyss, a dark fall into something beyond his comprehension. But then, he'd come up from an abyss. What he had in the middle was only the fact that he was alive, that he was seeing what he was seeing.

He glanced at the man, suddenly wanting talk.

"You like what you do?" Cody asked.

The man didn't seem to hear. He made no move at all. Cody waited for a moment, and then he gave it up and turned back to the fields outside the window.

Then the man took a breath, a slow, contemplative sound. " 'Like' probably isn't the right word," he said. He opened his eyes, smiling quietly. "It's more of a passion with me." He stirred slightly, leaning forward. "What do you see out there?" he asked.

There was no easy answer to that. The sky — not so much seeing as feeling — and the dirt in the fields and the stubble. And color, an incredible richness of quiet color — no single, unmixed color anywhere. And the shadows of the rocks and stubble and trees, falling into patterns, crossing the bright reality of the more tangible things.

"I don't know," Cody said. "I see everything." And then he tried to explain it, all of it, amazed at himself for talking so much, for seeing so much, as though he'd only just opened his eyes for the first time, and he couldn't keep quiet about it.

"Now," the man said. "How much of it do you understand?"

Cody was still looking. "None of it," he said, finally.

"Good," the man said, sounding satisfied. "Very good."

Cody felt unaccountably happy.

"Find something round. Round like a cylinder," the man directed.

It wasn't hard. "Okay," Cody said.

"You're sure it's round."

"Yeah," Cody said, half laughing. *You think I'm an idiot?*

"Okay. What makes you so sure the thing is round? How do you know it's round?"

And Cody had no answer for that. He didn't know. He knew the thing was round. Of course he knew it. But he didn't know how he knew it. He sat for a moment, understanding that he *was* an idiot. "I don't know," he said, finally. "How do I know?"

"You want to know?"

"Yeah, I want to know," Cody said, almost impatient.

The man grinned at him. "Okay. Keep looking at something that has that same shape, okay? You got a tree or something you can look at for a minute? Okay, now *look* at it. There should be a highlight there, on the sunside. A strip of color that's lighter than the rest. You see it?"

Cody nodded.

"And then there's a shadow, the darkest area, not quite opposite the highlight."

"I see it," Cody said.

"Your eyes see those two aspects of the thing, and your brain understands from them that the thing is round. That's why there's depth in a good photograph, because you use the light and the absence of light — or the colors that represent them — to make the brain understand. All shadow on something, and you've got a flat thing, no depth. It's the same with all light — all highlight, and you still have no depth. You need both. In the right proportion."

Cody was absorbed in what he was trying to see. And then, suddenly, he *understood*. As if he'd never had a thought in his life, this one exploded inside him, a flash of explosive insight. Something new out of something old. Something from outside of himself, like lightning, suddenly illuminating something in the dark inside.

He nodded slowly, a little short of breath, looking for the pattern in other places and finding it. "I can see it," Cody said, forgetting to be careful, letting the pleasure sound in his own voice.

"Good," the man said. And then he offered Cody his hand. "I'm John Hanks," he said, as if he were speaking to another man.

Cody took the hand. "Cody McClellan," he said.

"You have a good eye, McClellan," John said, sitting back. "What did you do to it?"

Cody looked at him, not understanding. John pointed to a place beside his own eye. "What did you do to it?" he asked again.

34

Cody touched his own face. The skin was rough and knotted beside his eye. And then he remembered. He'd never cleaned the blood off. Instantly, he felt uneasy.

"I was in a fight," he said. He said it with finality.

John nodded. "You know, last night, I didn't think you were going to stay on the bus. You almost got off."

"It was too late," Cody murmured. Last night, coming to his senses, finding himself on a bus with most of his money gone. Almost gave it up, then. But the driver started the engine and closed the doors up tight, and Cody let that be the decision. Too late for second thoughts.

Cody turned around and looked at John. "You weren't sitting next to me last night," he said. He was starting to get a strange feeling.

"I was a couple of rows back," John said.

"Oh, really. So, why'd you move?" Cody shut down his face, pulling back. Suddenly, he didn't like the situation.

John shrugged. "I can see better out this side of the bus."

And then, casually, all the time looking past Cody and out into the wide world, John said, "Being a photographer is kind of a weird thing. There are people who don't think it's an art. They think of it as mechanics, as chemistry. And it's true, you know —those are the tools we use. But that's not what photography *is*. It's a communication, just like every other art form. It's an understanding of the way everything is so fragile—the faces, the moments in time. A good photographer tends to see more deeply than most people, and his timing is almost instinctive— it's a matter of seeing in a moment, or in a thing, or in a face, the whole story. And then being able to get what you see down on the paper so other people can see it."

He nudged the bag with his foot. "I believe it's a gift, that kind of sight. You have to be aware of light and color and texture. But most of all, to the human condition. Both to the ones you see, and the ones who'll be looking."

"So? There's a point to this?"

John looked at Cody. "I think you could do it."

"Do what?" Cody asked.

"I think you'd be good with a camera."

"And you could tell that last night from a few rows back, right?" Cody said, icy now, anything but vulnerable. "What're you selling, man?" It was kind of a bitter thing, having the relationship sour on him that way.

"What do you mean?" John asked him. All innocence.

"I mean, what's the point. You want something from me?"

John was looking at him, half smiling, like he was trying to figure him out.

"What's the matter?" John asked. "You can't take a compliment?"

"That wasn't a compliment."

"Oh, no?"

"No."

"You want to tell me what it was?" John asked.

Cody turned his face away. "It was a line, man," he said. And what was it supposed to get him?

"It was a compliment, *man*," John said to him. "Not everybody who's nice to you wants to *buy* you, man."

"So, why'd you move over here?" Cody said, annoyed more than anything, annoyed and suspicious.

"Aren't *we* defensive?" John said. Cody turned his face away, staring out of the window at things he wasn't seeing. And John said, "What made you so scared of life?"

Cody turned around and stared at him. "You got a lot of nerve, you know?" he said.

"Am I wrong?" John asked, serenely.

"Why'd you move over here?" Cody asked him again. Insisting.

"Because I thought you were interesting. Okay? Because I thought I'd talk to you, and maybe see what you were. You had this *Photography*—why shouldn't I assume we could talk? Why does anybody want to talk to anybody?" He made an exasperated sound. "You *are* a New York kid." And then it was like, thinking about it made him mad. "You don't have to be so hard core defensive, kid. You make yourself into a walking stereotype, and then you're going to get ticked because somebody reacts to it?"

"You don't know anything about me," Cody said.

"Ah," John said. He leaned down and refastened one of the buckles on his bag. "Well, that's right," he said. "I don't know your story." He shifted the bag, poking at it with his foot. "You want me to do a little magic here, Dr. Privacy? Okay, we'll do a little mind reading." He closed his eyes and held his hands up, palms out. "Oh, yeah—" he said, grinning, "you do lousy in school, right?" And then he said, "Because that's the way you *want* it. Keep 'em guessing. And, of course, they're always on your back. Am I right? But everybody's always telling you how bright you are, right? And they're always saying, 'If you'd just *try*.' Am I close? It's nice, isn't it? Getting all that attention."

"Really," Cody said coldly.

"And you can't stand somebody telling you what you *could* do, because that threatens you. I mean, what if you try, and then you can't cut it? Maybe you don't believe you can."

"What are you, a psychologist?" Cody said.

"Am I wrong?" John asked, quietly.

Cody shrugged again.

"You're just not the only one, that's all," John said.

Cody snorted. He sat there, staring out of the window. Somehow, John's being such a smart mouth had made him feel easier.

"So, I suppose you went through the same thing, right?" he said.

"Not really," John said, sounding satisfied with himself.

"So," Cody said, and then he let himself smile.

John laughed. "You look like the devil, McClellan, but you see like an angel," he said.

"Really," Cody said.

"It's the truth. There's a poem that says, 'No man is an island unto himself.' And that's the truth, too. I just thought you looked like somebody who needed somebody to talk to." He parted his hands. "And I needed somebody to talk to, too. Is that a crime? Just two people, passing the time."

And he was supposed to stay mad after that?

"And it just happens, we have something in common," John finished. "There aren't that many people who ever see things the way we do. It's like finding a brother."

Cody held up a warning finger. "You're gushing," Cody said. "Don't do that." He was smiling now, won over and not denying it. "Can I see your camera?" he asked.

"I thought you'd never ask," John said, grinning, leaning over to unzip the bag.

"You study this in college?" Cody asked him.

John pulled a beautiful black camera out of the bag, handling it with a careless kind of reverence. He was still grinning. "I was an anthropology major, actually. But the two things seemed to fit together *very* nicely so . . ." He pulled the lens cap off the front of the camera, ran a piece of tissue over the lens, and then handed the whole thing to Cody.

"This is incredible," Cody said reverently, hefting the lovely thing and holding it up to his eye.

"The tool of the artist," John said. "Look through it." Cody did. "It makes you an oracle. You can see through people with

37

it. You can show a thing the way it really is. Or the way it should be. But if you want to see what's *incredible*, you've got to see what goes on in*side* this little hummer."

Cody reluctantly handed the camera back over. John accepted it gently and disengaged the lens.

From that time until late in the morning, John talked photography. He showed Cody how the camera worked; he told him theories of light; he even loosened up about the places he'd been and the things he'd shot. And then, before Cody'd learned enough to ask intelligent questions, the bus stopped at a tiny hamlet in the middle of a dark pine woods.

"Home, already," John said, surprised. "You're good company, McClellan." He pulled the bag over against his feet and quickly packed up the camera.

"Short stop," the driver warned.

John stood up, slinging the bag over his shoulder. He stuck out his hand and Cody shook it. "One more minute," John called to the driver.

"I got a schedule," the man said.

John opened a little pocket on the bag and pulled out a card. He held it out to Cody. "Let me know what happens," he said. "Send me some pictures."

Then he was gone. Cody watched through the window. There was a small crowd of people waiting, and it swallowed John up the moment he stepped out of the bus. They bore him away to a dark blue station wagon, and the bus began to move out onto the road. Cody looked back as long as he could, till the trees were all he could see, and then he looked down at the card in his hand. *John Hanks,* it said. *Freelance.* There was a New York address. Cody held it for a moment, and then stuck it deep down inside his bundle. The last thing Cody saw of that town was a white clapboard church, bright against the dark trees behind it.

The bus made another stop a little later, just after noon. This was a bigger town, a lunch stop. Cody got off to get something to eat. There were a lot of people waiting around in the station; Cody wondered if they were all waiting for this bus, if the bus would fill up. He wasn't excited about the idea of having to sit next to somebody new just now. He reboarded with sandwiches in hand, unwilling to give up his window seat.

It was a while before the rest of the group got back on. There were a few new people but not enough to fill up the bus.

One older lady came down the aisle almost hand-over-hand, looking for a seat. She paused at Cody's row, gave him one cursory glance, and moved on. It was so matter of fact; no nice old lady is going to sit next to any punk kid in a crummy beat-up jacket.

It wasn't even like he'd *wanted* her to sit there by him; she'd probably talk too much, anyway.

But he didn't like being passed up like that. And he was stung.

What was worse, he was missing John Hanks.

4

It was a long, hot, endless afternoon. They'd gotten down into a flatter country now, not so much to look at—telephone poles whipping by in rhythm, the lines tracing lazy scallops against the thin blue of the sky.

Half a slow lifetime later, the sun began to go down. Cody watched it, his face pressed against the window, trying to keep in his mind every word John had said.

The light was changing, rotating, spinning shadows—turning in Cody's mind like something lovely held up to a window, something held carefully in the hand. Every change in the shadows changed the shape of the world—the shape of things Cody had thought he'd known past having to learn—and now he felt like an infant with new eyes.

The bus stopped again just at dusk, a small town, a dinner stop. Cody sat alone at a tiny formica-topped table, eating a simple sandwich, scandalized at the price of it. The station was a small place, darkly paneled, with a jukebox in the corner and stuffed fish hanging on the walls. There was a counter with stools, an Olympia clock on the dark wall above it—the kind with the plastic waterfall on its face—and shadowy pinball machines in the far corner.

He rested his elbows on the table, wondering how a person could get so worn out just sitting all day, his body humming as if the bus was still underneath him. Eyes half closed, he floated in the noise of the people around him, the murmur of voices, the music, the rich sound of the grill.

There were colors in the room Cody had no names for, reds more brown than red, blues that ran to gray. He felt the texture of the room and the darkness and the sound, and he wondered how John would get all this into a picture.

Boarding call.

The screen door slammed behind the driver, and people began to rustle around, eating the last of their dinners, gathering their things up. Cody picked up his pillowcase and stepped out of the building. The air had cooled off, and he shivered, standing in the smoky amber cone of the station's single parking lot light, staring out into the huge and uncompromising darkness of the rural night.

He looked up and saw a hint of stars.

He glanced at the bus, squatting there in the skirts of the shadow, and then he wandered away from it, leaving the sanity of the light for the unnameable blackness beyond. He didn't go far—a few yards down the road—but it was like stepping off into space, worse than that expanse of morning sky, now not even a horizon to judge distance by—darkness, totally without limit.

He threw his head back. An immense dome of indigo, spangled with points of frozen fire—near or far, far away, he couldn't have told—but present they were, the million stars, more of them than he'd ever dreamed, and real—and he felt the empty distance between himself and their places, felt he was falling up into it.

He shivered, all of a sudden dizzy and more than a little disturbed.

"Coming?"

The bus driver was standing beside the bus, peering out after Cody. A bit of earth.

"Thanks," Cody called. Without looking up again, he trotted back to the bus.

The passengers were fussing around in their places, arranging things for the long night's drive. Cody found his old seat waiting, nobody next to it. He pulled his jacket on and held his bundle in his lap. The engine started, doors closed with a hydraulic sigh, and the bus pulled away onto the dark road.

He nestled down, shoulder against the body of the bus, and closed his eyes, wishing he'd looked at the clock before he left the station. He was gritty and weary, and the steady thrumming of the engine made him heavy in his mind.

He drifted between sleeping and waking for a while. Then his back was cramped, so he sat up, and crammed his bundle behind him, feeling the cold in his legs—they ached, and it made him restless and uncomfortable. There was a murmur of soft voices somewhere behind, nothing else but engine drone and quiet. A lady across the aisle had her reading light on. Cody sighed and turned his face to his window. There was nothing to see out there now, nothing but the reflection of his own face in the glass.

The face in the window was nothing but highlight and shadow, no detail. The eyes were lost in deep pools of dark, the cheekbones under them stark and sharp. It was a harsh face he saw there, and cold—almost cruel. For a moment, as tired as he was, and as fuzzy-brained, the image scared him.

But this is not my face, he thought. *It's just a trick of the light.*

The reflection stared back at him, unchanged by the protest.

He started thinking about the old lady who'd passed him up that afternoon—wondering what she'd seen to make her so sure she wouldn't like him. And those people in the station back in New York, what had been in their faces, looking at his?

Maybe it's more your face than you know.

"No," he whispered to the window glass. "You're not what I am."

But Parker had been saying to him—*doesn't matter what you are. People not going to see beyond what you show them. Most just can't do better than that.*

He shifted in his seat, still cold.

And it's just possible, the voice inside him went on, *the people know more about you by looking than you know about yourself. Maybe there's really nothing inside you. Maybe you're really empty after all.*

His heart jerked back from the thought. He rested his cheek against the seat, shivering.

All right, there were rules he followed, strictures he kept. Simple things. *You don't count on anything, you never get dis-*

41

appointed. And that was true. *You don't trust anybody, you don't get hurt; you don't care about anything, you don't get hurt. You don't let anybody know anything, because privacy is safety. Privacy is control.* All true. All absolutely true. They kept him away from people, okay. There's a price for everything.

Good rules. Good walls. And that face—the cold one. It was just part of the privacy—the face of the wall, blank and smooth with no toe holds. Because he knew what would happen if somebody should somehow slip past—and that was something he just could not afford.

He was too near bankrupt. But not empty. Not yet. And not cruel—never that.

He dragged his bundle back onto his lap and dug around inside it for the picture. He found it, pulled it free, and tilted it towards the light, squinting. *This is a nice little family. They're not like you. Look at those children. Look at that mother. What do you think they're going to do when they get a good look at you?*

For a moment, he was scared—to the depths of his stomach, he was scared. Tough kid who didn't know the difference between New York City and New York state. Stupid kid. Ignorant. *Streetwise with no street, eh? And where you headed? Another planet.*

So what did he expect to happen? He was going to march up there, knock on the door, and these people were going to throw open their arms and ask him to stay? Was he crazy?

Sure. You with the empty face. Come live with us. Come live with our children. Sure—we can see right through you. Never mind, you look like you could kill somebody and walk away, grinning. Never mind it's going to mean another mouth to feed and another body to clean up after.

This is not happening, man.

No job. No place, anymore.

You're lost in space, buddy.

He touched his uncle's face with the tip of a finger.

We're tough. We'll make it. Whatever comes—we'll make it. Very tough.

He glanced at his reflection again. Very tough. *Right.* A trick of the light.

He put his hand across the place on his wrist, the place his mama had touched. His eyes burned. He took a long, slow breath, half inclined to think she'd been right. There were always options. His heart hung in him like a stone.

He shoved the picture back into the bundle and crammed the whole thing in the space between the seat and the window. He rested his head against it, drawing up his legs as best he could against the cold.

One thing at a time, he told himself. *You don't know what's going to happen. No use guessing. You don't know half enough to guess. Maybe it'll work out. Maybe.*

Maybe it won't.

The lady across the aisle turned off her light, and the face in the window disappeared.

Cody closed his eyes and tried to get some sleep.

The next morning there was rain on the windows. Cody rubbed his face with his hands, trying to wake himself up. The bus had stopped. "Coffee and donuts," the driver was telling them. Cody sat up and tried to work out the kinks in his back.

Three more days of this.

One more day sounded impossible.

Rain all day. And on into the night.

Very chilly.

A million shades of gray.

He was tired of being cold. Late in the afternoon, he gave up on the world outside and pulled out the magazine, flipping on his reading light. He read the whole magazine, cover to cover—every word, down to the ads. He pieced together the technical stuff, going on what John had showed him.

The next morning, he woke up with the magazine still in his lap.

When he looked out the window, he saw plains stretched out flat and forever—fields ahead and on either side—and the bus was following a road that never changed, not all day. Just the stops at quiet little towns, short stops and more road.

Cody had no idea where he was. He'd lost track of how many days he'd been sitting in this seat.

And then the sun came out, and it got hot.

And it got hotter. And muggy.

And then the sun finally began to go down, taking its time until it finally slid the last little way and disappeared below the horizon, taking the light and the heat with it.

Cody screwed one eye open against the brightness of the early morning, sight bleary from the long, cramped night. His neck hurt, and the small of his back ached. He couldn't understand what he was seeing out of the window—and when it

43

finally did come into focus, he threw himself back away from the window — a reflex.

There was a solid wall of rock outside the window — not ten feet away from the side of the bus.

"Ex*cuse* me," a voice beside him said.

Cody swung around, surprised. Somebody finally sitting in the seat next to him, a skinny man, not too clean — trucking hat and cowboy boots. Reeking of cigarette smoke. He nodded slightly at Cody.

"Sorry," Cody said, settling himself back in his own seat, checking his belongings, a little more awake now, a little crowded.

Then he stole another look out of the window.

A mountain. Haven't you ever seen a mountain?

Pictures. Movies.

Not the same, eh?

Not the same.

Cody pressed his face to the glass, straining to look up. He knew his mouth was hanging open, but he didn't care. He'd seen buildings this tall before — it was the raw, solid rock that made this different, the *mass* of it.

The walls outside fell away, one mountain fading into the next, a little gully and a stream between.

They drove through mountains all that day, every so often breaking out into high, green valleys, then plunging again between the shoulders of more craggy hills, always heading up.

And then the sky opened up again, late in the afternoon — a big valley that spread itself wide. Trees and houses — a river. A Seven-Eleven. A big, old red barn like something out of a painting, big baskets of fruit out in front, and people buying.

More houses. Apartments. An intersection. Then down into the town. The driver called out the stop. Cody's stop. His stomach screwed itself into a tight little ball.

You didn't plan this very well.

A high school on the right. More trees — big old houses set back on a tree-lined street. Then little stores, tiny ones — no more than two stories — crowded along the sidewalk on either side.

This stupid trick is going to cost you.

The man next to him leaned over and picked up a bag.

Just how much do you think you can afford to lose?

The bus turned a corner, went down between a bank and a line of neat little brick houses, pulled up at the station, and stopped.

And that was it.

"This is you," the driver said, looking back at Cody.

Cody picked up his pillowcase and got off the bus.

The sun bore down in the parking lot.

Cody stood beside the bus.

The driver had opened up the baggage bay, and there were people milling around, meeting each other, looking for their bags. Women's voices, high and pleased, some hugging. There were a few people alone like Cody. But they knew what they were doing, going about their business.

Cody was a little light-headed.

The bus driver looked at Cody over his shoulder as he slammed the bay. He brushed his hands against his pants. "Good luck, kid," he said. And then he walked back towards the front of the bus.

"Thanks," Cody murmured, cold all over, standing in the sun.

The doors of the bus hissed shut, and the engine roared as the driver put it into gear and began to pull out. Cody stepped away. It was weird, hearing those sounds from the outside of the bus.

And then it was quiet. The bus pulled off down the street and went around a corner. Gone. All the people had left the parking lot.

Only Cody, standing there.

He looked around. Turned around once, slowly, full circle. *So, what do we do now?*

"Excuse me, do I have to go far to get to this place?"

The man behind the counter in the terminal looked up from his magazine and took the envelope Cody handed down. He looked at Cody and smiled.

5

"Not that far. *Right,*" Cody said, disgusted. He dropped his bundle on the grass and ran his fingers through his hair.

He was standing on a corner, forty-five minutes' uphill walk from that station, legs aching, back aching, hungry enough to die, the hot September sun beating down on his head like a punishment.

Fine. I thought I looked bad before.

He wiped the sweat off of his forehead with the sleeve of his T-shirt and looked around. Hunger or nerves—mild nausea, anyway—not much, just enough to make him slightly sloppy in the knees.

He looked up at the street sign, down at the envelope, up at the street sign again, then squinted down the street. "It's down there," he murmured. "About a block away." And his heart started hammering in his chest.

He picked up his bundle, swung it wearily over his shoulder, and started down the sidewalk. Tree-lined sidewalks, nice houses—very quiet neighborhood. The street was wide here, almost empty. He was glad for the trees; they kept the sun off. But the neighborhood—he'd never been in a neighborhood like this, graceful, full of quiet money.

The sidewalks were broad, set away from the street curb by wide stretches of sweet green grass, the lawns rolling up and away gently on the other side, deep green and cool, so that each and every house had its own little private park around it.

There were neat little walkways that came up two or three steps from the sidewalk and then meandered along up to the front porches of the houses. Big houses—Cody was thinking they were huge houses for just one family each. And there were trees all over the place, old ones with tops like bright green canopies. It was very beautiful. It was calm. Very intimidating.

He went along slowly, watching the numbers on the houses. And so he found his uncle's house.

It sat across the street, a beautiful white house with a steep slate-gray roof, set around with deep green shrubs and the rich, damp-looking grass, everything neat and clean and perfect, more like a picture than a real place. The sunlight came slanting down onto the grass, stained with the leaves. The little front walk was bordered with yellow and orange flowers.

Cody stood for a while under a tree across the street, leaning against the broad trunk, watching the house. His courage was gone. His energy was gone. The moment he'd seen the place, he'd given it up. He stank, he was filthy, he had nothing at all on his side. He didn't belong in a place like this. He couldn't ask them the thing he'd come all the way here to ask. He was defeated by the beauty of the house. And it was only what he'd expected.

So he had a little debate with himself, wondering what he should do next. For a while he thought about going back downtown, looking for a box to crawl into for the night, but the hunger finally made up his mind for him. That and the weariness. He was too tired to walk any more, and he had nothing with him to eat. So really he had no choice. At least he could meet his relatives.

At least there was the chance they might let him stay the night. He wasn't going to ask any more than that. Resigned, he slung the bundle over his shoulder once more and crossed the street slowly, hoping they wouldn't have a dog, hoping they hadn't moved since last Christmas, hoping they wouldn't just throw him out into the street.

He passed under the big trees, crossed the sidewalk, mounted the three steps, and then followed the walk, naked to his soul, hoping no one was watching him from the windows, wondering who he was and what he wanted.

He climbed the stairs up to the porch. He put the bundle down. Before he knocked, he took a long, slow breath, just to steady himself. And then he lifted his hand and knocked on the door.

The late afternoon was very quiet. He turned and looked out over the lawn. There were insects flying around in the last of the golden light, hovering over the lawn in bright shafts of sun. There were no people sitting out on their porches. That seemed a shame to him.

And then the knob turned, and the door came open.

A young boy stood in the opening, peering out from behind the screen door. He looked Cody up and down.

"May I help you?" he asked, politely but doubtfully.

"Is your father here?" Cody asked, wondering just what he would do if he *weren't*.

47

"Yeah," the boy said. "I'll get him."

Cody heaved a sigh, clasped his hands together for warmth, and tried to set his face. Then the door was pulled back further, and the man from the picture was standing there in front of him. The image came all at once—the short, light brown brillo hair, the sweater vest and oxford shirt, the jeans and the hiking boots. Immediately and unaccountably, Cody liked his uncle very much. *Very much.*

And suddenly, he understood how weary he really was.

"What can I do for you?" Erin asked, not unkind, but businesslike.

Cody took another deliberate breath. "My name is Cody McClellan," he said. "I'm your sister Susan's son."

It took a moment before either of them understood what had been said. At the same moment Cody was thinking, *I belong to you,* the surprise hit his uncle's face. Shock. Comprehension. Clear and plain to read. And then there was a brightness in his face, a happiness in his eyes that Cody had never in his life expected to see.

"*Cody,*" Erin said, like he'd known the name all along, like he'd been *waiting* for this. "Please, please come in." The door was opened as wide as it could go, and Cody was drawn inside the house.

"Charlotte!" Erin called. And then to Cody, "Is your mother with you?" Cody hadn't expected that, either. *Stupid,* he thought. *You should have known he'd think that.*

"No, sir," Cody said. "Just me."

"Well," his uncle said, just a little disappointment behind his eyes. "We're glad to have you." The man's voice was warm. So warm that it took Cody totally off guard—almost too much for him. It took everything he had, tired as he was, to keep his lower lip from trembling. He set his face hard, hanging on to his dignity.

"*Char*lotte," Erin called again. Children's faces appeared in a wide doorway off the hall; and then the children themselves, curious, the boys, and the one girl, wide-eyed, looking at him. Then a door opened somewhere and someone else was coming. "I can hardly believe this," Erin was saying. And down the hall came a pretty, dark-haired woman. She was dressed in new jeans and a plaid shirt, and she was wiping her hands on a towel.

"What is it?" she asked. And then she saw Cody and stopped. He saw in her face exactly what he'd expected to see all

48

along. She caught herself quickly, coming a few, slow steps nearer, and offering him a civil smile. But he'd seen her thoughts in her face, the way she sized him up, the instant distaste.

He didn't mind it, really. It was a lot like coming home.

6

It had been one of those rare days for Charlotte, a peaceful one, a successful one—the kind of Saturday that *is* suburbia: the whole family together all day, out working in the yard and doing odd jobs—*almost* no arguments, *almost* full cooperation. The yard was perfect, the windows were clean, and every single person in the family was sunburned and worn out with the work.

After that, hamburgers in the backyard, then baths, and now the kids were all tucked away into the den with a good Saturday night video.

Charlotte was doing the last touch-up on the kitchen, all alone, and—for this isolated moment—at peace with life.

Generally, things had been going very well. The kids were doing well enough in school, everybody and everything was healthy—including Erin's firm. Finally. Not that it hadn't been doing all right before now, but there was a difference between paying the bills and making a living.

So Erin was successful. He deserved it—he was a *good* architect. And something inside Charlotte—the worry thing, the *careful* thing, the how-are-we-going-to-manage, lying-awake-at-night thing—had finally let her go. Well, mostly. Old habits, especially basically *sensible* ones, tend to die hard.

They were doing well enough that they'd finally been able to tear off the back of this old house and put on a new kitchen—

Erin's design, Charlotte's specs—a big old-fashioned country kitchen, lots of oak and used brick in it, greenhouse windows, a good heavy table, and a big hearth on one end of the room. It had turned out to be rather a symbol of the life they'd been building—comfortable and pleasant, strong, orderly, wholesome and traditional, but not all tradition. And Charlotte was satisfied with it, as she was with very few other things, not the least because it made the kitchen work tenable if not completely pleasant.

It had never been easy for her, the ordinary business of running a household. She wasn't terribly domestic, or terribly patient, or terribly happy with herself. She was doing a job that was bearable to her because Erin loved her and was able to let her know it, and because he thought of her as a full partner, and because she loved her children.

Even Mickey. Mickey the problem. It was a ticklish thing, having a twelve-year-old girl who suddenly didn't want anything to do with anybody but her few Very Special friends. She'd turned materialistic on them lately, too—and it was expensive stuff she was after, jeans with the *right* label on them, shirts with the *right* label on them, Reeboks—money Charlotte wouldn't have spent on herself, and certainly wasn't going to be bullied into spending on Mickey. Which meant that things could get nasty. And when Mickey wanted to get nasty, she could do it up royally.

Charlotte shook her head, thinking about it, rinsing the last of the soap off her hands.

Erin called her. She pulled the dish towel off of its little hook and took one more look around the room. At least tomorrow morning when she came in here to get breakfast before church the place would be clean.

Erin called her again, a cheerful urgency in his voice. She wondered what was so important. Maybe a surprise; that would be nice. More likely, somebody had fallen down the stairs.

She pushed open the kitchen door and went down the hall, drying her hands on the towel.

The entire family was crowded into the front hall, the front door standing open. Visitors, obviously. She was a little too tired for visitors, a little too jealous of the quiet evening she'd planned.

Erin was beaming, looking very much like he'd just opened up a birthday present or something. There was a dark smell in the room, like old cigarettes. Erin stepped aside. And Charlotte stopped dead in her tracks.

50

There was this *person* standing beside Erin. A boy—a dirty, sick-looking, sullen-faced, ratty, punk-haired boy in clothes that looked as though they could use a good burning. She wondered what a kid like that was doing in this neighborhood, what he could be selling, and why in the sweet name of heaven Erin had actually asked him into the house. Still, she caught herself and came a little closer, trying to keep her face polite.

And Erin was *still* beaming.

Of course he was. Of course he was. The man was the most irritatingly *simple*, Christian person she'd ever *known*.

"This is *Cody*," Erin said, and she got the distinct impression the name was supposed to mean something to her. She felt a little stubborn, suddenly, a little resentful, because she knew that whatever was going on here—and there *was* something going on—it was going to cost her something.

"My sister Susan's son," Erin went on, explaining.

Charlotte's mental jaw dropped—Susan, the near legendary, the vanishing sister; Susan, the classic emotional black hole; Susan, who put her entire family through hell every day for nearly twenty years without batting an eye—and now, she had a son? And he was *here? Now?*

The question was, what did he want? That was the question she felt on her face, greeting him without Erin's enthusiasm, looking him over from the standpoint of this new information.

Shadowed smudges around his eyes, the horrible hair—he reeked of cigarette smoke. And that look on his face—cold and hard. He answered her greeting with a half smile anybody would have called insolent, *knowing.* He looked like a drug dealer. He looked like somebody who'd spent a lot of time lying in gutters. Or making trouble.

"Can you stay with us tonight?" Erin was asking. Of course, he would ask that. He would have asked *any*body; this was his nephew—he *had* to ask. But he could have had the decency to check with his *wife* first.

The boy gave her an appraising look, and then he turned to Erin and said, "Thank you. I'm not sure what I'm going to do."

The quiet of his voice took her by surprise. She hadn't expected him to be articulate.

"Well, you've got to be hungry," Erin said.

Charlotte was a very honest woman. She knew she didn't *want* to feed this person; she didn't *want* to mess up the kitchen again; she wouldn't have wanted *any* company this evening, let alone somebody who looked like he made a living making drugs in a basement somewhere. But most of all, she didn't want to

51

feel any of these things. She was ashamed. She understood that she was being selfish and unkind.

But her conscience couldn't argue her out of her reluctance. And guilt, if anything, only aggravated the feeling. It always seemed so easy for Erin—doing the right thing, the humane thing—and it was so hard for her. Maybe because she was the one who always ended up doing the work.

Well, the boy was hungry. He didn't even have to say so; she could tell.

"Okay," Charlotte said to the children. If she couldn't welcome him with her heart, at least she could feed him. "You guys get back in there and watch your movie." Erin was steering his nephew down the hall towards the kitchen, slapping him on the shoulder, saying, "I can't believe it. It's so *good* to see you."

"But, Mom," Sawyer, the nine-year-old was saying, "Can't I just . . ." watching his dad's back longingly. Mickey was lingering, too—staring after them as they disappeared into the shadows of the hall.

"Just get back in there," she hissed, giving them the eye so they'd understand she meant what she said. They went, but not very gracefully. She sighed. The last thing she needed was a bunch of little kids in there with that boy. The thought of it made her very nervous. She took a moment to settle herself, and then she followed Erin to the kitchen.

"We've got fried chicken . . ." Erin was doing an inventory of the fridge, ". . . mashed potatoes . . ." left over from last night. "What's in here? Naw. You won't want that. How about some salad . . ."

"Anything would be fine," the boy said. He was standing by the table, and he sounded slightly embarrassed.

"All right," Erin said, and he hauled out the plate of chicken.

"I'll do it," Charlotte said to him, taking the plate out of his hand and giving him a little shove towards the table. "You talk to your nephew."

"Sit down," Erin said heartily, pulling out a chair, and then one for himself. The boy put down what he'd been carrying—it looked like a lumpy pillowcase—and more or less sank into the chair. Immediately, he seemed to come slightly apart, filling the chair as if he'd been needing to sit down. Then he pulled himself upright, and she got the distinct impression he was *not* going to let them know he was tired. Then he yawned, and with an air of resignation, rubbed at his eyes with the palms of his hands.

Charlotte put the chicken into the microwave. She found the bowl of potatoes and pulled out several small plastic containers, some of vegetables, one of gravy.

"So, how did you get here?" Erin asked.

Charlotte opened the beans and emptied them into a bowl.

"I took the bus," the boy said.

She did the same with the corn. She put both of the bowls in the microwave with the chicken, and then stood in front of it with her hands on her hips, waiting. *Well*, she thought. *At least for once we'll use up the leftovers before they rot.*

"And how long did it take?" Erin asked. It was rather a one-sided conversation, but Erin was doing very well, keeping a lot of energy in it.

"Several days," the boy answered, his voice low, a little ragged.

"Whoo—" Erin said, "I'll bet that took it out of you."

Charlotte didn't hear what the boy said to that. She was digging around in the refrigerator for things that would make a salad. She carried the lettuce and the scallions and the celery over to the sink and got out the cutting board.

"So," Erin said, his voice gentle, the way it was when he felt like one of the kids needed to talk, "where are you headed?"

There was a tiny silence. And then came the lie: "I thought I'd go out to the west coast and stay with my dad for a while."

He'd said it with such lightness. She turned around and looked at the two of them. The boy had slumped casually back into the chair. It struck her that the lie had been told with consummate skill—just solid enough that it could have been real, but too transparent to pass without question. He didn't want them to believe it.

"Really," Erin said. "Your dad live in L.A.?" Charlotte smiled. The boy was going to have to be careful with Erin. Erin was too willing to believe what people told him.

"Yeah," the boy said, as if L.A. sounded as good as anything.

Erin nodded. The bell on the microwave went off.

"So, you decided to leave New York," Erin said, running out of inspiration.

Charlotte pulled the chicken and the vegetables out of the oven and shoved in the potatoes.

"Yeah, well," the boy said, quietly. "Sometimes you need a change of scenery." And Charlotte began to wonder what it was he was running away from.

53

"Yes, well, that can help," Erin said, talking like a man who was not sure where reality lay.

Charlotte put a plate out on the counter, and began to fill it up.

"So, how's your mother?" Erin asked. Charlotte paused, the head of lettuce in her hands. Erin had never given up on his sister. He was just as stubborn as she was, in his own way. Every year, he sent a Christmas card to New York. There had never been an answer. Never.

Now Charlotte was afraid of what Erin was going to hear. Until this moment, he'd been able to believe whatever he wanted about Susan, good things, hopeful things. She didn't want him hurt. There wasn't enough energy left in this house today to handle Erin's kind of quiet grief.

"Ummm," the boy said, shrugging. And then, again with the lightness, "She's fine."

Charlotte sighed. It was another lie. But Erin could still believe what he wanted to; this lie hadn't been quite as transparent. If he'd been a different kind of kid, she would have chalked up this particular lie as a sensitive gesture.

"Good," Erin said. "Good." And then he lapsed into his own thoughts.

The potatoes came out of the microwave, and Charlotte dropped a mound of them on the plate. "What do you want to drink?" she asked, filling in the silence.

"Anything, thank you," the boy said, without looking up. And then, "Not coffee, please."

"Too much caffeine," Erin murmured in agreement. "Keep you awake."

"Or maybe I should," the boy said, having evidently just remembered something.

"Milk?" she asked, offering what she had. "Water?"

"Milk, thank you," he said, after a moment.

Well, you couldn't fault his manners. And you couldn't fault the way he spoke. Every time he talked, he surprised her. The way he looked, you expected grunts. But then, he opened his mouth and out came this almost cultured-sounding Eastern-ish voice.

"I really wish you'd stay the night," Erin said. "It's kind of late to be going anywhere. Unless you already have plans."

She poured the milk, and then picked up the plate and ferried it all over to the table. She put it down in front of the boy. She was pleased with the plate; the steam was still coming off the potatoes and gravy, and there was butter melting on the corn.

The boy sighed, looking down at the plate with his hands in his lap.

Charlotte put a fork and a knife beside the plate.

"I don't have any plans," the boy said wearily, resignedly, his hands still in his lap. And it struck her then that he might not *want* to be staying.

"Great," Erin said.

Just great, Charlotte thought, but wondering, now.

The boy hadn't made one move towards his silverware.

"Is there something wrong with the food?" She hadn't meant to sound quite so irritated, but she was tired, and he was still sitting there, just looking down at his plate.

He looked up at her, and it was clear nothing in her tone had escaped him. "It looks very good," he said, quietly. The dark circles around his eyes took her down a little. He seemed very tired, spiritless. "It looks wonderful. Thank you."

"But you're not eating it," she pointed out. She could tell, even without looking at him, that Erin was giving her that puzzled, almost disappointed look.

The boy sighed and looked at Erin. "Actually," he said, all of the lightness gone from the voice, "I'm probably too tired to eat it."

"Well, you sure don't need people watching you eat," Erin said, standing up. The boy didn't argue. "Let's get things settled," Erin said to Charlotte, and then he came around the table, putting one hand on her shoulder, steering her out through the door.

"Don't," she said, out of earshot. She moved her shoulder and his hand fell away.

"You're mad," he said.

She folded her arms and started slowly down the hall. "Not really," she said, although she hated in the worst way being *steered*.

"Did you want me to send him away?" Erin asked.

She stopped, arms still folded. "I'm going to spend the whole night wondering if he's going to murder us."

"Come on," he said gently. "He's just a tired, hungry kid."

"On his way to California," she said, just to remind him in case he should start having other ideas.

"Maybe," Erin said. And that's when she knew he already *did* have other ideas.

"No," she said, poking him in the chest. "Forget it. One night with that kid in the house is more than enough. You don't know where he's been. You don't know who he is, or what kind of things he does, or what kind of trouble he's been in. We've got problems enough keeping our own kids from killing each other. There's no way I'm going to have this kid in my house more than one night."

Erin gave her that sad look.

"It wouldn't be fair to our kids," she said. "School's just started. I'm already stressed out as it is. I don't have the time or the energy to take care of a guest right now. He wants to go live with his father. Let him. Get his address and you can write."

Still the sad look. Sad with disappointment mixed in. She felt trapped, and it made her angry.

"He's my nephew," Erin said, the quiet voice. No reproach in the tone, and that made it reproach enough.

"He's Susan's son," she said. "Where's Susan?"

Erin put his hands out. Does it matter? he was saying.

She pointed at the kitchen. "I'm scared of that boy," she said.

"I don't think you need to be," he said. "Let's just play it by ear, all right? We'll just let him stay the night — or, if you want, I'll just drive him to a motel. I really don't think he's going to make any kind of trouble tonight. It looks to me like he can barely keep his eyes open. But it's up to you." *Sure it is.* "What do you want me to do? I'll take him to a motel if you want me to."

Of course she wanted him to. Of course, she wasn't going to say so. As if it hadn't been decided the moment Erin had opened the front door.

"What if he does drugs?" she asked.

"He's not going to do them tonight," Erin said, patiently.

"Where am I going to put him?"

"In the boys' room."

"I am not going to have my boys stay the night in the same room with a stranger," she said.

"The boys can sleep on the floor in our room," Erin said. All thought out. She'd already thought it all out herself, knowing she was going to lose in the end, but this was part of the ritual — the protest, the reassurance.

"All right," Erin said. "So, what do we do?"

"You go back in there," she directed, "and you keep an eye on that kid. *I'll* move the boys."

"All right," he said, a little more cheerful. He started back down towards the kitchen. "Charlotte," he said, turning.

She waited for what he had to say.

"Don't worry."

She shook her head and turned away down the hall towards the stairs.

"So, how ya doin'?" she heard him say as the kitchen door closed behind him.

It didn't take long to get things arranged: a clean pillow on the bottom bunk in the boys' room; the little boys' pillows, pajamas, and blankets transported to hers. She rolled the sleeping bags out onto the carpet at the foot of her bed, put the pillows down on them carefully, trying to avoid the inevitable fight later as to who would get which bag.

And after all that could be done had been done, she went back down to the kitchen. The room was empty. The table and the counters, however—they were not empty. They were still full of dirty plates and bowls and silverware.

And so it begins, she thought angrily, lifting the plate and its accoutrements off the table. *And it's* only *the beginning.*

Because, she thought as she turned the water on hard and let it run till it got good and hot, *Erin is going to end up keeping this boy here another night at least. And probably more*—I'll end up cleaning up after him for the next week. And then she stopped what she was doing, realizing that Erin had a heavy week this week, realizing that after Erin made the invitation—which he was going to do—there wouldn't be anybody in the house to honor it but Charlotte and the baby.

She scrubbed at the plate, mad at Erin for something he hadn't even done yet. *Just like a man,* she thought. *Say yes and then leave before the work begins.*

The door opened and Erin came back in the room. He didn't say anything. He just watched her for a moment and started puttering around, making little forays at cleaning off the table.

"I was going to do that," he said finally, meaning the dishes, straightening up and looking at her.

She didn't answer. She opened the dishwasher, letting the door fall just a little too hard.

She dropped the plate down into a slot on the rack, and then hauled the top rack out and put the glass in it. She dropped the silverware into its basket, all without a word, but with a certain amount of negative energy.

She started rinsing out the bowls.

"Why don't you let me finish?" he asked, moving to take a bowl out of her hand, a bowl she had no intention of relinquishing.

It was a stalemate. And then the kitchen door swung open and Sawyer, their oldest son, the nine-year-old, came in.

"Nothing else to eat," Charlotte warned him severely.

He stood there by the door, giving her a reproachful look, and then he turned to his father. "Hey, Dad?" he said. "Is that kid really our cousin?"

"He is," Erin said. She felt a little guilty at the sound of Erin's voice. He'd said it a mite defensively, as if he were just waiting for somebody else to say something uncharitable.

"Well, he's asleep."

"Oh, yeah?" Erin asked.

"He just sat down in the recliner, and a second later, I looked at him, and he was asleep.

Erin looked at Charlotte. *What did I tell you?* his eyes were saying. "I'll go look after him." Erin dropped his dishrag with some degree of triumph. He put his hand on Sawyer's shoulder and started steering him out of the kitchen. *Out of the direct line of his mother's wrath,* Charlotte thought.

And then the door swung shut behind them.

All right, she thought, *so he probably won't be making any trouble here tonight.* And then she thought about that last look in the boy's eyes, the emptiness. She didn't like it. It just made her feel guiltier. *Maybe it won't be so bad,* she thought, in the moment before she realized — there she was — the whole kitchen and the whole mess all to herself again.

"*Hey*—" A loud whisper.

Charlotte was just hanging up the dish towel for what was — hopefully — the last time. Erin startled her.

"What?" she asked, not much in the mood for games.

"I want you to see something," he said, very quietly, leaning around the door, just his head in the room. He looked thoughtful, disturbed.

"Why are you whispering?" she asked him.

Then he looked a little sheepish. "Can you come upstairs?"

She wiped her hands once more, not because it was necessary. "In a minute," she said.

"Come up," he said, and he disappeared.

She sighed. She did as he asked, but she took her time about it — one last inspection of the kitchen, lights out, down the hall to check the kids, putter around in the hallway, all the time feeling guilty for being so ornery. Up the stairs at last.

He was waiting patiently at the top. He led her down the hall to the boys' room, eased the door open, and slipped inside.

Wonderful, she thought. *I wonder what we're going to get to see.*

He turned Sawyer's desk lamp on, a brilliant little star of light, and then turned back into his own shadow.

"You're going to wake him up," she warned.

"*Nothing* is going to wake him up," Erin said.

"You're whispering," she pointed out. He gave her a look of mild disgust.

"Get over here," he said. So she did.

The boy was lying in the bottom bunk, asleep on his back under Grandma's good quilt. She was about to protest about the quilt, but gave it up as a futility.

His hair was dark across the white pillow slip. In sleep, his face had relaxed, all the insolence and the toughness gone out of it. His hand was thrown back on the pillow, palm up, the fingers slightly curled beside his cheek. He could have been one of their own boys lying there, he looked that young. There was a sort of wild sweetness about him now, about his face, and the hand that curved so gently.

"Looks dangerous, doesn't he?" Erin said, smirking.

"They all look like that when they're asleep," she said, straightening, figuring they were finished.

"Wait," he said, forstalling her. He leaned over, gently pulling the covers back. The boy stirred.

"Erin," Charlotte whispered, giving him her wife-to-idiot-husband look. "All you put on him was bottoms? He's going to freeze."

"That's all I've got," he said, unruffled.

"You've got tops somewhere," she said. "You can't buy pajamas with just bottoms. You could at least have found him a T-shirt."

"Will you stop?" he said. "I'll get him a T-shirt. Just hush and look, will you?" He pointed down at the boy. It was a good, lean, strong-looking body, muscular, well put together. That's all she saw at first. Then she leaned a little closer, feeling that something wasn't right . . .

And she saw what Erin had brought her to see—the boy's body was peppered with scars. Some looked like they'd been cuts; others, on his arms, were tiny circles that could have been burns. The most appalling thing was one very long, ugly slash—the boy's chest had been ripped from just over his right breast all the way across his stomach to his left side, down to below the waistband of the pajamas.

Charlotte drew in her breath and put out a hand, then pulled it back, straightened up, reached for the upper bunk, and leaned against it.

"How do you suppose?" she asked. She was thinking about her own boys, how unmarked they were, how unmarked she hoped they'd stay. "It could have been an accident."

Erin didn't answer, but he looked unhappy.

"You don't think Susan did any of that?" she asked, dead cold inside at the thought.

He still didn't answer, looking down at the sleeping boy.

"She may have been a lot of things . . ." Charlotte said, her own motherhood refusing the thought. "She couldn't have done this."

He shook his head. "Only God knows," he said.

He turned around to turn off the light again.

"What's this he's wearing?" she asked. A thin gold chain glinted in the light at the boy's neck.

Erin came back, leaned over, lifted the chain, and found a tiny round medal hanging from it. He turned it in the light, considering. "It's a Catholic thing," he said. "Saint Christopher. He was the patron saint of children and travelers. Somebody must have thought Cody needed some looking after."

Erin gently replaced the medal and pulled the covers up over it. Then he went over and picked up the bundle. He rummaged through it and came up with a worn-out stuffed dog. This he placed on the pillow by the boy's head.

"You want to know what else was in there?" Erin asked her. "Clean underwear—" he raised his eyebrows, indicating that this was something she should be impressed with—"some other clothes, a copy of *Modern Photography*, a photographer's business card, and a picture of us. The one from last Christmas. And the envelope with our address. And that's it."

He gave her a long, almost absent look. "There is no father in Los Angeles," he said.

"You don't know that," she told him, chilling a little.

"I think we both know that," he said, and he went over to turn out Sawyer's lamp. "Out," Erin directed, and followed her out of the room. He pulled the door closed carefully, silently. "I can't imagine what that child has been through," he said.

"Well, I'll tell you what," she said, keeping it practical, burying herself in the expediencies. "Find him a T-shirt. The last thing he needs right now is pneumonia."

"I will," he said, but he didn't do it then. He went into their bedroom first, and she knew well enough why. He was going there just to look at his own children. Just to touch them.

She took a slow, careful breath, standing there a moment more, fighting with herself. And then she went back into the room, feeling for the desk, for the clothes that had been left draped over the chair, thinking they could stand to be cleaner than they were. When she was satisfied she had them all, she left the room again, pulling the door closed as carefully as Erin had.

I haven't got much, she thought. *But such as I have . . .* And with her arms full of smelly clothes, she followed her husband down the stairs.

7

Cody swam up through his sleep, viscous stuff, weaving slowly, slowly upwards like some heavy fish, the light glinting off his sides with every sinuous sweep. There had been a dream, but it passed, forgotten and buried in the darkness somewhere below him. He was very warm, and deeply, absolutely comfortable.

There was light against his eyelids. The sleep rumbled in his throat and he shifted, pulling the heavy covers up over his shoulder. More blanket than he was used to; he began to try to remember where he was.

He let his eyes flicker open for just an instant, just long enough to test the light, make a grab at the surroundings; then he let the eyes close again, something they wanted very much to do.

He was in some kind of compartment, or maybe a berth. But no, because what he'd seen was definitely a bedroom. He lay flat on his back and opened his eyes again. It took a moment, and then he understood; he was in the bottom half of a bunk bed.

He took a deep breath and let it out slowly, and then he curled up on his side. The light was like buttered air, bright and golden, and it came pouring down through a window on the far wall. There were dark shapes in front of the window that eventually resolved themselves into model airplanes—hung from the ceiling, two or three of them.

It was a nice room, blue and brown and papered with more airplanes. Then he remembered all of it, where he was, the whole sad situation.

He lay on his side, staring dismally at the cheerful shafts of light where they made hot pools on the floor of the cool room.

He loved his uncle.

It was a problem he could have done without, but it was too late to do anything about it. He loved his uncle and he needed his uncle. It was beyond question, certainly beyond reason.

The good night's sleep hadn't helped anything, or the comfort of the covers, or the good mattress. Whatever had done it to him, Cody was too heavy, now—with a lassitude and a hopelessness that ran all the way down into his deepest soul. His energy was gone, and so was his courage. Completely. Nothing left. Nada. If he couldn't stay here . . . but he couldn't even face the thought.

If it were up to his uncle, there wouldn't be a problem. Erin would do anything, give him anything he needed; he had understood it from the first moment last night—the moment he had seen behind his uncle's eyes. He wondered at that, how a person could live long enough to grow up to be a man—a fairly *rich* man, from the way it looked—and be as open and guileless as his uncle seemed to be.

But this wasn't just a matter of what Erin would do. There were children involved here; there was a routine here, a life. And there was Aunt Charlotte.

And it was not going to work.

You knew that last night. You knew that before you ever knocked on the door of this place.

Cody felt himself balancing on the edge of despair; he'd come as far as he had strength to come.

He screwed his eyes shut and rolled over on his back.

"Please," he breathed, Erin's face in his mind, "Please don't let me go."

There was a slight rustling behind him. His reactions were still good; he came up on his side, immediately aware, immediately ready to move.

There was a young boy, one of the ones from last night—the one who had answered the door. He was sitting at a desk, just far enough back that Cody hadn't been able to see him before. He seemed to be waiting for something, and he was watching Cody.

Once it was clear that Cody was finally aware of him, the boy smiled.

"Hi," he said.

"Hi," Cody answered, disarming himself—and suffering a little embarrassment.

"I'm Sawyer. Your cousin."

"Hi," Cody said again. "I'm Cody."

"I know," Sawyer said, and he smiled again.

"Why didn't you say something before?" Cody asked, rubbing the sleep out of his face.

"I wasn't sure you were awake. And then I thought maybe you were praying."

Cody smiled. "I was, kind of. This your room?"

Sawyer nodded.

"This your bed?"

"Tyler's," Sawyer said. He pointed at the top bunk. "That's mine."

"Well, thanks for letting me use your room," Cody said. He threw the covers back and sat up. At first, he was dizzy. He sat there blinking, leaning over slightly. But the cool air in the room braced him up a bit, giving him a little chill. He yawned and shook himself and gave Sawyer another smile. Sawyer was staring at Cody's chest.

Cody looked down. It was a reflex; he'd known what Sawyer was looking at.

"How'd you get that?" Sawyer asked, almost reverently.

Cody blew wearily. "It was kind of an accident."

"Did it hurt?" Sawyer asked.

Cody laughed. "Yeah," he said. "It did, actually. Look . . ." gently now, "it's something that's kind of hard for me to talk about. If that's okay."

"Sure," Sawyer said. "I probably shouldn't have asked you. I think I may have a problem with asking the wrong questions all the time."

"Well, don't worry about it," Cody said, grinning.

"Are we really cousins?"

Cody nodded.

"Are you going to stay here for a while?"

Cody tilted his head thoughtfully. "I don't think so," he said. And then he smiled his weary best at Sawyer.

"That's too bad. I was kind of hoping you would stay for a while."

Kind thing to say. "Why?"

"I don't know. I think you're interesting."

"You do, huh?" That was nice.

"Yeah. How come your hair is cut so weird?"

"You like it?" Cody asked, shaking the hair out.

Sawyer wrinkled up his nose. "It's kind of weird."

"Yeah, well, that's the idea," Cody said. There was a robe lying aross the foot of the bed. He reached for it.

"Did you do it for a party or something?" Sawyer asked.

"Something like that," Cody said.

"A concert," Sawyer said, like he'd finally figured it out.

Someone knocked softly at the door. "Sawyer?" Charlotte's voice came, whispering.

"In here, Mom," Sawyer called.

"What are you doing?" she asked.

"Talking to Cody," he said.

"I don't want you in there disturbing him," she said, maybe a little annoyed.

"He's fine," Cody spoke up.

"Well, you come on out of there, Sawyer," she said, a little louder. "You can help me in the kitchen. When you want to come down, Cody, there's breakfast." They heard her go down the hall, and then down the stairs.

Cody folded his arms and blew again. "Listen, Sawyer," he said. "I don't think you should hang around with me unless you check with your mother first, okay?"

"Why not?" Sawyer asked, sounding slightly offended.

"Well, it's just—I don't know. I don't think she's real comfortable with me, is all."

"Why not? I'm comfortable with you."

Cody shrugged. "Would you be comfortable with me if it meant having to give up your bed?"

"Sure," Sawyer said. "I don't mind the floor. Anyway—it's probably because of your hair," he went on, thoughtfully. "And your earring. She hates boys with earrings."

"She does," Cody said, amused.

"She thinks it's stupid," Sawyer said.

"Well, she's probably right," Cody said.

"I don't know," Sawyer said. "Sometimes she's just a little out of touch."

"I think you'd better go," Cody said. Sawyer sighed and stood up. "Do you think it would be okay if I took a shower?" Cody asked.

"Oh, sure," Sawyer said. "We have our own bathroom up here." He began to look a little uncomfortable.

"What is it?" Cody asked.

"I was supposed to clean up the bathroom yesterday," Sawyer said.

"And you didn't do it?" Cody asked, grinning and giving Sawyer the reproachful eye.

"Not exactly," Sawyer admitted.

"Don't worry about it," Cody said. "It won't bother me. And I'll take care of it when I'm done. But I think, right now, if you don't want to be in a lot of trouble—"

"I know. I know," Sawyer said resignedly. "I'm going. The bathroom's through that door just right there down the hall. See you."

"See you," Cody said, feeling a little less taut. Kids. With them, it can be very simple. Whoever you are, they just assume you're okay. Whatever you say, they think you know what you're talking about.

Cody lay back down on the bed, pulling the robe up over his chest to keep the chill off.

If you really want to stay here, you're going to have to do something about it, his voice said.

"I know," he murmured.

What's it worth to you?

He put his hands behind his head.

Your aunt's the key to this. She sees what she sees and she doesn't like it. If you don't show her something better than that, you don't stay. She's not impressed by machismo, man—she'll say, "You can take care of yourself." So fine. Go do it. You got to give her something else.

He made a hopeless face. Cody had a lot of useful gifts: manipulation wasn't one of them. The only thing he was really good at was making people dislike him. He didn't have much skill the other way.

Maybe it's time to put some things on the line. Some real things.

Maybe not. *We going to forget the rules?* he asked himself. *For what? On a chance? Since when do we gamble like that?*

Are you kidding? You're going to take care of yourself? What chance have you got? These people could take care of you. You think about that. But you're so tough, you don't need it, right?

You think about it. You can't have it all your way—if you want something from these people, you're going to have to put it on the line. Not everything, maybe.

But more than I want.

Yes. More than you want.

He sat up.

He ran his fingers through his hair; it was gritty.

She doesn't like earrings.

He sighed. He picked up the robe and put it on, and then he looked around for his clothes.

He found them hanging over against the closet door, very clean and smooth as new. He touched them, lifted them up to his face. They smelled very sweet. He took them in his arms and sat back down on the bed.

And sat there, trying to figure her out.

He'd seen her face last night. There'd been no charity there.

He put his hand up to his ear and touched the earring. He took it out of his ear.

He knew enough about women, about the ways they could be socially abused; his mother had given him a thorough education.

Maybe . . . maybe he could make a deal with Charlotte.

Maybe he could show her he knew how to be useful.

But it wasn't that simple. She'd had him sorted out and classified in two seconds last night; he had that to deal with.

Put it on the line.

He got off the bed and padded out into the hallway.

He found the bathroom, pushed open the door, and felt for the light switch. And then he stood there in the doorway, totally amazed. He made a low whistle, and then grinned, feeling very pleased.

She could definitely use somebody like him. Definitely.

Suddenly cheerful, he cinched up his belt and pushed up the sleeves of the robe.

8

Charlotte had been in the kitchen for a while this morning, getting supper ready for the afternoon, standing at the sink, gazing out the window at the green, green earth. The morning had been warm; the afternoon would be hot. Early September was such a strange time. There was all the spiritual promise of afternoon haze and chilly evening, but still came these earthy hot days, a terrible thing for the pregnant and the allergy prone, people who waited so impatiently for the first frost, the end of the heat, the end of the lawn mowing.

She loved autumn. With all her heart and soul, she needed the turning, the harvest. To Charlotte, it was like the beginning of life.

"He'll be down in a minute," Sawyer said, dancing back into the kitchen the way young boys will, flouncing himself into one of the chairs at the table.

Charlotte had been lost somewhere under the trees in the back yard, a carrot half peeled in her hand.

"I still don't know why you wouldn't let me go to church," Sawyer complained. She glanced at him over her shoulder and then finished up the carrot.

"You have a cold," she pointed out.

"I had it Friday, too. But you didn't let me stay home from school."

And that was true. But somebody had to stay home with this boy of Erin's, and Erin couldn't do it because he had extra meetings to go to, and Charlotte had thought that having two people here with the boy would be better than one—wiser, at least.

"It wouldn't be terrifically Christian of us to give everybody at church your cold, now, would it?" she asked. He made no answer, but in her mind's eye, she could see him rolling his eyes at her, and she had to smile.

"He won't let me hang around up there with him unless you give me permission," Sawyer said, meaning the boy upstairs.

"He won't?" Charlotte asked. She dropped the carrot into the pot with the roast and potatoes, and covering the pot, shoved the whole thing into the oven.

"He thinks you're not comfortable with him."

"Really," she said. Not surprised. A little dismayed that she should have been so transparent.

"Why aren't you?" Sawyer asked.

"Who said I wasn't?" she asked.

"Mo-om," Sawyer sang. She looked at him, grinning, ready for that look on his fine, freckled face.

"I don't know, Sawyer," she said then, because Sawyer was her friend. She went to the refrigerator for eggs and bacon for their guest.

"Is it because of his weird hair?" he asked.

It was. Partly. "It shouldn't be, should it?" she asked him. Because that's the way they'd tried to bring the kids up, not to judge anybody, not to discount anybody because of the way they looked.

"And his earring?" Sawyer went on. And that was true, too. "A lot of guys wear earrings now. It doesn't have to mean you're weird or anything."

"I know," she said.

"Well, why don't you like him?" Sawyer asked, pursuing the point as only a nine-year-old can.

"I didn't say I didn't like him," she said, wishing he'd just drop it. How could you explain to a child that it was all a feeling, an instinct about what people were like, about what they were going to need from you.

"We'll just have to wait and see," she said. "You know, Sawyer—your dad and I have always tried to teach you not to decide about people till you've given them a chance. But that doesn't mean you have to trust them right away. That boy is your cousin, but we don't know what kind of person he is, or what he believes, or what kinds of things he'll do. He's a stranger. I believe we've taught you something about strangers."

"I haven't let him give me any candy," Sawyer said disgustedly.

"Well, now, that's good," she said. "At least you're not an idiot." She put the frying pan down on the burner. "What's he doing up there? It's been ten minutes since I sent you up there to get him. How long can one person shower?"

"He had to clean up the bathroom," Sawyer said, swallowing the last syllable as if he hadn't meant to say any of it.

She turned around and looked at him, hands on her hips. He squirmed on the chair. "I got busy and forgot," he explained.

"So, you didn't clean it last night," she said.

"Well, you didn't tell me you were going to check it," he said. And she riveted him with her you've-had-it-chum look. "Is that supposed to be an excuse?" she asked. She let her breath out, exasperated. "So, how bad was it?" she asked, embarrassed to think of that kid up there getting intimate with their bad habits.

Sawyer made a face. "We all took baths last night," he said.

"Tell me you didn't play otters," she said.

He didn't answer.

"Oh, Sawyer," she moaned, turning back to her work. "You'd better be thankful it's the Sabbath day." She scooped a bit of butter out and flicked it into the pan, turning the heat up under it. Then curiosity got the best of her. "And what does it look like, now?"

"What? The bathroom?"

She gave him an exasperated look. "Yes, the bathroom."

He shrugged. "It's clean."

"My clean or your clean?"

"It's clean. Just the way you like it. He even got out some clean towels and folded them all *that way*." He looked at her as if to say, *So there.*

"Okay," she said, a little impatiently. *So the boy can clean a bathroom.*

"You really ought to like him, Mom. I really think you ought to. I think he's interesting."

And there it was, the major problem. He was interesting. And heaven only knew how interesting he was going to turn out to be.

"Go make your bed," she said. He groaned, but she heard the chair move, and the door swing shut behind him. And then she remembered he hadn't slept in his bed.

She hissed through her teeth.

Get home, Erin, she thought. *Just get home, and let's get it over with.*

The boy was standing there when she turned around to get the cheese out of the refrigerator. It startled her; she hadn't heard him come into the room. The brightness of the late morning sun filled the whole kitchen and danced around him like an aura, and him blinking and looking awkward in the midst of it.

She had to take a second look.

He had on the same T-shirt—but clean, now, of course—
and the same pants—dark khaki. They hadn't been as dirty as
they'd looked last night. They'd washed up well, clean and
pressed now, the pleats sharp, and he looked better in them
than she would have supposed, fresher. His hair, still wet from
the shower, for the moment seemed a bit more at peace with
itself, and his eyes had lost some of their deep shadows.

He stood in the doorway quietly, as if he'd been waiting for
her to turn around. And when she did, he smiled at her, a hesitant, almost shy smile. It made his face very beautiful, very
gentle seeming, and she smiled back before she realized she
had.

"Good morning," she said, not able to keep all of the surprise out of her voice.

He smiled again. Unsure.

He looked down at his feet, and then back up at her—just
like the boys; he had something he wanted to say. She flipped
the dishtowel up over her shoulder and leaned with her hip
against the counter, waiting.

He laughed a little, embarrassed, rubbed the end of his
nose, and shifted his weight. She had to turn her face down because he was almost too funny.

"I don't think I made a terrific impression on you last
night," he said, suddenly straightforward, suddenly throwing
his eyes up, straight into hers. They were Erin's eyes, she realized with a little shock, that clear, startling blue. She wondered
why she hadn't seen it last night.

She didn't answer him. She didn't have anything to say to
that. But she didn't shut him off either.

"I thought it might be nice if we could start over." There
was something in his voice—something that pulled at her. But
he was speaking with a lot of self-possession, and that covered
it. For a moment, she couldn't tell how old he really might be.

"I don't know that we need to do that," she said, but it came
out stiffer than she'd meant it to be, and rather unrelenting.

Ghost of a smile on his face. He closed his eyes, just for a
moment.

"Thank you," he said, starting over, glancing down at himself, "for taking care of my clothes." He was working on her.
She had sons of her own; she knew how it went.

She dismissed the clothes with a little wave. "Why don't
you sit down," she said, pulling the towel off her shoulder and
getting back to business.

70

His place was set at the table, the Sunday dishes, the Sunday napkins; he stood where he was for another moment, and then went over to stand behind the chair, looking down at the dishes. "You have nice things," he said, quietly. It sounded to Charlotte like an indictment.

"We've worked hard for them," she said.

He nodded and sat down.

She broke the eggs into the pan and put the strips of bacon on paper towels for the microwave.

"Where is everybody?" he asked. There was only the one place set at the table.

"They're all at church," she said, and then quickly, "except for Sawyer, because he's not feeling too well. They'll be home in a few minutes." She couldn't see his face, because she'd set the table so that he would have his back towards her.

He was sitting with his hands in his lap.

"Church," he echoed. "Is it Sunday?"

"It is," she said.

He nodded. And then he said, "I knew you'd be religious."

The eggs sizzled in the pan, and the microwave was humming. She put two pieces of bread into the toaster.

"Oh, really," she said. "And how would you have known that?" The information wouldn't have come from Susan, at least not kindly. She started wondering what Susan had told him about the family.

"I don't know," he said. He'd half turned in his chair so that he could see her as they talked. It made her feel a little guilty. "It probably has something to do with your taste in Christmas cards."

She glanced at him. His eyes were all for the window over her shoulder.

She followed the direction of his look. "It's a beautiful day, isn't it?" she asked.

"You can see so far out your window," he said.

Not far, really; across the back to the trees. She stood there for a moment, trying to see it as he did. The bell on the microwave sounded. Her mind shifted back inside and she picked up a hot pad.

"So, are you a Catholic?" she asked. He looked up at her, a startled movement. She glanced at him. He was amused.

"No," he said. "Why do you ask?"

"You have that medal you wear," she said without thinking, glancing over her shoulder at him.

71

He had the most amazing face. It was like there was a shutter behind it. Now it closed, and she realized what she'd done. He had put his hand to his chest, over where the medal must have been hanging under his shirt. It was a simple gesture; all at once it made him seem very vulnerable. She had violated his privacy.

She was embarrassed. A casual observer couldn't have known about the medal.

"We saw it last night when Erin put you to bed," she said, explaining, apologizing.

He looked up at her as though he'd forgotten she was there. He rubbed the place over the medal thoughtfully.

"I'm sorry," she said. "It was none of my business."

She kept working. She could feel him watching her.

"A good friend gave me this," he said after a little time. "She thought it would keep the evil away. She was a very religious woman."

And did it work? Charlotte wanted to ask.

"It's just a medal," he said as if he'd heard the thought. "But I never told her that."

Charlotte nodded.

"You're not Catholic," he observed.

"How do you know?" she asked.

"Not enough kids," he said. She looked at him. He was grinning. She smiled and turned back to the eggs.

The bell on the microwave went off a second time. Charlotte scooped the eggs out of the pan. The toast popped up. "She must have been a good friend," she said, asking a question that didn't have to be answered. She pulled the toast out and the butter over.

He was half backwards in the chair again, resting his chin on his hands.

"Kind of. It was her husband who was really my friend."

"Was he a Catholic, too?" she asked, keeping up the talk, assembling the plate.

"No," he said, and he laughed softly. "No. Not really. It used to drive Mrs. Guicci crazy. But she never could get him to go to Mass. She was afraid he was going to end up in hell for sure." He fell silent.

She went to the refrigerator for jam.

"But he was religious in his own way," the boy said.

She looked at him. He was lost somewhere inside. She picked up the plate, and then she stood there and studied him.

She hadn't forgotten the vulnerability she'd seen a moment past. It had been very disconcerting. He wasn't turning out to be what she'd expected. Still, she couldn't help but feel that there was going to be more to this. It was going to get harder.

He came to himself, and when she felt his eyes through her own thoughts, she shook herself and held the plate up. "Your food," she said. And she carried the plate and the glass of milk over to the table.

She went back to the counter for the jam.

She put it on the table with the other things. He was sitting there with his hands in his lap, just like last night, not touching anything.

"You don't like my cooking, do you?" she asked.

He looked up at her, surprised. "I do. It's very good. I was just waiting for you."

"Ah," she said. "We've already eaten."

"Oh," he said.

She gave him a perfunctory smile and went back over to start cleaning up the counter, his small graciousness not entirely unmarked.

"You didn't go to all this trouble just for me," he said.

"What trouble?" she asked. But that was a lie; in her mind there was a whole list of Troubles Taken. "It's just breakfast. Doesn't your mother ever feed you?"

He didn't answer.

"Are you going to eat?" she asked.

"I am," he said. "Thank you."

She smiled to herself and picked up the frying pan.

"This is *very* nice," he murmured around a bite of something. It seemed like he was going in fits and starts, as if he had to start all over every so often.

Now there was an honest cheerfulness in his voice that made it seem as if this breakfast must be some kind of big novelty for him. So maybe his mother didn't usually feed him in the morning. Or maybe they always had cold cereal. Whatever it was, Charlotte was beginning to get this very pleased-with-herself, appreciated sort of feeling, as though she'd really done something extraordinarily nice, actually feeling a little warm and sappy. She put a little glass of juice down beside his milk.

"Well, thanks for the thanks," she said, thinking it would be nice to hear something like that from her own kids.

And then she caught herself. *The way to a woman's heart* . . . She turned around and leaned back against the sink, folding her arms and watching his back. She wasn't going to be manipulated.

"Look," she said. "It's not like I'm making any unusual effort here. You're my nephew," she told him. "You're my guest."

His back straightened, and he put his hands down on the table.

"I'm Erin's nephew," he said quietly, "And I'm Erin's guest." Correcting her. Reminding her.

"You're my guest, too," she said, a little impatient with the clarity of his perceptions. *And I'm just doing what I have to.* "Your food's getting cold."

He picked up his fork. She turned back to the sink. The kitchen grew uncomfortably quiet.

"So," he said after a while; there was a doggedness in his voice. So okay. If he wanted to force the conversation, then let him. He'd made Erin do it last night; now he could do it himself.

"What do you think? Can you call a man religious if he doesn't have a church?"

"I don't know," she said, running the water in the sink. "It depends on how he believes, I guess."

"It wasn't like he was always talking about religion," the boy said. "It was just his attitude. Mr. Guicci, I mean, the man I was talking about. He treated people like they were all a part of God."

"You want another peice of toast?" she asked him.

"Yes, please," he said, sounding a touch weary.

She got the bread out of the bread box.

"He was very careful about God," the boy pressed on. "He told me, no honorable man uses the name of God for swearing. Of anybody's God. He said, 'In the first place, you don't have the right to use such a name unless you believe. And if you believe you could never be so rude.' "

"He was right," she said, slapping the towel over her shoulder and sticking the frying pan into the sink. "So, do you do it?"

"Do I do what?" he asked.

"Use the name of God for swearing."

"No," he said. And then, "Not very often."

She pursed her lips, nodding. "That's good," she said. It was as if they had set up some kind of secret scoreboard between them—he needed her to hear good things, and she needed to remember she'd heard them. So mark up another point in the kid's favor; he doesn't misuse the name of God. It was a strong point, especially alongside the good manners, the gratitude, the shy smile, and the fact that he could clean a bathroom.

Charlotte ran the scrubber around the inside of the pan.

"He had a good God," Cody said, and he took a long drink of his milk.

She rinsed the pan off and shook it out over the sink.

"And what about you?" she asked. As long as they were keeping score. "Do you believe in God?" She pulled the towel off her shoulder and wiped the pan with it.

He stopped for a moment, the fork suspended just above the plate. Then the fork went down on to the plate.

"There've been times I hoped there was one," he said.

"And why was that?" she asked.

"Sometimes you need a miracle," he said. She could hear him smiling. He picked up his toast and took a bite.

"But what about it?" she asked.

"You mean seriously?"

"I mean seriously," she said.

He shrugged, the toast still in his hand. "I don't know. Does it matter? Whatever happens, happens. What difference does it make what you believe about it?"

She could hear Sawyer calling her from upstairs. She made one last swipe at the pan and put it down on the drainboard.

"But don't you think it's a comfort," she asked, threading the towel through the handle on the refrigerator door, "knowing that whatever happens, at least there's a reason for it?" Sawyer called again.

Cody was picking up his juice glass. He paused, and he asked very quietly, "Now, how would that be a comfort?"

"Excuse me," she said. She pushed the hall door open and yelled, "Sawyer, if you want something, come down here and—" but he was hollering again, from the top of the stairs, and she had to go to the foot of the stairs to get his attention.

"Will you stop yelling?" she asked, glaring up at him.

"I can't find my soccer socks," he said.

"You could come down here and ask me without yelling, couldn't you?" she said. "You don't need your soccer socks anyway. It's the Sabbath."

"For tomorrow," he said, insisting.

"Get down here," she said. "Why don't you just come in the kitchen with us, and forget about that until tomorrow?"

The phone rang.

"I'll get it," Sawyer announced, and came thundering down the stairs.

"Sawyer—" she said, but it was too late. He was gone. She shook her head, feeling just a little as though things were never going to be under any kind of sane control in her life, ever again. She wandered back down the hall into the kitchen.

Cody was standing at the sink, washing off his plate.

"You don't have to do that," she said.

"You want me to leave it for you?" he asked, the half smile, the slightly knowing look, back on his face. It was a straight question. A legitimate one.

For a moment, she was suspended between polite protestation and honesty. "Not especially," she said finally, opting for the straight answer.

"Okay," he said, and continued with the plate. So she went over to clear off the table.

The kitchen door flew open and slammed against the wall behind.

"*Sawyer*," she said.

He came in and threw himself on one of the kitchen chairs. "It's such a *rip*," he yelled.

"You want to not do that to this door, please?" she said. "And you want to not yell anymore? We're standing right *here*."

"I can't help it," he shouted. "I'm *mad*." He shook his fists in the air. "I can't *believe* it."

"What?" she asked.

"It's not *fair*," he lamented.

"Saw-yer," she sang, and she went over and took hold of him. "You're not making se-nse. Look at me. What's not fair?"

Of course, he didn't look at her. He folded his arms on the table and put his head down on them. She threw an exasperated look at Cody. He was watching them, rinsing off his plate and smiling to himself.

"What is it?" She shook Sawyer's shoulder gently.

"Brian Evenstin's dad was going to take us to the Galleria Wednesday night for laser tag, remember?" His voice was muffled in his arms.

"How could I forget?" she asked. As if it hadn't been *the* topic of discussion for the last two weeks.

"And now we're not going."

All things considered, she could understand how disappointed he was. She patted his shoulder. "I'm sorry," she said. "What happened?"

"I don't want to tell you," Sawyer said, still into his arms.

"Really." She tapped him on the head. "Well, now, obviously you're going to have to."

"Don't make me," he whined.

That suspicious *feeling* started creeping in. She pulled out the chair next to Sawyer and sat down facing him.

"Let's hear it," she said, her serious voice on.

Sawyer half lifted his head and looked at her. "Promise you won't get mad at me?" he said.

"*Saw*yer."

"Okay, okay. Brian got caught ripping off candy at Seven-Eleven after school Friday, and he got grounded for the rest of his life." He ran it all together, as if saying it faster would help.

"Sawyer," she said quietly, really surprised.

"Well," he said, "*I* didn't do it."

"Were you with him?"

"Well, yeah—but I tried to tell him not to do it."

"*You* didn't do it . . ." she said, enough of a question in her voice that he gave her the most disgusted of looks.

"What do you *think*?" he said.

"Well, I hope you wouldn't," she said.

"I can't *believe* this," Sawyer howled. "I *knew* you were going to get mad at me. I *told* him not to do it."

"Okay," Charlotte said. "Okay. You're right. I'm sorry. I'm not mad at you. Brian really did that? He really did steal the candy; I mean, he didn't just forget to pay for it."

Sawyer rolled his eyes. "He did it on a bet," he explained.

"I thought he had more sense than that," she said, angry now.

"Well, it's not the first time he did it."

"What are you *telling* me?"

"He takes little stuff from Woolworth's all the time."

"He does not."

"Yes, he does." Sawyer was looking at her with something like pity.

"I thought he was a nice kid," she said.

"He *is* a nice kid, Mother. He just does stupid things sometimes."

"I trusted that kid," she said, almost to herself. And then she looked appraisingly at Sawyer.

"Well, don't look at *me*," he said.

"I just don't want you doing stupid things," she said.

"Okay, I promise you. I'll never, *ever* steal anything from a Seven-Eleven. Okay? I *promise*."

She realized she was studying his face, feeling a little scared inside. "You know," she said. "I happen to know that Brian's parents think he's a pretty good kid. I think they've really trusted him. If you can't know your own kid any better than that—I mean, if you can't trust your kid not to steal *candy* . . ."

"I'm not going to take drugs, Mom," Sawyer sighed.

"Yeah, well, that's probably exactly what Brian said to *his* mother . . ."

"I can't believe this. I *knew* I shouldn't tell you. Look, he got caught, okay?"

"Well, it's a good thing he did," she said. And she got up and picked up the little bowls of honey and jam and took them over where she could empty them back into the jars.

"Does your mother ever treat you like this?" Sawyer asked, directing the question to Cody, who was now scrubbing down his placemat with the dish rag.

Cody laughed as if the question had surprised him. "No," he said.

Sawyer threw her a See-I-told-you-you-were-weird look. Charlotte was watching Cody's face. It had been a strange answer, considering the rest of this morning's conversation.

Sawyer watched him for a minute, too. Then he asked, "Have you ever stolen anything?" Charlotte froze, spatula in hand, her eyes still on Cody's face.

Cody was wiping at the placemat absently, now. He looked at Sawyer and smiled. "Yes, I have," he said.

It's only what you expected, she told herself. *So why are you suddenly so disappointed?*

"Did you ever get caught?" Sawyer asked, looking very interested. *And there's our problem,* she thought to herself. *That was what I was afraid of. Why do children have to be so interested in the wrong things?*

Cody was smiling to himself, one last wipe with the rag. "Yes, I did," he said. "But only once." He lifted the mat off the table and looked at Charlotte for instructions. She cleared her face immediately, opened a drawer for him, and then screwed the top down on the jar she was holding.

"What did you steal?" Sawyer asked.

"Oh, I stole a lot of things," Cody said, trying to get the mat to lie flat in the drawer.

78

"It won't go flat," Charlotte told him. "It's too wide."

"But what were you stealing when you got caught?" Sawyer asked, evidently quite riveted by the whole thing.

Cody closed the drawer. "A cheese," he said. He shook the rag out over the sink.

Cody looked at him, the smile flickering around his eyes. "Yeah," he said. *So?* He rinsed the rag and wrang it out.

"Why did you steal a *cheese*?" Sawyer asked.

"Because I was hungry," Cody said simply. He took the rag over to the table and began to wipe that.

"For a cheese?" Sawyer said, incredulous.

Cody stopped wiping and fixed Sawyer with his eyes. "It seemed like a good thing at the time," he said, and started in again on the table.

"Sawyer isn't real fond of cheese," Charlotte explained. The sound of her own voice startled her. Cody nodded, acknowledging the explanation.

"You *must* have been hungry," Sawyer said, grimacing.

"I was," Cody said. "I was starving."

"Not starving," Sawyer said. It was only what Charlotte had said to Sawyer a hundred times—*You don't know what starving is, buddy.*

"Yeah. Starving. I said it—I meant it. It's not something I'd expect you to understand, Sawyer," Cody said, gently.

"You're right. I don't," Sawyer said, thinking of a whole cheese and screwing up his face.

"Well, the problem was, there was no food in my house, and I didn't have any money." Cody put the salt and pepper back in the center of the table where they were supposed to go. Which, Charlotte realized, meant that he had *noticed* where they were supposed to go.

"Why didn't you just tell your mom to get some?"

"My mom wasn't around," Cody said. He took the rag back over to the sink.

"Where was she?" Sawyer asked.

Cody was rinsing out the rag again. He began to seem a little uncomfortable. "I don't know," he said. "But she'd been gone a couple of days."

"Who was staying with you?" Sawyer asked.

Cody smiled. "Nobody," he said. He dried his hands on the towel and sat down at the table again.

"Well, how old were you?" Sawyer wanted to know.

"I don't remember. I think I was about five."

Charlotte screwed the top on the jam, her lips tight. She should have stopped Sawyer's questions, but she couldn't do it.

"Your mom left you all alone in your house when you were five, and she didn't even leave you something to eat?" Sawyer asked, open mouthed.

Cody nodded, sliding back into the chair, folding his arms across his chest.

"Why?" Sawyer wondered.

"I guess she had her reasons," Cody said. "It wasn't like it was the first time."

"I didn't know moms could do that," Sawyer said, and he glanced over at Charlotte. She found herself grinning at him, not because there was anything funny about it—just because of the thoughts she saw chasing around his face.

"It happens," Cody said. "I guess they have the option."

"Not really," Charlotte murmured.

"Where'd you steal the cheese from?" Sawyer said, resting his chin on his fists.

"There was this little market down the street," Cody said. "I'd go in there every so often and just kind of walk out with a little piece of fruit or something. All that food, just sitting there out in the open, out on the sidewalk, big boxes of fruit—I guess I felt like I probably needed it as much as anybody did."

"But somebody caught you."

"Mr. Guicci caught me. He owned the shop. This one day, I tried taking out this—" he held his hands up, making a fat round in the air—"big cheese. I tried running for it, you know? Right out the door, but I guess he was waiting for me. He caught me, grabbed hold of me by the hair. I remember I dropped the cheese I was so scared.

"And he hauled me up on the counter, and he began to yell at me. He gave me such a lecture. He said to me, 'Where would I be if everybody just came in here and helped themselves without paying? How would I feed my own family?' There was all that food around, I couldn't believe he would ask such a stupid question.

"So then, he asks me, 'Why do you steal from me?' So I told him: I was hungry. So he asked me a lot of the same questions you just did, and then he took me upstairs and had Mrs. Guicci give me some lunch. He was a nice guy. I guess he did some checking around after that, anyway—he ended up making me a deal—"

Cody took a quick, hooded look at Charlotte.

"He told me that if I came back every day and did some work for him, he'd make sure I got a good dinner every time.

"So that's what I did. And then, see, he made me understand what you do to people when you steal from them. So I didn't steal things anymore. But then, I didn't have to after that. I never got that hungry again."

He looked at Charlotte. "How's that for a moral tale?" It was almost a challenging look.

"I worked for him every day of my life after that," he went on. "Till about six months ago."

"What happened then?" Sawyer asked, even though Charlotte had been willing him not to.

"He died," Cody said.

"Why don't you go up and find your soccer socks?" Charlotte said.

Sawyer looked at her like she was crazy. "Go *on*," she said, giving him a look that told him he'd better do it. He got up from the table. But he didn't leave.

"Get," she said.

"I'm sorry he died," Sawyer said. Cody glanced up at him, smiled at him. "He was old," he said, making it all right.

"But I bet it made you sad, huh?"

"Well," Cody said, staring down at his hands. He glanced up at Sawyer with the little smile. "I wasn't really a member of the family."

"Get out of here," Charlotte said to Sawyer. He finally went.

Charlotte put the honey jar back into the cabinet, crossed to the sink, and rinsed her fingers off carefully, buying a little time. She dried her hands slowly, watching Cody. He sat at the table so quietly. The boy with the shutters behind his eyes. The boy with private grief.

She went over and sat in a chair across from him.

He swallowed, then he glanced up at her and shifted in the chair. "It's the first time I've talked about that," he said. It almost sounded like an apology. His face was very still.

"If you left here this afternoon," she said, "where would you go?"

He looked up at her, not having expected the question. It took him a moment to answer. "I told you last night," he said. "I thought I'd—"

She held up her hand, cutting him off.

"I know what you told us last night," she said. "That's not what I'm asking."

He studied her face, his face showing nothing.

"So you want the truth," he said, finally.

"That's what I usually prefer." At least, that was what she was asking for now.

He dropped his eyes. "Okay," he said.

Then he looked straight at her. "*When* I leave here this afternoon," he spoke carefully, "I don't know where I'm going to go."

"Do you know where your father is?" she asked him.

He shook his head, still meeting her eyes, but telling her nothing with them. It wasn't that his face was hard or cold; it was simply unreadable, completely private.

"Do you know anything about him?"

He shook his head.

"What did your mother tell you about him?" she asked.

"Nothing," he said. "Not even his name. It was not something she talked about." And then there was a break in the smoothness of his control, a seam, and there was something in his eyes. "Is there anything you can tell me?" he asked.

It was too cruel a thing. "I don't know anything either," she said. "I'm sorry." And she was. Very sorry, she realized.

Charlotte took a long breath and let it out slowly. "Why did you come here, Cody?" she asked. "I mean, really."

He reached for the salt shaker and then sat back, the shaker on the table in front of him, his hands cupped around it. "I've been in some trouble," he said, carefully. "I hoped I could come here and maybe pull it out before it was too late."

"Trouble with the police?" she asked, scared of the answer.

He laughed. "No, ma'am," he said. "I managed to avoid that. It's mostly school. It seemed to me that going to college would maybe be a good idea. Without doing that, I don't have a lot of options. But I figured that out a little late in the game; back home, I have a grade point average of about point four, and a kind of—you could say, unpleasant reputation. Which is all my own fault."

"I see." She stood up. She went over to the sink and poured herself a drink of water. When she looked at him again, he still had his hand around the salt shaker. His eyes were closed.

"I don't like being lied to, Cody," she said, not meaning to recriminate. She was just telling him.

"I know," he said.

"And I don't like being manipulated," she said.

He nodded. "I know," he said.

She stood over by the sink and looked out of the window.

"And the hard thing is, I'm not sure I can tell when it's happening to me. I'm not that sophisticated."

She heard him take a breath. "You know, there's a certain amount of risk involved in this for me, too," he said. "Why should I be honest with you? You don't like me."

"It's not that I don't like you," she told him. "That's not it at all. Last night, I didn't like you. Today, I think you'd be surprised how I'm feeling." *It surprises me.* "The problem is . . . I don't know what the problem is. I'm scared of you."

"Have I done something to you?" he asked.

"When Erin hears the things you've just told me, you know he's not going to let you leave here."

"I know that, too," he said. "Remember. *You* asked me these questions. I only answered you."

"I've got four little children in this house, Cody," she said.

He looked up at her, a quick look, hurt. "I've never hurt a child in my life," he said softly.

She sighed. She pulled her chair out again and sat down with him. "That's not what I'm afraid of," she said, lying again, but only by so much. "I'm afraid having you here will be too much for me. I'm afraid of what they'll learn from you."

"My bad habits," he said.

She shrugged. Whatever. Whatever it was.

"We're so careful about how we've brought them up," she said. "About the attitudes, and the morals. You have to understand . . . your mother . . ." but she didn't know how to finish it.

"My mother was not the best of all possible people," he said doing it for her.

"She had different ideas than we do," she said, carefully.

"I probably do, too," he said.

She put her hands in her lap and looked at him.

"Aunt Charlotte," he said, and he said this now as clearly and as plainly as he had said anything, "I didn't come here to hurt anybody. I didn't come here to mess up your life. I didn't come here to make a lot of work for you. I came here because I didn't know what else to do."

He gave her a long look. "If you don't want me to stay, I'll understand. It's no more than what I expected. If that's the case, I don't know what I'll do—but I've taken care of myself before. And I'm sure I can again."

He sounded so weary. "But if you let me stay, I promise you, I'll never lie to you. And I'll never manipulate you, not on purpose, not any more than your own kids would, probably.

And I'll help around the house and do my share of the work; I'll get a job, and I'll pay my own way. All I want is a chance. Just one last chance. A place to sleep. A name. That's all. I've got to know for sure about myself. Whether it's worth it to me to keep going."

A car turned into the driveway, scraping bottom over the gutter.

"It's Erin," she said.

He sat back in the chair. "That's everything I have," he said. "It's way more than I meant to say. But that's giving it to you straight. I'm not trying to talk you into anything, and I'm not trying to make you feel guilty. I'm just . . . but then, you know . . . maybe it's really not worth it. Maybe I've been kidding myself for a long time."

"About what?"

"About me being able to *do* anything." He dropped his hands into his lap, and she saw his jaw tighten.

"I doubt that," she said. She shook her head, pulling her mouth over sideways, looking at him. "You've messed up my life already," she said. She stood up. The car pulled even with the back door and stopped. The engine stopped, and the car doors opened up.

"I don't know what's going to happen, Cody," she said and then pulled a breath in through her teeth. If she'd been scared before, she was terrified, now. "I have the feeling it's going to be okay."

He closed his eyes.

She could hear the voices now, the family coming up the back steps.

"Do you think we can be friends?" she asked, quickly.

He looked at her.

"Both ways," he said, putting a condition on it. "I'm just as scared of you."

The back door opened.

"Hiya!" Tyler called.

"How's it going?" Erin asked cheerfully. He had the baby by the hand, all dressed for Sunday with his tiny bow tie. Mickey was hanging back in the doorway, looking at Cody with eyes at once enormous and hooded.

Charlotte glanced at Cody and then gave Erin such a look of pure despair. The earth had just shifted under her feet, and life wasn't ever going to be the same again. This she knew. And it had been by her own timorous choice.

84

"What is it?" Erin asked her, reading the look.

"Dinner," she said. "It's not going to be ready for another hour."

Tyler groaned.

"Well, that's all right," Erin said, looking as though he couldn't imagine why that should be so awful. He pulled off his tie and crammed it into his jacket pocket. "It gives us plenty of time to change."

"Tell me about it," she said.

9

"This'll have your mother in it," Erin said, handing down a heavy notebook that turned out to be a photo album, "when she was about your age."

Cody took the book in both hands and went to sit down in the big recliner. They were all—except Tyler and the baby, who were napping upstairs—in the den after Sunday supper, half asleep in the warmth of the afternoon, just sort of contentedly puttering around.

Cody opened the book and looked over the pictures on the first page.

"Who are these people?" he asked, pointing.

Erin leaned over the back of the chair, peering over Cody's shoulder.

"Your grandparents."

Cody dropped his palm down on the page. "Really," he said, softly.

"Really," Erin said. And after a moment, "You didn't know you had grandparents?"

"Everybody has grandparents," Cody murmured. This had taken him completely by surprise.

There was a moment's silence.

"Well, these are yours," Erin said, a little sadness in his voice. "My folks."

"Huh," Cody said, running his hand lightly across the picture and leaning down to take a better look. He was nursing a little heartache. "Are they still alive?"

"Yeah, they're alive," Erin said, looking at Charlotte. "I've got to call them."

She nodded.

"They're going to be here at Christmas," he said.

"Your dog?" Cody asked. There was a black mop of a dog in the same picture, its pink hanging tongue the only discernible sign of a face.

"Black Sambo," Erin said. "Long gone."

"Cute dog," Cody said. It had been an incredibly heartless act, his mother stealing these things from him. His eyes stung in the looking; he kept them down and turned the page.

There was a picture of his mother—same face, but younger, and not quite so hard. Showing off a little in the picture, actually. She was wearing hip-hugger pants, purple with big flowers on them, a simple sweater—not tight, but shaped to her—and a rough, suede jacket with beaded fringe. Her hair hung down straight and long, very dark. Way over her shoulders.

"Different, and not," Cody murmured. "Is this you?" Another picture. This one of a boy. Blond afro and outrageous sideburns—rimless glasses, striped bell-bottoms, and an acoustic guitar.

"That's me," Erin said.

Cody laughed. "Incredible," he said. "What were you, a hippie?"

"Oh, I dunno," Erin said, smiling. "Not really. I was way too normal a kid."

"You do sit-ins and stuff?"

"Kind of. We did one at school once. It was to get the school to start a black history class. And we did it. We got the class. We didn't get into too much trouble over it, either—there were too many of us. We felt really *good* about it, you know, even though nobody much took the class after the first semester. Like we'd *done* something. But all that stuff was really more your mother's style."

"My mother."

"Yep," Erin said.

There was another picture. Cody's mother, graduating.

Standing there in a black cap and gown, looking sideways into the camera, lifting her hair away from her face.

"What happened between you and my mother?" Cody asked, quietly.

"I'm not sure," Erin said. "It's more like, what happened between your mother and herself."

Not an answer, really. But something Cody understood.

"What was she like?" he asked.

Erin sighed and straightened up. "She was an interesting person," he said.

"She still is," Cody said.

"She was," Erin went on, "what you might have called a 'political activist' back then. She did a lot of protesting, and—I don't know."

"Woman with a cause," Cody said, dryly.

"Well, not really," Erin said. "More like a woman looking for an excuse to be angry. I don't think she ever really had a cause. She just objected to everything generally. She hated having to be part of the family; we could never do anything right for her. She had our parents totally bewildered. She didn't believe in God. She hated church. She hated the law. Always angry. Always."

"And so she left," Cody said.

"No. It wasn't that clean. She graduated from high school with honors. Got accepted into Johns Hopkins. Graduated from there with honors—which is something, by the way—and got accepted to Harvard Law."

"What?" Cody turned around and stared at Erin.

"You didn't know that?" Erin asked quietly.

Cody shook his head, had to remember to close his mouth.

"She hasn't told you very much," Erin observed.

"Not very much," Cody agreed. "Not much." He let go of a breath, sat back down into the chair.

"She was a very bright girl," Erin said.

"Articulate," Cody said. His mother's word.

Erin laughed. "You could say so."

"Why law school?" Cody asked. "You said she hated the law."

"She hated the law because it was power. You learn the law, you become the power."

"Ah," Cody said. He dropped his head against the back of the chair.

"But she never got her degree," Erin said. "She dropped out

at the end of the first semester, and that was the last we heard of her for a long time.''

"She just disappeared?''

"Off the face of the earth.'' Erin went over and stood by the couch where Charlotte was sitting. "My parents didn't understand; they'd done everything they could for her. Same as they did for me. They even took out a second mortgage on the house to pay for the first year of Harvard. Then she disappeared. Not a word. So my dad figured something must have happened to her. He went out there and poked around, but he couldn't come up with anything. All the evidence said she'd left under her own power.''

"So, how did you finally find her?''

"Well, that was kind of strange.'' Erin sat down next to Charlotte. "About a year after that, an old high school friend of your mom's ran into her in New York. Your mom was clerking in a law firm—'' he made a question with his face.

"Not anymore,'' Cody said.

"Anyway, she was then. And they went out to lunch together or something. The friend ended up staying the night at your mom's place, and the address got back to us.'' Erin put his feet up on the coffee table, laced his hands together and rested them on his chest, all the time with his eyes on Cody. "There was a baby living with her at the time,'' he said.

Cody looked up.

"With your mother,'' Erin said, clarifying, his face impassive.

"Me?'' Cody asked.

"One would assume so,'' Erin said.

"I see,'' Cody said. And he did, suddenly—he saw a lot of things. "So, that's why she dropped out of school.''

Erin opened his hands. "Who knows, Cody?'' he said.

"Well, certainly not *me*,'' Cody agreed acidly.

He closed the cover of the book, his eyes gone very dark. "I mean, my mother and I never were what you'd call emotionally close. But, you know, I start to wonder; maybe she never told me about my father because she wasn't really sure who he was.''

Cody caught the quick move of Charlotte's eyes. Checking on the children. Careful of what they were hearing. "Go check the baby,'' she said to Sawyer.

Erin had dropped his eyes.

"So," Cody said. "Why the Christmas cards? You thought she'd care?"

"My folks wrote to her," Erin said.

"She didn't answer," Cody guessed.

"No," Erin said. "They were going to go out there and try to make her come back with them."

"They didn't do it."

"No, they didn't."

"They gave up on her." Cody had no problem understanding that.

"What could they do? She was a big girl."

"And then, there was me," Cody said bitterly.

Erin's eyes met Cody's square on.

"What do you mean, there was you? You mean, you think they gave it up because of you? Because she had you? You think they wouldn't have wanted to have you?"

Cody didn't answer.

Erin was a little angry now. "It was because of you they thought about going out there at all. If they'd thought for a minute they could've gotten you away from her, they would've brought you back here and brought you up themselves."

Cody fixed a look on Erin, his face closed up and carefully empty. The thing Erin was saying had made an unexpectedly quick wound.

Erin shook his head, his eyes still on Cody's. "*You* know her," he said.

Oh, yes. She might have hated her baby, but she wouldn't have given him to them. Not if they'd wanted him.

"So, why did you bother with the cards?" Cody asked, his eyes stinging again. It was the old, dark feeling inside, almost like she was standing just behind him.

Erin looked surprised. "Because we love her," he said, simply.

And then Cody was surprised.

"You loved her," he echoed.

"We *love* her," Erin corrected him.

"*Why?*"

Erin sighed.

"It's the way things are," he said. "It's just the way things are."

Cody rested his elbow on the arm of the chair, his fingers against his lips.

And then he looked at Charlotte. "And do you love her?" he asked, his eyes and his voice both still very dry.

Her face was cool. "I never knew your mother, Cody," she said. But it was very clear in her voice; she didn't like the *idea* of his mother. She was just as glad not to have known her.

He nodded.

"So, I owe your parents," he said to Erin, knowing how cold it sounded.

"Your grandparents," Erin corrected him. "Owe them? For what?"

"The money they spent on Harvard. I owe them that."

"*Susan* owes them that," Charlotte said.

"She's my mother."

"Does that make you responsible for what she did before you were born?" Charlotte asked. She had coals for eyes, sometimes, his aunt.

"In this case," he said, in spite of her look. "I think it does."

Charlotte's eyes flashed.

"Well," Erin said. "It was a long time ago. I don't think they're going to be asking for it." He dropped his feet off the stool and onto the floor. "You wanted to know about the cards. That was the story."

"And you thought, if you kept sending them, someday she'd turn around. And maybe end up on your doorstep."

"Even as you did," Erin said, making a ghost of a smile.

Cody glanced at Charlotte. She was watching him.

"Yeah," Cody said.

"*Well,*" Erin said, slapping his hand down on Charlotte's knee. "Want to take a walk?"

"*I* do," Tyler said, standing in the doorway, drowsy eyed and tousled.

"Your mother and *I,*" Erin said to him, a firm apology. "Get Cody to play checkers with you."

"Checkers," Cody echoed.

"You'll love it," Erin said, pulling Charlotte up off the couch. "See you in a while."

"You'll love it," Sawyer echoed, a very wicked gleam in his eyes and the game box already in his hands. "But you're going to *lose.*"

And that was true enough.

Cody had pulled Tyler up into his lap. Sawyer chortled as he set up the checkers for the third game. "You're really rotten at this," he said. "I start again."

For some reason, Cody had begun to feel uncomfortable. He shifted Tyler onto his other knee.

"You go," Sawyer said.

"You guys," Cody said, pushing a checker forwards with the tip of one finger, "haven't found anything of mine lying around in your room, have you?" He had an itch between his shoulder blades, like somebody was watching him.

"No," Tyler said.

"Nope," Sawyer said. He made his move and waited, grinning. "Did you lose something?"

"Yeah," Cody said, squinting, and finally looked around the room to figure out what was bothering him so. His eyes caught Mickey's. She dropped hers and blushed. She'd been staring at him.

Oh-oh, he thought. *Not good.*

She looked up again and more or less batted her eyelashes at him. It was very unpleasant; he saw his chance with Charlotte fading as the color came up in Mickey's cheeks.

The boys were one thing. The girl was another.

"Your move," Sawyer said, impatiently.

He moved.

Sawyer chuckled with satisfaction.

Cody glanced back at Mickey again. Eyes still on—full bore.

Cody sighed.

Mickey sighed.

"Your move," Sawyer said. He had all the look of somebody who'd already won.

"You know," Cody said, moving his man. "It's nice to have cousins. All you guys are my cousins. You too, Mickey."

"You moved right into it," Sawyer cried, satisfied to the bone.

Cody glanced at Mickey again, making an older-brother smile. She fluttered.

"What?" she said.

"We're cousins. You know that."

"No, she doesn't," Sawyer said. "Your move. She thinks you're a *boy.*"

Mickey sat straight up in her chair. "I do not," she said, and her cheeks went bright red.

"Yes, you do," Sawyer said, leering at her disgustedly. "I heard you on the phone after dinner— '*Eewwwwww!* You should *see* him, Allison. He's so *cuuuuute.*' "

"I did not," Mickey said—this, with dignity, and straight to Cody.

91

"You did too," Sawyer said.

"I wasn't talking about *him*," she said to Sawyer. She stood up, her nose in the air.

"You were too," Sawyer said, making a move. "I heard you."

"You can just shut up," she said. And then to Cody. "You don't know what it's like having to have little brothers. Sawyer is just a nasty little immature brat. Believe me—I have better taste than to be talking on the phone to anybody about *you*."

Cheeks still flaming, she flounced out of the room.

"Well," Cody said, moving another man. *"That* went well."

"You're losing again," Sawyer said.

"Why did you do that, Sawyer?" Cody asked him. "You had to embarrass her?"

Sawyer shrugged, unrepentant. "She's a dope."

"She's going to tell," Tyler told him, solemnly.

"No she won't," Sawyer said. "Are you kidding?"

"You shouldn't do things like that to your sister," Cody said. He put Tyler down and stood up.

"We're not done," Sawyer said. "Anyway, she deserves it."

"Nobody deserves that," Cody said.

"She does," Tyler corrected him, still solemn.

A door slammed upstairs.

Cody sighed.

"Come on, Cody," Sawyer wheedled. "We got to finish the game. You haven't lost yet."

"You don't think so," Cody said. But he sat down again. Tyler climbed back into his lap. Cody sighed once more and made the move Sawyer was wanting him to make.

Just off the front hall of the house, Erin had a study. An office, actually, lined with bookshelves and cabinets, art prints on the walls, pottery in the corners—and the whole place hung with blueprints to the point that there wasn't a patch of plain wall to be seen anywhere.

And the books.

Cody had never seen so many books in one place, not outside an actual library.

The desk in the middle of the room was heaped with paper. There was a huge brass pot on the floor next to it, long rolls of paper springing out of it like the leaves of a fern.

Here they brought Cody when the children were settled and occupied for the evening. And Cody had that familiar gripping of the stomach; there was no mistaking the solemnity of this meeting.

Erin, standing behind his desk, offered Cody one of the chairs across the desk from his own. Charlotte took a chair off to the side. Cody tried to settle himself as he sat, but the chill got to him, and he heard himself beginning to talk.

"Before we start," he was saying, the coldness in his chest coming right through in the words, right through all the defense systems, "not that I want to change your minds, but I just—" He stopped unhappily. "May I say one last thing?"

Erin folded his hands. "Sure," he said.

Cody let his breath out and sat back into the chair, not sure now what it was he'd wanted to say. He folded his hands, too, and looked down at them. "I'm not like your kids," he said. "There's not much I haven't seen. And not much I haven't done. But I know what responsibility is. I've taken care of myself for a long time. I know how to mind my own business. I can keep my mouth shut. And I know how to clean up my own messes.

"Even if we don't see life the same way, I can respect what you believe. I won't interfere with your children. And I'll live by your rules." *And listen to me begging, here, and believe that I'm not trying to change your minds.*

There was pain in Erin's face. It had brought Cody to a halt, and now he was aching for what he was about to lose.

"Let's try it," Erin said.

Cody didn't understand him at first. He opened his mouth, and then shut it. "What?" he said.

"He said 'Let's try it,' " Charlotte said.

It shouldn't have come as such a shock.

Cody screwed his eyes shut. He dropped his face into his hands. His eyes were dry, but suddenly he was very, very tired. It was quiet in the room. If he'd looked up, he might have seen them looking at each other—but what their eyes would be saying, he couldn't guess. He was surprised, and not surprised. And he was unbelieving.

He sat up straight and looked at Erin.

"This is going to cost you money," he said, finally, finding rational ground. "I told Charlotte I was going to get a job—"

"No," Charlotte said, cutting him off, scaring him. His accepting of the situation had just given her the right to do that.

"You came here to get your grades up," she said. "You can't do that if you're trying to work at the same time."

"But—" he said.

"You have to understand," Erin said. "This wasn't an impulsive decision. We considered a lot of very fine points. If we're going to do this, you're just going to have to trust us about some things. It's going to cost us some money; it's going to cost you some autonomy."

"I haven't got any clothes," Cody reminded him. "I'm going to eat more than Sawyer."

"Already, he's arguing," Charlotte said, wryly.

Cody stopped, gave her a look.

"It'll work out," Erin said. "We've been doing pretty well financially for the last little while. It'll work out."

Cody sighed.

"Okay?" Erin said.

Cody said very softly, "I didn't expect you to do this." He looked at Charlotte. "Thank you."

"Let's just hope you don't end up sorry you came," Erin said, cheerfully.

"The rules," Charlotte said, the voice of reality. "You respect us. We respect you. You make a mess, you clean it up. Nobody in this family ever lies. You want something, you ask. And you be very careful of the children. *Very* careful. Because that's the one thing I have no flexibility about."

"Yes, ma'am," Cody said.

"And while you're under our roof, you don't get into any trouble—not with girls, not at school, not on the street."

Her eyes met his.

"Yes, ma'am," he said again. And he meant it.

A howling broke out, coming from the den.

Charlotte rolled her eyes and got up out of the chair. "That it?" she asked, looking at Erin.

"That's it," Erin said. "The rest, we just play by ear."

There were a few awful shrieks.

"*What* is going *on*?" Charlotte yelled, heading out the door.

Cody stood up.

"Just one more second," Erin said, still sitting. "Close the door, would you? Maybe you'd better lock it."

Cody hesitated for a moment, and then did as he was told.

"Sit down," Erin said. He pulled open the drawer of his desk, rummaged around a bit, and drew something out. He closed the drawer, leaned forwards, his elbows on the desk. The knife was on his palm.

Cody's hand went to his empty pocket. "I wondered where that was," he said. "I was afraid the kids would get hold of it."

"I picked it up last night," Erin said. "I apologize. I didn't want Charlotte to find it." He turned it over in his fingers. "How does it work?"

"Don't you try it," Cody said, quickly. "Give it to me. I'll show you." Erin handed it over across the desk. Cody fitted it neatly into his hand and with one deft move had the blade out and set.

Erin's eyebrows went up.

Cody tucked the blade away again.

"You seem to know how to use it," Erin observed.

"Yes, sir," Cody said, and he put it back down on the desk. Out of his own hands.

"Have you ever used it?" Erin asked him. It had come out a casual question, but Erin was watching him closely.

"Yes, sir," he said, meeting Erin's eyes.

Erin nodded.

"You want me to explain?" Cody asked.

Erin took a thoughtful breath and sat back, rubbing one ear. "I think," he said, "I think I'd like you to explain your attitude towards it."

Cody picked it up again, weighing it in his hand. "You do what you have to do," he said. "Whether you like it or not, sometimes."

Erin considered. "What is it," he asked, "you have to do?"

"Get home without getting cut up." Cody smiled at him. It was really just about that simple, in the end.

"It's got a beautiful handle," Erin said.

Cody looked at it, ran his fingers across the surface. "You see the irony there," he said. Erin nodded. He saw.

"Does this worry you?" Cody asked. He was quite frankly amazed that Erin hadn't asked more.

Erin shrugged. He wasn't sure.

"Because there's blood on it," Cody went on. He kept his eyes on Erin's. "I lived in a rough neighborhood. I didn't look for trouble."

"That the truth?" Erin asked.

He actually expects an answer to that.

"What if it wasn't?" Cody said. "You think if I lied to you once, I wouldn't lie to you about the lie?"

"What else can I do?" Erin asked.

Cody laughed, ruefully. "Yeah, it's the truth," he said. "I'm very good with this knife. I had to be on the street at night. I'm alive. But if I were you, that would make me nervous."

Erin folded his arms. "You think you're going to need it here?"

"I don't know," Cody said. "I don't know what it's like here."

"If I tell you I don't think you will?"

Cody put the knife down on the desk, very carefully. "Then I'll take you at your word," Cody said. "The same way you're taking me at mine."

Erin was staring absently at the mess on the desk. "You know," he started, still lost in his thoughts," whatever happened between you and Charlotte this morning, you made a friend out of her." Erin was looking at him, now. "Last night, she'd just as soon have tossed you out into the street. This afternoon, she's worried about your welfare."

The longest shot I ever took, Cody was thinking. *And I'm not dead yet.*

"Anyway—whatever happened, it's made *my* life easier." Erin reached for the knife, held it on the palm of his hand. "If she sees this," Erin said, "I'm not sure what'll happen. I can *guess...*"

"I understand," Cody said. But he didn't really. He didn't understand Erin.

"The knife is a fact," Cody said. "The knife is a part of me. How could I lie to her about that?"

Erin nodded. "Maybe we'd just better not bring it up at all," Erin said. "We won't need to..." and that was a question.

"Why don't you keep it for me?" Cody asked him. "Unless it really bothers you. I don't know—maybe this changes your mind. I could understand that. This is what I was trying to explain in the first place, that keeping me has its risks."

"It doesn't change my mind," Erin said. "It does scare me."

"Then you keep it," Cody said. "You keep it. And I'll do my best not to bring you shame." But he was still scared. "Erin, you've got to understand something. I want you to trust me, but look—I'm a long way from perfect, you know? I'm going to mess up sooner or later. Probably sooner. I'm just a stupid street kid from New York. If I can believe you understand that, if I think you won't come to pieces if I blow it, then I won't be so scared. But if you think I'm going to be perfect, we're both going to get hurt. I can't stand up under that. I mean, I'm not going to hurt your kids or kill anybody, but I don't know how well I'm going to do."

Erin picked up the knife and slid the drawer open. He put the knife way back in. "You know where it is," Erin said. And that didn't bother Cody at all, because the one thing he did know was that he'd never betray this man's trust in him.

"You want me to tell you everything?" Cody asked.

Erin looked at him.

"You want to?" he asked.

And Cody would have done it. But the thought of how a lot of it would sound — it was too fragile a thing, their accepting him. He was giving them his honest face. If he talked too much about what had been, he'd be talking about the Cody that wasn't the real one. He'd be talking about the face, and it would be bad. He didn't have that much faith in the resilience of this situation. And something in him didn't want to tell Erin the truth about his mother, not any more than Cody himself wanted to know it.

"No, sir," Cody said, finally.

Erin nodded.

"I never hurt anybody that I enjoyed it," Cody said. "I never looked for fights. I would never hurt a child. I don't get violent when I'm angry. I don't get angry much. I don't do drugs. I don't drink. I just — try to take care of my business."

Erin nodded again. "Okay." And he leaned across the desk and stuck his hand out. Cody took it and shook hands with him. "We'll just have to trust each other," Erin said. Very simple.

Erin smiled at him. "There's something about you I really like," he said.

Cody accepted that with a little pain. "Same," he said, from his soul. "I promise you. You'll have my best. I may not be good, sir. But I'm not bad, either."

Erin looked at him evenly.

"But I worry about Charlotte," Cody said. "I get the feeling . . . I'm not sure she can forgive very much — not to offend you."

"No," Erin said. "In some ways, she doesn't forgive very easily. Well, ultimately she does. Sometimes. Well, no. Most of the time. But not at first."

"So, what if I do something wrong?" Cody asked, a little worried.

"We're just going to have to see how it goes," Erin said.

"Well, can you explain some of these things to her?" Cody asked him.

"Are you *kidding*?" Erin said. "She's still expecting *me* to be perfect."

"She is?"

"Yes, she is."

Cody whistled. "What if we start messing up?" he asked.

"Well," Erin said, grinning. "That's part of the beauty of your being here. From now on, at least we'll have each other."

Late night rounds. She always did it, woke up at least once in the night and had to go around through the whole house and check on the kids. And usually, at least one of them had kicked all the covers off; he'd be lying there — or she, because it was still so with Mickey — all curled up in a tight, shivering little ball. The moment Charlotte tucked the covers back over the child, the little body would relax happily, legs untuck, everything slowly, blissfully uncurl.

Tonight, and it was *very* late, there was a light under the boys'-room door — Cody's door. She peered up through the gloom at the clock in the hallway. Two o'clock in the morning. She stood in the hallway for a little time, listening, before the maternal part of her had to find out why that boy was still awake.

She tapped softly at the door. There was a stirring behind it.

"You can come in," she heard him say. So she turned the knob and pushed the door open, all very quietly, as if she were afraid of waking him.

He was sitting at Sawyer's desk, wearing Erin's pajamas and robe. There was money spread out on the desk, a lot of bills. He looked up at her and smiled. He looked tired.

"Come in," he said. He got up out of Sawyer's chair and stepped aside for her, pulling Ty's chair out from under the other desk for himself. She sat down.

"What are you doing?" she asked.

He leaned over and gathered up the bills into one pile, and then he sat down again in Ty's chair, the money in his hands. The moon was framed squarely in the window behind him. In the dim light, the shadows under Cody's eyes seemed very deep.

"This is all I have," he said, putting the bills down on Ty's desk. "I've worked all my life, and this is all I have. A hundred and fifty dollars." He tapped it. "That's all. It's not even enough to get me back to New York." He pushed the chair back so that he could stretch his legs out and look out the window into the night.

98

She studied him silently for a moment, still sleepy and slow. "You want to go back to New York?" she asked.

"No," he said, and he smiled at her, the same smile from this morning. The one that wasn't sure of anything.

She shrugged. "So. Here you are."

He waved towards the bills on the desk. "But it's not like I have a choice."

"Sure you do," she said. "You've got us."

He smiled, giving her quiet gratitude for that. Then he turned his face away, back to the window, sighing. "I just . . ." He parted his hands slightly. "I guess I'm just a little worried about my mother."

He rested his chin on his hand. The moonlight fell through the window and lit a tiny rhyme of brightness on his hair. It was funny how familiar he seemed to her, now the thing was settled. It didn't hurt any that he was the kind of kid who would worry about his mother.

"I left her without any food in the house," he said.

"She can't get herself some food?" Charlotte asked.

He lifted a shoulder.

"What's the problem? She doesn't have any money? She can't get to the store? What?"

He gave Charlotte a long, thoughtful look. "Grocery shopping is the kind of thing that never enters her mind," he said, a strange mix of disdain and sadness in his voice. She got the feeling he was choosing his words carefully.

"If money's the problem," she said, "I'm sure Erin would want to send her whatever she needs."

"That's very kind of you." He shrugged. "But if you did it, she wouldn't buy food with it."

Now it was Charlotte's turn for the long look, wondering what it was he was saying. "What would she spend it on, Cody?" she asked, not sure she wanted to know, but sure she could probably guess.

He looked at her. "Not food," he said. Very careful, indeed.

"I see."

"I don't know what to do," he said softly. "I probably shouldn't have left her."

But that made her angry. "There does come a time," she said, "when people have to take a little bit of responsibility for themselves. She's a big girl, Cody. She's your mother. You've got to remember, *you* are the kid."

"I know it," he said, his eyes flashing a bit. "But that doesn't change the fact that there was no food in the house."

She sighed. He was right. The words didn't change the reality. "Okay," she said. "Does she have any money?"

He shook his head slightly. "I don't know," he said.

"Okay," Now she was casting around for ideas. "Okay. Is there somebody up there you trust? Somebody you know well enough, you could trust them? I mean, you know—like with money. Somebody who wouldn't mind doing you a favor."

"Yeah," he said. "There is. There's a guy upstairs. Parker. Mr. DuBois." And from the way he looked at her, she could see he was figuring it out himself.

"Okay. What if we sent him a little money each month, and maybe he could make sure she had some groceries? You know, just—maybe he could pick up a few extra things when he went shopping—oh, I don't know. It sounds like probably too much work."

"Not really," he said, pulling himself up straighter in the chair. "I think Parker would do that. I've done it for him. He doesn't have any family anymore. I think he'd do it."

"Well," she said, opening her hands.

He was looking at her closely. "Aunt Charlotte," he said, something like respect in his face. "Are you rich?"

Big smile. Quite funny, actually. "Not really."

He tapped one finger on the arm of the chair. "I think you are," he said. "How else could you do this—take care of me, send a little to her. I don't know; I don't like to ask you for this much."

Another point on the plus side for him. "Look," she said. "We do all right. We do well enough." *If we're careful. If we don't get too silly.* "This whole thing is important to us. To Erin, especially."

"He's a nice man," Cody said. But there was more in his eyes than he was saying.

"He's a *very* nice man," she said.

"You love him."

"I'd be stupid not to, don't you think?"

He smiled, and then he asked, "Does he ever make mistakes?"

She laughed. "He wouldn't dare."

He nodded. "I do," he said, solemnly.

She smiled, stood up, leaned over, and patted his shoulder. "So do I," she said. "A lot. Now, why don't you go to bed? And don't worry. I think it's time you started taking care of yourself."

He smiled again, but his face had gone unreadable. "Thank you," he said again. He switched off the light, and she stood by the door, just until she heard him pulling up the covers. *We're going to have to take care of this,* she thought, feeling nice. Very nice. *This just may work out.*

And then she went on and finished her rounds, just in case Mickey should be lying there freezing in the dark.

10

"Hullo," Erin said, glancing up from his work. Charlotte dropped herself into one of the wing-backed office chairs, feeling fine and satisfied, and a little walked out. "How'd the shopping go?"

"It was *wonderful*," she said. She raised an eyebrow, looking at his desk. "I don't know how you ever find anything in that mess."

"How much did you spend?" He sorted through the brass pot collection of rolled-up plans, picked a roll, pulled it partway open, let it draw itself closed again, and stuck it back into the pot.

"Too much," she sighed happily. "You know, I don't think anybody's ever bought him anything before. Everything he has, he's paid for himself. And I don't believe he's ever had anything extra."

"It's kind of fun, isn't it?" he asked. "Suddenly being somebody's benefactor."

"Yes," she said, stretching. "It is." She closed her eyes, pulling the kinks out of her back, relaxing against the chair.

"One of the things that made it so pleasant," she mused, "was that he doesn't *expect* anything. With him, everything is surprise and gratitude and embarrassment. *Nothing* like going with Mickey. You feel like you're practically *forcing* it on him."

Erin glanced up at her.

"The other very most fun thing about it is that *every*thing looks great on him. He really is quite a beautiful boy, once you get him cleaned up a little—you'll like the haircut. We didn't take anything off. We just shaped it a little, and it looks good. He's got good hair, a little of your curl in it." She rubbed her hands together, making eyes at Erin. "Such terrific raw material—and today I had him all to myself."

"Made him over in your own image, did you?" he said.

There was something in his tone she didn't like. "*Right*," she said, slightly disturbed by it. She *had* been kidding about that last thing.

"So you had a good time," he said, finally finding the plans he wanted. It was beginning to sound like he was being just a little patronizing. Tolerant—as though he suspected she was being a little silly about all this.

"Yes, I did. Should I not have?"

He glanced up at her innocently, unrolling the plans, smoothing them out on the desk. "No. I'm glad you did." It was her *job* after all, the procuring of the wardrobe. "This is that building we did for Prime West," he murmured.

"Something significant happened today," she said, talking to him, not talking to him. "I think we sort of made friends."

It had been a silly kind of a thing—a salesman with too many airs, explaining to them that all the other stores in the mall buy in Los Angeles, but *his* buyers bought in New York. Proof-in-point: "*These* pants are what *everybody* in New York is wearing," and the salesman had hauled a pair of pants off the rack, an exact duplicate of the pants Cody had on.

Cody and Charlotte had looked at each other, and in that moment there had been a total sympathy of mind, a shared joke —the pants, the salesman, the mall, and the two of them buying *fashions*. A door, open. And in that moment, she'd *liked* him. And Cody saying, so soberly—"He's right, you know. They *do* wear those in New York."

"What are you doing?" she asked Erin.

"I was thinking . . ." Erin made a few rapid marks on the plans. "We could probably use some of this floor plan for the Smith's research building."

"Labs or offices?"

"Offices. So, do you feel like you got enough stuff?"

"Oh, yeah. We bought him enough for two kids. He'll fit right in with everybody else in school tomorrow."

"You sure?"

"I asked around," she said. "He wants to be unobtrusive. So, we bought unobtrusive, but extremely *classy* unobtrusive." She looked down at her hands, humble, but not actually repentant. "We did get a lot of stuff. I was just having too much fun to stop. I know he was embarrassed."

"He'll get used to being spoiled," Erin said, and he turned the plans slightly, squinting at them.

"He doesn't like money, Erin." She'd seen it in Cody's face, studying himself in the mirror, all dolled up and looking quite fine. At one point, he'd muttered, "I look just like the East End," and he hadn't said it with any pleasure. She'd seen it in the way he gauged other people, too; the preppie types he didn't like—you could see that in his face. "I think he maybe resents it a little."

"I don't think that surprises me," Erin said, tapping the eraser of his pencil against his lips.

"The funny thing is, this morning he asked about the utility bill, how much it costs to run a house like this. What does a kid know about utility bills? *You* don't even know about utility bills. I didn't get the feeling Susan paid that much attention to his domestic education."

Erin looked at her, tapping at the plans now. "I keep wondering what Susan's doing," he said. "I wonder what she looks like, how she lives."

"You could ask Cody," she said.

He shook his head, still absently, still unfocused. "No," he said, suddenly pulling himself back in. "He doesn't want to talk about her." And maybe Erin didn't want to hear.

"You know that photography magazine he has? We passed the camera store in the mall, and he *lingered* there. You ought to show him your camera, kiddo. Maybe he'd appreciate the thing."

Erin smiled.

"I like him, Erin," she said. "I never thought I would. But I do. We talk, and I like a lot of the way he thinks. He's just kind of lost. You know, it's just not fair—you get these sensitive, gentle little souls, and the world gets ahold of them—it just makes me sick, what the kid's been through."

"We don't know what he's been through," Erin reminded her.

"We know some of it. We know he's been hurt. We know he's been grieving for his friend, the old shopkeeper, and that he hasn't been able to talk about it. We know he's had to take care of himself. And we know he had the courage to come all the way out here on a chance—What are you *smiling* at?"

"You."

"Why? I hate it when you smile at me that way."

"What way?"

"Like, whatever I'm doing, it's so *cute*."

"Two days ago," he reminded her, "You were afraid that kid was going to murder us in our beds. Now, suddenly he's a battered innocent."

"So?" she asked, incensed. "Isn't he?"

"I doubt it," he said.

"Really," she said, heat in her face.

"You have to remember, Char. This kid was brought up by my sister, the anarchist. He told us himself—he grew up on the street. He *said* he'd been in trouble. You think he didn't generate at least some part of it? For all we know, he might have been part of a gang. He might have hurt somebody in a street fight. We just don't know that much about him." He raised his eyebrows meaning, *Doesn't that make sense?*

"I don't believe he's that kind of kid. I don't believe he'd hurt anybody."

"I wouldn't be too sure of that."

"I thought *you* were the one who was so *comfortable* with him."

"I am," he said. "I feel fine about him. It's just, I don't think we ought to be making assumptions about anything—about his past, about the way Susan treated him, about his personality. I think we ought to just sit back and see what develops, let him be what he is. And for heaven's sake, I don't think we ought to be thinking of him as an innocent. I don't think there's probably been a heck of a lot of innocence involved in his life."

"Really," she said, tightly. "Well, I think he's probably been done *unto* far more than he's *done*."

Erin parted his hands: Maybe yes, maybe no. "But I'll tell you, we've gotta not romanticize him. I mean it, Char. You give that kid something to live up to that he just can't do and somebody's going to get hurt. If we're going to love him, we have to love him for what he *is*, not what we hope he is or what he could be."

"Well, then," she said, hearing the stiffness in her voice, and satisfied with it. "At least we'll have your extremely mature perspective to guide us along, won't we?" She stood up, making no secret of her anger. "Dinner in twenty minutes?"

"Charlotte . . ." he said.

She held up her hand. "Just come when you're ready," she said, and she was gone.

Erin heaved a sigh, watching the door close behind her.

The room was dark, only the moonlight drifting in through the window. Quiet. Cody could hear Sawyer's breathing, sweet and regular, up above in his bunk. Cody should have been asleep himself—Charlotte had nearly worn him out, walking him all over the mall like that. He was feeling it, his legs aching slightly, lying in the bed that was now *his* bed. Because now he was a member of the family. At a cost.

Tonight they'd told the kids he was staying—had a family council about it. All the boys had voted an emphatic yes. Mickey had voted no. She'd pitched a fit, is what she'd done, an amazing, incredible fit. It hadn't lasted long—Charlotte wasn't the kind of mother to stand for something like that. But she'd made her point: "You can't afford to buy me one crummy pair of Reeboks, but you can buy *him* more clothes than he could wear in a year."

Charlotte *had* spent too much on him—nice things, *very* nice, beautiful things—and Mickey had lost her private bedroom because Ty had to sleep somewhere, and now Cody for sure had made one very certain enemy in this house.

He sighed and curled up with his back to the wall.

There was school tomorrow. Thinking about that, he hadn't been able to eat much all day. And he couldn't sleep, lying here wide-eyed when the rest of the house had been silent for hours.

It was the not knowing. Wondering what it was going to be like, whether he could really pull it off. One thing he did know —he wasn't going to get another chance after this one.

11

"You sure you don't want me to go in there with you?" Charlotte asked.

Cody was in the front seat of the car, studying the indifferent brick face of the school through the window. New notebook, new pencils, new pens, new clothes, new haircut—but the old Cody, getting the unhappy devil in him, looking at that building.

"No, ma'am. Thank you," he said.

"Are you going to be okay?" she asked him.

His hands were shaking, and his stomach gone all cold and knotty. "Fine," he said. He smiled at her, and then looked out at the building again.

And then he said, carefully, "I probably won't be telling them the absolute truth in there. Not at the very beginning."

"Oh?"

"No, ma'am. Not at first."

She didn't like it, of course.

"I need the right classes," he said, looking at her. "I can't take a chance with that."

"Why don't you just tell them the truth?" she asked. They could hear a bell ringing inside the school, and the sound of it made his stomach tighten.

"There isn't any," he said. "Just because the lies are old, that doesn't make them the truth." He smiled at her. *Relax.* "I won't make it any worse than it has to be."

"I think you're making a mistake," she said. "I think you may be underestimating them." And he admired her restraint. He could see it in her face, the parent wanting to speak out.

But he knew what he was doing. She'd probably never even seen the inside of a resource room. She didn't know what it was like to be a "problem." She wouldn't understand the attitudes in there. "Why don't you let me come in and explain things?" That's all he needed—somebody speaking for him, a *mother*, for heaven's sake.

Because you'd end up frustrated after—because you'd find out they don't listen. And, okay—you'd understand why I wanted to do it my own way; but it'd be too late by then.

106

"If I make a mistake," he said gently, "I'll abide the consequences. I just wanted to keep it straight between us." He smiled again, a little apology. "You don't have to like what I do, Aunt Charlotte. But I'm not going to lie to you about it." He popped the car door open and climbed out. "Thank you," he said, leaning over and smiling good-bye but avoiding that last, parting don't-do-it-look.

He stood on the sidewalk until she drove away.

He turned around, gazing up at the building. *I should have let her come. I know I don't want to do this alone.*

In the end, it was good she hadn't. She wouldn't have liked it, listening to how smooth he could be. He'd always been a very good and gifted liar when he had to be, and as he saw it, sitting in that counselor's office, this was one time he absolutely *had* to be.

He called up his mother's bored academic vocabulary, mixed in his own male savvy, and, in spite of the cold in his stomach, before too long he had the heavy woman behind the desk thinking he was the most earnest, intelligent, *charm*ing young man she'd ever worked with. Even Cody wasn't so comfortable with how well it went.

All college prep classes. No questions.

Very impressive. Quite an asset for the school.

She asked for his old address. He gave her an East-side address, a smoke screen, a time-buyer, and he made up some story about having to go live with his grandmother, shifting schools, the name of a school uptown—all confusion, a postponement of the inevitable. The longer he could hold off his old records, the more chance he had of survival.

She gave him a list of electives. "Just *one*, now," she said, lifting one finger, smiling at him from behind it. Then she stuck a form into her typewriter. He scanned the list, whipping by the shops and the home ec's until he stopped, unbelieving, halfway down the list.

"You have a photography class here?" he asked.

"Yes, we do," she said.

The excitement made him cooler inside. "Do you have to have your own camera?"

"I don't think so," she said, swinging around in her chair to check her notes. "Why don't we just put you in there and see what happens?" she asked, charmingly. She really liked him. *This is not good,* he thought, embarrassed and beginning to feel a little guilt—not because of the lying, but because of the poor, silly lady.

There was a lot at stake here. The one thing he couldn't afford was the consequence of his own altruism. So he sat back, giving her a little smile of his own. "That would be wonderful, thank you," he said, not believing his luck, apologizing to her silently.

She finished what she was doing, pulled the form out of the typewriter, tore off the top copy, and then the next, and handed the pink sheet to him. "This is your schedule," she said. "And here—" she added a small pile of things—"are your student code book, umm—there's a map of the school there—your inoculation form—this form, you need to have your parents fill out—and this form, you have to have each teacher sign. You can leave it with Mr. Allen at the end of the day. This is your bus assignment. And, I think that about does it."

She beamed at him. "Well, we're very pleased to have you with us, Mr. McClellan," she said, putting out her hand for him to shake. "Now, you've missed a week. You shouldn't have too much trouble catching up, but you'd probably better go on to your first class before you miss any more."

And then he was out in the empty hallway outside the office, the little pile of papers in his hand, trying to sidestep his nerves. He studied the schedule—first period/homeroom: English with Ms. Hunsaker. And there was a map; Cody kept trying to turn himself so that he had the map and the school and his body all lined up the same way.

In five minutes, he found himself, uncomfortable and suddenly most *terribly* reluctant, outside the door of his homeroom class. The smell of the place was getting to him, the scent of blackboards, maybe, of lockers and acoustical tile and years of so many people in one place. It triggered a serious fight-or-flight inside of him, and he wasn't sure what he would do—what he *should* do—once he had actually opened this door and started it.

But the thing had to be faced. Or else, not—but it was a little late for that. So he took a deep breath, opened the door, and went inside the room.

The brightness took him by surprise; the whole wall opposite the door was windows, and the diffused sun came dancing through them making the room a confusion of light. He blinked once, turning a bit to the side. The illusion passed.

He was standing at the front of a full classroom. And everyone—*everyone*—was staring at him. Understandable. But unpleasant.

The teacher had been leaning back against the front of her

108

desk, a young woman with an almost bored professional voice. A college type. He could feel his mother coming up inside of him as he looked at her. *Well, you've got yourself another dedicated, intellectual teacher, son. Dedicated to making you use your little brain.*

Ms. Hunsaker put her hand out for his pink form. He gave it to her. She smiled at him, not a warm smile, perfunctory. Maybe preoccupied.

While she looked over his information, he looked over the class. Middle-class kids, neat as Barbie dolls, clean room, chrome and wood desks, posters on the walls. And the old feelings that had been coming up inside him surfaced with a vengeance. It was an old fight in him, to be hoping for anything, and at this moment it was that this middle-class disguise of his would hold—and at the same time, to detest the world that held what he didn't have.

He was looking over the population of this room, drowning in his own disdain. *Too much money, here. Too soft.* The college-bound. The privileged. *I can't believe you're actually messing with this.*

There was a ferret-faced kid smiling up at him from the first seat, middle row—the perfect, classic nerd. The kid had on a plaid shirt with one of those pen caddies stuck in the pocket, heavy glasses, half-curly hair cut short—like he was in a disguise of his own, a nerd disguise.

And a little cheerleader, front row, right in front of Cody— silver-blonde halo of curls like a fur hat around a face that was far too cute, too clean to have anything but a vacuum behind it. And the uniform—lots of leg, tanned legs.

And the rest of the room, a cluster of guys in letter sweaters, girls in expensive colors, faces he couldn't see with any clarity. He held the sneer in his mind, all the time, his palms sweaty, afraid somebody'd figure out the truth and throw him out on his face. He was studying the cheerleader's legs again when Ms. Hunsaker spoke to him.

"Take the seat second row back, just behind Mr. Getts in the middle there." Behind the nerd.

"People," she said as he sidled his way to his seat. "We have a new class member." He dropped his notebook on the desk and slid in. "I'm sure Mr. McClellan would appreciate your indulgence and your assistance. I expect you to make him feel welcome here." She was standing behind her desk, now. She flipped something open and began to write in it.

The cheerleader turned around smiled. *Nice*, he thought

with distaste. *She must be popular.* He raised one eyebrow at her. *Didn't your mama ever tell you not to smile at strangers?* Her smile faded when she got no better answer than that.

Then the nerd turned around and stuck out his hand. "Marty Getts," he said, pleasantly. Cody took the hand, but with undisguised reserve.

"All right," the teacher said—she had that arrogant tone his mother used to use when she was presenting a strong point— "So, we have Descartes on the one hand: 'I think; therefore I am.' We have a seventeenth-century dualist here—a man who attributes existence to God, and this is his proof.

"On the other hand, we have the existentialists; we have Nietzsche, nineteenth century—and what is his feeling about existence? Can you define existentialism for me in one neat little package? Mr. Ersle?"

Silence in the room.

"Ms. Forrester?"

The black girl across the aisle from Cody. "It's like," she said, her voice sounding disappointingly like the rest of them looked, "that an individual—that in your life, there's like no way to know exactly what's true and what's not true, because for everything, there's evidence for either side of any question. So, when it comes down to it, you just have to do what you think is best. You have to make your own choices. You have to decide what's right."

"Okay," the teacher said. She came around to the front of the desk, leaned back against it, folding her arms. "But that's not all of it." She surveyed the room. "Ms. McCall?" she said.

There was no answer. Then the cheerleader looked up, glanced over her shoulder at the rest of the room, got suddenly very red in the face, then looked contrite, folding her hands on top of her desk.

"I'm sorry," she said.

"It would be nice if you could join us," Ms. Hunsaker said, pushing off from the desk and beginning to articulate. "So, no one can tell me? You read the story. There are two aspects to this concept, here." The little cheerleader's shoulders slumped a bit. Cody could still see a bit of her legs from where he was sitting.

"On the one hand, as Ms. Forrester told us, the definition of truth—and of morality—are ascertained by the individual. But there is another factor—and if you've missed that, you've missed the meat of it."

110

The cheerleader raised her hand.

"All right, Ms. McCall," the teacher said. "If you would be so kind."

"It has to do with responsibility," the girl said, but very quietly.

"Would you say that again?" the teacher asked, facing the rest of the class.

The cheerleader cleared her throat and said clearly, "If you're the only one who can choose, then you're the only one who can take responsibility."

"Nice to have you back," the teacher remarked. "Okay? You hear what she said? The *essence* of it is that life is a matter of *choice* rather than destiny. Choice or the relinquishment of choice, which is also a choosing. *But*—what happens to you after you choose is—to put it simply—your own darn fault. Nobody else's."

Cody realized he was sitting at this desk the old way, face locked on bored, body totally disengaged; it was a defiant posture, and he knew it. He hadn't meant to put it on. He pulled himself upright in the seat, cleared the look off his face.

But he couldn't clear his discomfort, because something about the discussion was bothering him.

"All right, now," Ms. Hunsaker was saying. "Now, we have the statement of a seventeenth-century dualist: 'I think; therefore I am.' And that means?" She pointed.

"He heard himself thinking," the voice came from the back of the room, "and so he figured that proved to him that he had to exist."

"Okay. We're talking about a totally different philosophy here. Descartes took his own *self*, his thinking, as evidence of the existence of God and of the universal reality of *law*, that there is a right and wrong, predetermined by God, that has little if anything to do with our perceptions of it. That if a thing is wrong, it's wrong, regardless of how you may *feel* about it. Can you feel that difference here? These are two quite opposite theories. Now, what I want you to do is to reconcile them for me. Can you find a middle ground? Can you bring them together?"

The teacher started prowling around the room, watching the faces. There was a great silence. She let it go on for several minutes. And then a voice from the middle of the room hazarded a guess.

"It depends on how you define *think*. It can mean conceptualize, visualize. The statement could read, instead of 'I *think*,'" maybe 'I *want*.' And that would mean that your thinking gave you direction. And that would mean choices. That what he could see in his mind, he could go after it, *be* it. That he formed himself.''

"All right,'' the teacher said with satisfaction, and she moved slowly, thoughtfully, back up to the front of the room.

They all agree, Cody thought. Somehow it made him angry. *That makes it so antiseptic.* And he put up his own hand, almost before he'd known he was going to.

"Mr. McClellan?'' Hunsaker said.

"But what if we *don't* exist?'' he asked. And he liked that. It was a real question; it made him uncomfortable. "What if we're nothing more than the by-product of a philosophical argument some mind is having with itself somewhere?''

"Ms. Jenson?'' There were hands up now.

"But we *do* exist.'' Almost angry there. That was better.

"How do you know?'' Ms. Hunsaker asked, cocking her head just a bit, her face enigmatic.

"We do have independent thought. We make our own choices. We're individuals. I mean, we do *exist*.''

Ms. Hunsaker looked to Cody, waiting for an answer.

"How do you know that? You don't know that. Okay, it's what we *think*. But what if it turns out we don't know what independent thought *feels* like? We think we're individuals. We think everything we feel is our own. But what if it's not? What if we're just characters in a story? What if somebody else made up, everything—our world, the people in it, our feelings. We wouldn't know the difference. What if we're preprogrammed, and we never did make an independent choice? What if we just *thought* we wanted what we wanted—how would we know the difference? There are too many possibilities here. It's irresponsible to settle on one when you can't be sure.''

"Really,'' Ms. Hunsaker said.

It was a concept Cody had never thought of before. He didn't like it; it made him feel worse than his first real look at the sky had done. But it was different than what everybody else had been saying, and that made it satisfactory.

"And what do *you* think, Mr. McClellan? What do you believe?''

The question was, of course, out of line.

"What do *you* believe?'' he asked, throwing it back at her, knowing full well she was going to have to be careful about her answer.

"What do you think I believe?'' she asked, and she had a

112

kind of private smile on.

He sat back in his seat. Ping pong. They were playing ping pong here. Okay. So, she'd asked him a question. So, she was going to have to take responsibility for the answer.

"I think you probably believe in God," he said, not necessarily meaning it as a positive observation.

She conceded with a slight nod. "And that means . . . ?"

"It means you must have a very busy mind," he said, well aware of how flippant he must have sounded, but not worried about it. She'd set the tone. It was her responsibility. *Just remember, you still have to live with this. You don't get an A out of somebody you insult; you should know that by now.* The tension in the room was proof enough that he'd crossed the line, and he began to wish he'd kept his mouth shut.

But Ms. Hunsaker, perched against her desk again, arms folded, was still smiling her private smile. Actually, you could have believed she was almost laughing.

"You're right," she said. "I do." She pushed herself from the desk, still amused — if that's what it was — and went around behind the desk. She looked up at the class, smiling broadly now, pleased as punch about some private thing. "Okay," she said, and she rubbed her hands together. "Let's get down to Thomas Hardy."

Elise McCall had troubles on her mind, and Ms. Hunsaker hadn't helped; the woman had an unerring instinct for people who were preoccupied. But then, these were troubles Hunsaker probably wouldn't have had much respect for — not in the face of Descartes and Nietzsche.

It was a simple enough thing; one of the cheerleaders had had to drop out of the squad, and something had to be done about it. Not that that was going to be hard. Finding someone who could fill the opening, anyway — there were about three hundred girls who would have loved to move right on in and take up residence.

And that was the problem.

How do you choose one girl out of so many without making a mess of all the ones who didn't make it?

This really wasn't Elise's problem. It was Mrs. Jacowski's because she was the advisor. But Elise couldn't help worrying about it, wondering why they couldn't just go ahead and let everybody who wanted to do it, do it. Why should anybody have to be hurt over such a stupid, insignificant thing?

Not that Elise knew that kind of hurt firsthand; she'd never lost anything in her life. And that wasn't to say she'd always *won*, either. It was just that, in her mind, losing was a way you thought about yourself, and you could do that whether you'd gotten what you wanted or not.

Still, she had a *very* good imagination, and an instinctive empathy, and she couldn't stand it when people were suffering. She sat there at her desk, a little chilly in her squad uniform —why they had to wear them all day, every game day, she never had been able to understand—and she was hoping that for once Ms. Hunsaker would just ignore her this morning. Vain hope.

The classroom door had opened at a propitious moment: the class had gone silent, and Elise was only just understanding that Ms. Hunsaker had asked some question she was expecting Elise to answer—

That's when the new boy had come in.

Elise could feel the general female gasp at her back the second he stepped through that door. He was a magnificent boy. Her heart went out to him right away, having to stand there while everybody—including Elise herself—gave him a good looking over. She knew he was uncomfortable. She could see it in the set of his face.

But he handled himself well, very cool, very dignified. She tried to make things easier when he sat down, turned around and smiled at him, thinking to make him feel a little bit more at home. But he just about cool-and-dignified her to death when she did it.

Aha, she thought. *Maybe we'll just leave this one alone.*

But she'd ever been a glutton for punishment, so she chalked the spiny response up to first-day fear, thinking *We won't be put off.* And then she began thinking about all the different ways people had of dealing with their fears.

The class had gone quiet again.

Elise felt an awful sinking of the heart. Sure enough, caught daydreaming again. *Nice, Ms. Hunsaker. Spare me no embarrassment. I know you won't.*

After that, she'd kept her mind riveted on the discussion. Which wasn't bad—Hunsaker's discussions tended to be interesting. And then there were suddenly a few added fireworks. Whatever it was that this new boy was afraid of—assuming he was afraid of anything—it wasn't Hunsaker, and it wasn't speaking up. He was turning out to be a feisty, argumentative soul with uncomfortably interesting ideas. And imagination. And you could tell Hunsaker liked it. Elise liked it, too.

She'd stolen a little look at him over her shoulder—something he hadn't noticed. He *was* very beautiful. *A little dangerous, maybe,* she warned herself. *Certainly not over-nice.* Altogether rather interesting. And she felt a little warmth inside, thinking about it.

The bell rang. She had a little squeeze of nerves; she was going to try to talk to him a bit.

"What's your next class?" she heard Marty asking. She looked up, her books in her arms. The boy was checking his schedule.

"World history," he said. "Mrs. Bruecher."

"That's where *I'm* going," someone said, a voice full of lights, surprise, and velvety pleasure. Angela Hernon came oozing around Marty's far side, her big brown eyes turned full on the new boy—sooo casual, so utterly physical.

"Actually," Elise said, too loudly, appalled at herself, "I was going to take him there myself."

Angela turned the look on her. *Really,* it said. *Aren't we nervy today?* And the new boy was staring at her, surprise and amusement written all over his face.

But it had been worth it. Nobody should get turned over to Angela the first day; it would have been like watching him put a gun to his head. Nobody needs to start out with *that* kind of problem.

"Anyway," Angela said to him with that *look,* "I'm Angela."

Oh, and he was interested. His eyes were full of her. "I'm Cody," he said. He had a hard, intelligent look to him, and Elise suddenly had a suspicion he might have been very capable of taking care of himself. As Angela moved away, he gave Elise the strangest look.

Well, she thought. *So much for making friends with him.*

Warm hands on her shoulders. She looked up. Steven, smiling down, solid and comfortable. "See you at lunch," he said, patting her cheek lightly.

"Okay," she said. And then, remembering, "Steven. This is Cody."

She couldn't see Steven's face as he looked at Cody, but she could see Cody's face, looking at Steven. They were not going to be friends.

"Nice to meet you," Steven said.

"Come on, Hewlette," the Turk was saying, pushing up behind Steven. Steven looked down at Elise, a little annoyed and

115

sharing it. "We're going to be late again, and coach is going to kill us," Turk said, sliding past Steven and standing restlessly at the head of the aisle, waiting with the rest of the guys.

"See you," Steven said again, quietly. "Nice to meet you," he said to the new boy. And then he was gone.

Fine. Now I get to be all alone with Al Capone here. She turned around and gave the boy a smile. "Shall we go?" she asked, keeping it light.

"After you," he said, still with that look.

She went out of the door first, taking one long, slow breath for ballast. She had the feeling she was going to catch it now, and good. She turned, waiting for him to catch up, deciding the best defense would be a good offense.

"Where're you from?" she asked brightly.

He glanced at her out of the corner of his eyes, a bored-amused look settled solidly on his face. They started off down the hall. "New York," he said.

"Really," she said. "City or state?"

"There's only the city," he said.

O—kay, she thought. "McClellan is a good Scottish name. My name's McCall. So, I guess we're both Scots."

"Hmmm," he said.

They were getting looks. And it was no wonder. Holly Brewster went by the other way, and her eyes got as big as saucers, throwing questions with her eyebrows at Elise as she passed. Too bad things weren't the way Holly must have been seeing them.

"Look," he said, his voice level, not bothering to look at her. "You want to explain to me why you felt like you had to rescue me back there? It was a rescue, wasn't it? From *Angela.*" He rolled the name off his tongue, the corner of his mouth turned up slightly—he *could* have been kidding.

"I just thought you might like to meet some people," she said, fully aware that she hadn't answered his question, that she was sounding idiotic, but not at all inclined just now to want to discuss the advantages or disadvantages of Angela's aquaintance.

"Like Mr. Letter Sweater?" he asked.

"Who?"

"Your friend, Steven. What is he? Captain of the football team?"

There's something wrong with that? "He's the quarterback," she said, beginning to feel a bit cautious. She wasn't willing to discuss Steven with him, either.

116

"Why am I not surprised?" he asked. "And you're probably the head cheerleader."

"No," she said, going very carefully, now.

"That must be nice, going to games together. Gives you something to talk about, doesn't it? Gosh, it must be thrilling."

She stopped dead. They were just outside of Bruecher's class. She felt like she'd been slapped. He looked at her, an amused—*not* good-humored—inquiry in his eyes.

"I'm sorry if I offended you," she said, her cheeks feeling high and flushed. "You don't need to be insulting."

His eyebrows went up, but the look in his eyes didn't change.

"If you think I had some *motive* for being nice to you, you're wrong. I just thought you might be more comfortable being able to walk with somebody."

"I believe Angela had already volunteered," he said. And then her whole face went to flame.

"That would have been a little bit more like being walked *on*," she said. "This is your next class. Enjoy it." She pulled the door open, slipped inside, not exactly in the mood to sit through an hour of world history.

She didn't turn around to make sure he'd made it inside, or to see if he seemed the least repentant—she had a feeling he wouldn't. He'd made her feel like an idiot, like a lightweight, air-headed idiot.

And what's worse, she thought as she dropped her books on the desk and sat down, *I told a lie.* About her motivations. *It wasn't exactly altruism on your part, was it, your concern for him?* But it could have been, she argued. I would have done the same for anybody.

And that was true.

It was just that this particular anybody had been awfully nice to look at.

That's what you get, she told herself. *Act like a fool, and you get what you ask for.*

The room had gotten very quiet. Too quiet. Elise looked up. Everybody was staring at her, including Mrs. Bruecher, who was standing at the front of the room, waiting patiently for an answer.

12

"So, how was it?" Charlotte asked. She was standing at her little kitchen island, slicing meat. He dropped his books wearily on the kitchen table and himself into a chair.

"I think I'm going to die," he said.

And then she was leaning over his shoulder, putting something down on the table in front of him. Milk and cookies. He laughed, picking up a cookie. Homemade. A lot like Mrs. Guicci's, actually—with nuts.

"A little respect, please," she said. "There's calcium, there. Carbohydrates. Just the thing if you think you're going to die."

"Well, thank you," he said, nibbling the edge of his cookie.

"So tell me about it," she said. "Did you end up not telling the truth this morning?"

Carefully, now. "Only for the first half-hour," he said. "Kind of."

"Kind of?"

"Well, I had to go around all day like *this*," hands parted, meaning the *image*. "Like I knew what I was doing. I've never brought a book home from school in my life—until today." He slid back in his chair, eying the small mountain of books ruefully.

"You'll live," she said, lifting a strip of meat and placing it in a pan just so. "Tell me about your classes."

"It's just college prep stuff."

"Like?"

"Well, English, world history, pre-calc—"

"Precalculus?" she asked, sounding a little doubtful.

"No big deal," he said. It was his old gift, the one Mr. Guicci had always been after him about, his understanding of the workings of mathematics. Along with his eyes, it was the true gift. "It's the one thing I have some experience with," he explained, and then quickly, before she could ask any more, "and P.E., physics, *photography*. They have a photography class." Not much of anything but theory today, but a lot of that had been mathematics. And it turned out you didn't have to have your own camera. He picked up the glass of milk and sat back again.

118

"Just remember, the first week'll be the worst," she said. "That's normal."

"I'm amazed I made it through the first *day*. I'm *tired*. That school bus is a *nightmare*." And it was nice, saying those things. He couldn't remember talking like that to anybody before. And now, here he was sitting in this kitchen with milk and cookies, griping—just *schmoozing*.

The kitchen door flew open. "Can I have something else to eat?" Sawyer asked breathlessly. "For me and Kent?"

"No, you can't have something else to eat," Charlotte said. "And I thought you were doing your homework."

"We are," Sawyer said indignantly, and disappeared again. Charlotte gritted her teeth and made a low, frustrated sound.

"Don't ever have children," she said.

Cody smiled into his milk.

"So, did you make any friends?" she asked.

He popped the last bit of cookie into his mouth and sat up straight, putting the glass down out of the way and pulling the history text over.

"Nope," he said.

"You didn't talk to anybody?" she asked.

He lifted one shoulder slightly. "Not a priority," he said.

She harrumphed.

"Okay. One person. I talked to one person. A *cheer*leader." With whom he had been supercilious, to say the least. He was a little repentant about that now; if she'd been a customer in Mr. Guicci's shop, he never would have spoken to her that way. It was his mother in him, and he hated it.

"Name?"

"McCall." He opened his book, settled it against his chest, and looked over the first page.

"McCall. What's her first name?"

"I don't remember. Lisa or something."

"Elise?"

"Could have been that." He shifted in the chair impatiently.

"Well, if it was, we know her folks. Nice people." She turned on the water.

"No doubt," he grumbled.

The door slammed open again. "Just a graham cracker?" Sawyer begged.

"Get out of here," his mother warned.

Cody heard the door swing shut.

Cody dropped the open book face down across his chest and reached for the last of his milk. "I'm not concerned about making friends. What I'm worried about is catching up." Glass down, book back up. "I must have read this page over five times in the library today, again in the bus coming home, and *I* don't see how you're supposed to remember any of it. What are you supposed to do, memorize the whole page?"

"Cody," she said, sounding disgusted. "Didn't anybody ever . . ." but she trailed off.

He pointed over his shoulder at her. "Nope. Nobody ever did," he said.

She turned off the water, and next thing he knew she was sitting next to him, wiping her hands on her towel. "Fine," she said. "Well, somebody's going to. Right now." She put her hand out for the book. He gave it up to her.

"You're not having problems with the actual reading, are you?" she asked.

"No, ma'am. I know all them words."

"Funny. Well, I saw you reading Erin's *Ender's Game* last night. I figured you could probably read. This stuff is really no different than that."

"Yes it is," he said. "It's boring."

She shook her head.

"Well it *is*. And you have to remember everything. Nobody's going to grill me to make sure I remember the dates and the names and the geographic locations in *Ender's Game*. But she's going to *test* us on this stuff. How are you supposed to know what she's going to go for? Which things are you supposed to remember? Or are you supposed to memorize the whole stupid book?"

She gave him a long look. "Frustrated, huh?" she said.

"Yes, I am. My life only *depends* on this." He scowled at the book, taking a quick glance at her, not sure just how gripey he could get before she got tired of it.

"All right," she said, patiently. "Tell you what. I'm going to tell you how to do this. And then I want you to go sit in the back-yard with a novel, or take a walk or something, okay? Just a little distance on the day. Okay? Because you can't learn any-thing when you're frustrated. Okay?" She was wanting his eyes. So he looked at her.

"Okay," he said. And he closed his eyes and took a long breath.

"Good," she said, smiling. She was satisfied.

And she taught him some good things — all about topic sentences, and concept flow, and time lines. *"Imagination, Cody,"* she'd said. *"Put some life into the story. Think about it."* And it helped.

There had been a strange moment between them that afternoon, and he thought about it hours and hours later, lying in his bed, alone in the dark. While they were working together, Charlotte had put her hand on his arm. She hadn't even noticed she'd done it, not until she'd noticed that he'd noticed. Then she took her hand away.

"I'm sorry," she said to him. "Does that make you feel uncomfortable?" And she was embarrassed.

But it hadn't made him uncomfortable at all. Actually, it had been *very* comfortable, companionable. Just strange to him, that's all. He'd tried to explain it to her, tried to tell her that his mother hadn't been like that, that he just wasn't *used* to it. And she'd understood, but she hadn't touched him again.

He watched after that—through dinner and into the evening; she touched her own children a lot. But not him. Not again. And now, all he had of it was a restless memory of the touch.

He turned over, pulling the covers straight, trying to straighten the bed clothes out.

Why can't I sleep? Hours of history, trying to catch up. And physics—a little easier because there was so much math in the structure of it. And the rest of it. Photographic theories, shutter speeds, and f-stops to memorize. Hours, he'd been working—till Erin and Char had gone off to bed themselves, and now he couldn't turn his mind off to rest.

You're a walking time bomb, his voice warned him. *If you don't get a decent night's rest pretty soon, you're going to come apart all over the place.*

I know, he told it. *Don't you think I know?* He turned over on his other side.

The last thing he heard was the clock striking three.

"I looked for you yesterday." Marty Getts, the Classic Nerd, sidled up behind Cody in the lunch line. "I figured you must have pulled second lunch." He picked up a tray and leaned over after a milk carton.

"I didn't eat yesterday," Cody said, getting his silverware. "I went to the library."

"I know what you mean," Marty said, pushing his glasses up on his nose with a knuckle. "I hate eating by myself. So, why don't you come sit with us?"

"That's okay," Cody said, a firm refusal. He wasn't sure he was going to be able to eat, anyway. But, as Marty'd said, eating alone . . .

"No, come on. You gotta meet the guys." No taking no for an answer. *So, okay.* Cody sighed and followed Marty out into the lunchroom.

The *guys* turned out to be an entire table full of nerds — tape on the glasses, calculators, pens bristling out of their pockets — the kind of guys Cody had never in his life had anything to do with. *Swell,* Cody thought, and Marty steered him so that he ended up right in the middle of them all. *All this and cafeteria spaghetti, too. Wonderful.*

There were introductions. The guys turned out to be friendly enough, nothing immediately repulsive about them besides their looks. Soon enough they'd forgotten he was there, and they started to talk. Cody pulled back into himself, poking at the spaghetti doubtfully, letting the talk buzz along around him without listening to it much. Then they all laughed. *A joke. It must have been a nerd joke. I should have listened. What kind of jokes do nerds tell?* Cody cut a bite of the sauce with the edge of his fork.

"It doesn't taste as bad as it looks," Marty told him. "And the salad dressing isn't too bad." Cody nodded, ate the bite. It wasn't horrible, and he was hungry.

The talk flowed cheerfully on. Cody was surprised. The guys were really getting animated. They were getting into it, talking about some computer program somebody was working on. The talk changed, going along from thing to thing, and then, suddenly, they were talking about girls.

Girls, Cody thought. *Really.*

It turned out to be pretty much just the normal stuff: they liked girls who didn't like them, girls liked them, but they were always the wrong girls — stuff like that. Cody tried to work up an image in his mind of the kind of girls who'd hang around waiting for these guys, but he couldn't do it.

And Marty. Marty was *love* sick.

"Where?" Cody asked him.

"Over there," Marty said. There were a dozen girls over there.

"Which over there?" Cody asked him, squinting.

"In the pink sweater. With the red hair."

"Red *hair*," Cody said, raising one eyebrow at Marty.

"Well . . ." Marty said, looking humble.

Cody located her finally. A regular-looking girl, nothing special. Just okay. Except for the hair. The hair was good, lots of it, chestnut red and soft looking.

"She's great," Cody said, and then he started picking at his salad. "It's the hair that got you, right?"

"Makes you want to touch it, huh?" Marty asked sadly.

"Yeah, it does," Cody said, surprised. It truly did.

"But that's not the only reason," Marty said, dabbling around in the yellow pudding. "There's just something about her. She has a good sense of humor."

"So, why don't you ask her out?" Cody asked him.

"You think I haven't? I've tried. A guy like me, with these glasses and my grades, I have to be very careful. I go about it the wrong way; all she sees is the nerd."

Cody stared at him.

Marty's heart and his wistful eyes were focused across the room. "Anyway, she likes somebody else."

"Oh, yeah? Who?" Cody wiped his hands with his napkin. He, personally, hadn't been able to face the pudding.

"The Turk." Marty didn't say the name with much affection.

"The Turk," Cody repeated, going for the last of his milk.

"Yeah. You saw him this morning. He's one of those guys on the football team. He sits on our row in the back." Cody was trying to remember. "Kind of a skinny guy," Marty went on, "dark hair—feral eyes, arrogant, vapidly good-looking."

"There're about twelve guys in that class who look that way," Cody said. And then, on second consideration, "I thought football players were supposed to be big."

"Not some of them," the kid on the end said. "Turk's a receiver."

"A receiver?" Cody said blankly.

"Oh, yeah," the same kid answered him. "That guy has great hands." Everybody laughed.

"What?" Cody asked, definitely missing something.

"He's *phalangoid*," Marty said, even more sadly.

"Flange-oid?" Cody asked, feeling like an idiot.

Marty held up his two hands and wiggled his fingers. "With girls," he added. "Everybody knows it. She's lucky she's only got unrequited love. It could be worse."

"She ought to be smarter than that," Cody said.

"Yeah, well," Marty sighed. "Anyway, she can't see me for the wall."

"Forget it, Marty," one of the others advised. "She'll come around when tennis comes on."

"She didn't last year," Marty said dismally.

"Come on. You can't tell us that. She was at all the games, Marty. She's not stupid. You're the champion of the entire region; it's got to make some kind of impression."

Marty shook his head dismally.

Cody was staring at Marty.

"What?" Marty asked him.

"Champion of the region?" Cody repeated.

Marty laughed; it was an embarrassed laugh, almost an apology.

"We're not just nerds, you know," one of the guys said, using an Ed Wynn voice. Evidently, not the first time he'd said it.

After that, they talked about sports for a while, then they started in about competitions. Bridge-building contests, egg-dropping contests, honors, scholarship possibilities — the way other people talk about football teams. Then girls again. They didn't talk like jerks; they talked like guys, intelligent guys. And they made jokes. Not rude jokes. Funny jokes. Intellectual jokes. Poking fun at themselves, even. It was stuff Cody could smile at, even laugh once or twice.

And then, "What do you do?" came the question, tossed right at him, unmistakably. And everybody was listening. He looked blankly at Marty.

"It's not like everybody *does* something," Marty said.

But by then, Cody had an answer. It had come to him very clearly. "I'm interested in photography," he said, feeling very satisfied, almost complete.

The answer satisfied them, too. Not altogether surprising. The bit about Turk was the only negative thing he'd heard through the whole lunch. Marty and company seemed fairly willing to be satisfied with people. They were *nice*, Cody realized. He *liked* them. He was comfortable sitting there. He *liked* sitting there. He was going to want to sit there again tomorrow, if they didn't mind. It was shocking, but it was true.

"You have your own camera?" someone asked.

"No," Cody said. "Someday . . ." They all nodded; they understood *someday*.

124

"Cody's a pretty sharp guy," Marty said, slapping Cody on the back. "He's got Hunsaker on the run. He's got every girl within ten miles in love with him, and on top of all that, he can calculate logarithms in his head."

"Oh, yeah?" grins all around.

"Not really," Cody said, giving Marty the eye.

"Soon—the bell," one of the boys said, and stood up with his tray.

"Don't want to be late for math," Marty said cheerfully. "You coming?"

"Yeah, I'm coming," Cody said. He stood up with his tray and followed Marty over to the dump station. He understood now that Marty had taken him in, that this lunch had been a deliverance, an act of charity.

"They're a nice group of guys," Marty told him, dropping his milk carton in the trash. "They liked you."

And the strangest thing about it was that Cody was grateful for that.

"Okay," Mr. Allen said, "Don't you think we've had enough theory? Yeah—see—McClellan thinks we've had enough, and he's only been here one *day*. So . . ."

He disappeared around the corner of the darkroom door and reappeared with a box in his arms. " 'Hands on' theory," he announced, grinning. He was a strange kind of guy, but you couldn't fault his good humor. He dropped the box onto his desk.

"Lesson number one: *This* is a film cannister." He held up the little metal capsule. "If you use a thirty-five millimeter camera, *this* is where the film is kept. If you use a two and a quarter—like our Mamaya Secores, here—" he lifted a little paper roll, "*this* is how you get your film. With this, getting to the film is a simple matter of unrolling paper. With *this*," he held up the cannister again, "you need a can opener."

He showed them how it was done. The film, once free, fell away from his hand in a long, lazy spiral, dull gray, "It's a little bit difficult to manage, until you're used to it."

He showed them the developing tanks, and the shiny silvery reels the film had to be loaded onto before it went into the tanks—and then he gave them all a reel and some practice film, and let them work.

"Don't *crimp* it, now." He stopped and showed Cody how to hold the film so that it arched up under his palm. "*Smooth* motion, you want," he said to them. "I'll bet you never thought you had to be *coordinated* to be a photographer, did you?" Looking at Mr. Allen, it was not the kind of assumption you would make.

He took them into the darkroom later and gave them a bit of a tour, ending with the film development rooms and a sketchy lecture about chemical processes. "Tomorrow," he said, most of them crammed into the tiny black film room, "we'll go over this in more detail—agitation and times and temperatures." Cody's eyes were wide, standing in the back where he wasn't quite inside the little space. He was wondering whether he could stand that little room in the dark, wondering whether this would be the end of his career, because the room was so small.

"And this weekend, I want you to be out there shooting some *film* . . ."

So the days began to fall into a sort of pattern. Cody spent the day at school, having to prod his mind to keep it awake half the time, but doing all right, carrying it off, so far. His afternoons he dedicated to making sure Charlotte wasn't inconvenienced having him there—vacuuming, folding laundry (*she* did the laundry, and she didn't have to leave the house to do it), anything, *anything,* to make it easier. And his evenings were all the same—sitting at the kitchen table, trying to catch up, trying to make it through the work.

Hunsaker had slapped a paper on them the first day. He didn't have any idea in the world how to write a paper. He'd always loved reading ever since Mrs. Guicci had opened up those secrets for him, but writing he had never really done. He got a few sketchy ideas from Charlotte, but he hated to ask her for any more help than he had already, figuring he could muddle through this. How hard could it be?

And his nights—they weren't getting any easier. He never could get to sleep. He'd lie there in his bed for hours, every bit of him vibrating, his mind going around and around until he wanted to scream with it. When he'd think about the bus trip from New York, which he sometimes did in those private, dark hours, it seemed like a lifetime ago. The days of his new life were long—each one of them *years*—and he wondered when he'd finally get so used to things, he could relax at night.

When you catch up, maybe, he told himself, turning over in his bunk for the fortieth time, eyes dry, mind hot. *Maybe then.* Meanwhile, he made it his business to avoid stressful situations, not an easy thing with Mickey and Sawyer and Tyler around.

Maybe you ought to get some pills or something, he decided. *You're going to have to do something.*

He lay there, feeling completely isolated in the silent house. He almost wished that Charlotte would come around, checking on them all; that maybe she'd stop and sit down and talk a little, ask him about how he felt. Maybe touch him, pat his hand, move the hair out of his eyes. But she never came.

He thought about Parker, wondering what he'd thought when Cody hadn't showed up at work that first night. And then he thought about Elaina. He was homesick for a moment, homesick for what had been no home at all. He tried to call Elaina's face up in his mind, but it was gone. All he could remember was a memory of the touch.

This quilt and these covers—they were heavy, and they folded around him comfortably. They would keep him from flying apart, but they had no warmth of their own to give him.

"Elaina," he whispered. And his soul cried out inside of him for what he remembered of her. *I'm so tired. I'm so tired. And what if I can't pull it off? What if I just can't?*

He was beginning to hate the sound of that clock downstairs.

13

"I don't like this," Charlotte said, squinting at Cody over the scrambled eggs. "Look at your eyes. You look worse than you did last week. You aren't getting enough sleep."

"I'm fine," Cody told her, but it was a gentle lie.

"And you're not eating." She looked at his plate significantly.

"It's hard for me to eat in the morning," he said, annoyed at her for noticing, but not really unhappy that she had.

She breathed out her motherly disapproval and started in on Sawyer instead. Cody sighed. How anyone could have expected him to eat with Mickey glaring at him dolefully across the table, he didn't know.

"How far away is the school, really?" he asked, pulling Charlotte's attention back his way. Sawyer glanced at him gratefully. "I mean—like, how many blocks."

"I don't know," Charlotte said, trying to get a spoonful of the eggs into little Matty's mouth. "Eight or ten blocks, maybe. I really don't know exactly. Why?"

"Oh, I don't know," he said, half-heartedly picking up his toast. "It takes forty minutes to get home on the bus. They drive all over the place before they get here, and they pick up kids from the junior high. It's a zoo. It just seems like such a waste of my time." He sighed.

She looked at him thoughtfully over her shoulder.

"I thought maybe I could walk it," he explained.

"You want me to pick you up this afternoon?" she asked.

"No." He put what was left of the toast back down on the plate, and he drank his milk. "Thank you. I just wondered."

"You wouldn't want to walk it with all those books," she said, wiping Matty's mouth and casting a warning eye on Sawyer and Tyler.

"We're almost *done*," Sawyer said.

"Well, you better be," she told him, nodding at the clock. "You've got about three minutes. And you better brush your teeth this time, buddy."

Cody took his plate over to the sink.

"The junior high," Charlotte murmured. "I bet it *is* a zoo."

Last day of the first week. *Endure,* he told his soul. *Stay upright in the desk, and take notes on everything, because you won't remember anything you hear today longer than five minutes.* Cody could feel the shadows under his eyes like they were weights. When he sat down at his desk in English, he became part of it, wood to bone.

"Your papers," Ms. Hunsaker announced the moment the bell rang. She held up the stack and gave the class an enigmatic look, then she started circulating, dropping a paper here, a paper there. They couldn't help but watch as she went; the little groans, the poker faces, the big eyes, the self-satisfaction. It was too interesting, what she left in her wake, until you got your own paper and everything else in the world disappeared for the moment.

But Cody didn't watch, only long enough to see the cheerleader get her paper; she looked it over briefly and then slipped it quietly into her notebook. She had her uniform on again, and he was far more interested in her legs than in her grade. Then his own paper came floating face down onto his desk top. He put a hand on it and turned it over. He pulled the first page up, surveyed the second. No grade. Nothing but a note in red pencil: *"Stop by after class."* Was this good or bad? *Are you kidding?* he asked himself. *Where've you been all your life?*

It made him nervous, and he stayed that way through the whole class, restless and quiet.

When the bell rang, Cody sat back in his desk and waited for the room to clear. He could have fussed around with his books to make it look like he was leaving, too. But he didn't like apologies and heaven knew he was used enough to the kind of looks he got, just sitting there, so he cleared his face, leaving a trace of pleasantness there, careful about seeming defensive, and he waited.

The little cheerleader checked in at the desk for a moment before she left. He shook his head and tapped his desk with the eraser end of his pencil. And then the room was empty.

He was far from comfortable. For one thing, he wasn't sure about Ms. Hunsaker's attitude towards him; he'd been playing the minor league iconoclast, and she'd seemed tolerant enough of it — sometimes, even pleased — but for all he knew, she'd been lying awake at night, trying to figure out how to shut him up. The probability was that she didn't want him in the class, that the paper would be the crux of it, the excuse she needed.

He gathered his books and stood up. She didn't appear to notice him until he was standing in front of the desk.

"Don't you have a class coming in?" he asked when she looked up at him.

"This is my free period," she said. And then, looking to either side of her desk, "I wish there was someplace here for you to sit." Funny thing to say in a room full of desks. He leaned back against one of them, hoping it wouldn't tip over on him. Ms. Hunsaker was watching him, studying him, thinking her own thoughts. He wanted to say, *Just tell me what you're going to tell me*, but he didn't. He just waited.

"I think this may be the wrong class for you," she said, finally.

And there it was.

"Why?" he asked, his nerves all humming.

She looked down at her desk and pursed her lips. Then she looked up at him. "Can I be honest with you?" she asked. Not hostile. Just asking.

He shrugged. "Sure," he said, but leaving a reserve in the word. She narrowed her eyes a little, studying him again, still thinking.

She sat back into her chair. "Here's the thing. You're bright. You're quick. Your thinking isn't remotely conventional, which is not a bad thing; you don't accept things without giving them a good once-over." She sat up straight again, resting her elbows on the desk. "But your writing is lousy." She spread her hands.

"It surprises me," she went on, "because you're so articulate about your ideas otherwise. But your writing is really lousy. Everything from the grammar to the organization of the paper. That paper was a mess. And the thing is, most of the grading in this class is going to come from your writing.

"I'm thinking, maybe another class would suit you better, something that isn't going to be so heavy on the writing end, something that would give you a chance to learn how to do it."

He sighed and looked out of the window. If he'd been tired before, he was infinitely more so now. He looked at her. He'd come to an impasse.

"Give me a reason to keep you," she said, looking him right in the eyes.

"Can I?" he asked. More or less a challenge. A calling out.

"What does that mean?" she asked.

"Wouldn't you just as soon have me out of here?" he asked, keeping the bitterness out of his voice.

She shut her mouth and just *looked* at him. "No," she said. "Is that what you think?"

He parted his hands. *Stands to reason.*

"I thought I might be disruptive," he said.

"You?" She was still looking at him. "Not really. Why? Because you speak up?"

He didn't answer.

"No, Cody. If that's what you think, you're wrong." She folded her hands together. "Actually, you kind of keep things moving along. This class was awfully dull before you dropped in. No. I don't want you out of here. I just want you to be where it's best for you."

Really. He was standing right on the edge, now, looking down into the dark, wondering what would happen if he took one more step forward.

"May I be honest with *you?*" he asked.

"Sure," she said, giving him back his own answer.

Now he studied her, scared of opening up something he wouldn't know how to close once things got out of hand. With her, you couldn't tell—she was hard, but there was that look behind her eyes . . .

"Can you keep a confidence?"

She smiled to herself. "I think I can do that," she said. He believed her. And she hadn't been using that hard-lady college attitude with him here. Not even patronizing.

"It's not just a personal matter," he said. "It may involve school policy."

"If you don't deal drugs and you haven't killed anybody," she said, "I think I'll be able to handle it." She got a tight little smile out of him.

"Okay," he said, and he took a slow breath, then let it out all at once.

"I really need this class." He started slowly, watching her face. "*This* class. I lied to get into it. And I'll do anything I have to to stay in it. Anything."

She refolded her hands carefully. "Why?" she asked.

He shut his mouth and looked away from her for a moment. This was the box he didn't want to open.

"Because where I come from my grade point average is below failing, and my reputation is even worse than that. Because I believe I can do this, and I always have believed it, even though there are precious few other people in the world who do. I've been stupid. I thought I could have things my own way and still make it work out." He shrugged. "I was wrong. So, I came here."

She blew quietly, pensively. "To see what you could really do," she said, finishing it for him.

"Yes, ma'am. And I lied to the counselor."

"Which counselor did you lie to?" she asked.

He told her.

She made a face, one of those I-wouldn't-want-to-take-the-heat-for-you-if-you-ever-got-caught faces. "There are easier ones to work with." She looked down and patted her roll book. "What about your school records?"

"They won't get here for a while," he said.

"I see." Then she met his eyes levelly. "And what if it doesn't work out? What if it turns out to be harder than you thought? What if you find out you can't do it?"

131

What if?

"I think I can," he said. "If it turns out I can't . . ." he shrugged. It was something he would face when he had to; the answer was too dark for now.

"I know this makes me a special case. And I know you probably have enough work already. But you show me how to do it right, and I'll do it right. I'll make you a deal—you give me a chance, and if I'm not up to level after the next, say, two papers, then fine. Then I'll transfer out." He turned cold inside as he said it. "Unless you think it's not worth your time."

She smiled at herself.

"This is funny?" he asked, and the hurt in his chest surprised him.

"No," she said, quickly. She leaned her cheek on her hand. "You're not funny." She picked up a pencil and looked up at him.

"You really did that?" she asked. "You really left home to start over?"

"It seemed like the only option."

She nodded.

"Well," she said, "I hoped all along you wouldn't give up. You seem to be a good kid, Cody. You're a fighter. I like that." She gave him a long look. "The lying probably wasn't the wisest thing. But the rest of it—you just might pull this off."

"I'd prefer you didn't say anything to anybody."

She held up one hand. "What you do is your own business," she said. "But do understand—it's all going to hit the fan, sooner or later."

He nodded.

She put her palms down flat on the desk. "So, okay. Here's the deal," she said. "I'll assign you a tutor. I have one all lined up. Best student I've got. Easy to work with. A very clear communicator. If you're willing to work with this, and if you're serious, I'm willing to give you the time you need—up to a point, of course. If you *are* serious, Cody, I don't think you're going to have too much trouble with this. And it'll do you some good to have to put some structure on your thinking." She watched him. "So. What do you say? You up for it?"

He nodded. *All this time, she was hoping you'd want to make it work. She had a tutor lined up.*

Then she did the most disconcerting thing. She smiled at him, *grinned* at him. It caught him off guard, and he smiled back at her, same way, no hesitation.

"That's nice," she said. "I wasn't sure you knew how to do that." She stood up. "Stay there," she directed. She went over to the door, opened it a little, and leaned out. She was talking to somebody in the hall. When she came back into the room, she left the door opened behind her.

"Your tutor," Ms. Hunsaker said, back to business—the little cheerleader had followed her into the room— "will be Ms. McCall. You work with her, and I think you'll do just fine. But it's going to take some effort."

His mouth must have dropped completely open. The girl stood there by the door, looking at him impassively. He could feel his face go hot.

"Is there a problem?" Ms. Hunsaker asked.

You could say that.

"No," he said, tearing his eyes away from the girl and fixing them on the teacher. "No problem. Thank you." He was lying now, not very well, either. The thank you had had no heart to it at all.

"Good," Ms. Hunsaker said. She scribbled something across the top of her pass pad, tore off the pass, and handed it to him. "This will get you past Mrs. Bruecher with a minimum of suffering. You'd better get going." Then she smiled at him again. "I'm glad you're staying," she said. "It would have been so dull without you. Take good care of him, Elise," she said to the girl. "You never know what he's going to turn out to be."

It was a dismissal.

And then they were out in the hall, the two of them—she with her legs and her grievances, him with his chagrin—alone together. *What was it Parker had always said? "Your chickens sure going to come home to roost, sooner or later."*

Cody sighed. *So, how do we start now?* he wondered.

"So, when do you want to start?" she asked, her voice fairly flat, as if she wasn't feeling so hot about it, either.

"As soon as we can," he said. And then, a little bitterly, "Obviously, I'm going to need as much help as I can get."

"It happens to everybody, sometime," she said, looking at him. So, she was going to be nice about it. So, maybe she was a nice girl; that didn't help things any. She looked away.

"What about tonight?" she asked.

"Don't you have a date?" he asked.

She glanced at him, sidelong. "No, I don't have a *date*," she snapped. "I don't always have a *date*. I have a game this afternoon," she said, daring him. He didn't say anything, so she went on, with a little less energy, "But it'll be over by six-thirty or seven. You can come over after that."

They had come up on Bruecher's door.

"I'd rather that you came over to my place," he said. He tore a piece of paper out of his notebook and balanced against the wall, writing down his uncle's address for her.

Her eyes flashed on him. "Look," she said. "I don't know you. I don't even particularly *like* you. And I don't know your parents. I'm not coming to your house."

"Fine," he said, masking his anger. This was going to mean walking back and forth between their houses with all his books. "Where do you live?"

He handed her his slip of paper. She glanced at it, and then looked it over again, carefully. "This is out where *I* live," she said. "You just moved in there?"

"I'm staying with my uncle," he said, letting nothing but the edge sound in his voice. "And I don't have a car."

"Who's your uncle?" she asked.

What's it to you? he was thinking, but he told her.

"Really," she said. "They're good friends of my parents—I mean, like *old* friends." She pursed her lips thoughtfully and studied his little paper a moment longer. "I'll come to your place if that's what you want," she decided.

"Oh, *thanks*," he said.

Her eyes flashed at him again. "But only if your uncle's going to be home," she said, coldly. She pulled the door open, passing him with dignity.

"I wouldn't *worry* about it," he whispered at her, and then he followed her into the class.

Using the dining room was Charlotte's idea. "The kids never come in here," she'd said. "It's the quietest room in the house." And then she'd warned the children, "You stay out of there while Cody's friend is here, you understand?"

"Tutor," he corrected her glumly, pushing open the kitchen door. The only good thing that had happened to him all day was Mr. Allen's letting him take a camera home for the weekend.

"It's probably his *girlfriend*," Mickey said acidly from over by the sink. Cody picked his notebook up off the kitchen table, and, for the first time, he allowed himself the luxury of glaring back at Mickey.

"Is it your girlfriend?" Tyler asked, coming over close and

looking up into Cody's face, dropping his hand gently on Cody's knee.

"No, Ty," Cody sighed, patting the little boy's cheek. "Just my tutor."

But Charlotte was giving him the good study-over. Everybody could tell he was nervous. Just having a tutor come by wouldn't make him so nervous, would it?

"This girl and I don't particularly like each other," he explained reluctantly, dropping his notebook on the big oak dining table and going back for the books.

"But she's tutoring you," Charlotte pointed out, following him, surely meaning to be helpful.

"Ms. Hunsaker asked her to," he said, heaving up the pile of texts. Charlotte held the door open for him.

"You bring home enough books," she said, sympathetically, as he carried them past her and put them down on the notebook. Char was right; it was quieter here than it was in the kitchen. But maybe that's because everyone in here was giving him the silent stare.

"It's really no big *deal*," he said. The boys looked as if they were giving him his final good-bye, and he wondered what on earth they were seeing in his face. He put his hands on his hips as he surveyed the table. There *were* a lot of books.

"Well," Charlotte said after a moment, "let's get out of here." She went over and slid open the door into the front hall. "Out, out, *out*," she commanded. Sawyer and Tyler and Matty all trooped out in a little row. "And I don't want you anywhere near this room while Cody's working, you understand?"

"Can't we even look at her?" Sawyer asked.

"*No*," Cody said, with visions of the little kids peeking around the edges of the doors, turning the awkward into the untenable; it would have been the wrong message to give that girl. *We don't need any weaker position than we already got.*

"Good luck," Charlotte said, still sympathetic. It was all instinct, of course. He hadn't really *talked* about any of this. He did a smile for Charlotte, a little wave. That should be reassuring. She laughed and shook her head as she pulled the door closed.

This really is stupid, he told himself. *So, you thought the girl was an airhead. And you acted like a pig the only time you ever talked to her. And you embarrassed her when she was trying to be nice to you. And she hates your guts. And you're*

135

so stupid, you need a tutor. What's the big deal? So, is she per-fect?

One thing you want to remember here, he reminded him-self. *She is in control tonight; she can do anything to you she wants.*

He sighed, pulled the chair out, sat down, and started ar-ranging the books.

He opened his notebook. He picked up the world history book and put it down in front of him, his hand down flat on the cover. For a moment, he got a vision of big Mrs. Bruecher, her glasses hanging by their ear pieces from that little black cord, bumping her chest when she walked — she and her pointer and her black orthopedic shoes.

Mr. Guicci used to say, "You can tell a lot about a person, looking at their shoes. It's a sad person pays a lot of money for sore feet." He'd laugh after he said that, remembering maybe an uptown customer, looking good but not walking so hot.

Cody rested his chin in his hands and gazed out of the win-dow on the other side of the room. Through the space between the fancy white curtains, he could see leaves pressing in against the glass. It was nearly dark outside. He was remembering the feeling of the store, and it made him heavy inside.

The clock in the kitchen struck seven-thirty. Somewhere in the house, little Matty was yelling. He had a good, lusty yell. Cody liked that, babies who could yell made you feel like there was life around you. He sighed and put the history book away from him.

If I'm going to have to wait for her, he thought, *I'd better do something I know how to do.*

He opened the math book, running his hands over the pages. He was on familiar ground now, and the heaviness lifted somewhat. He checked the assignment sheet, and he pulled two pieces of paper out of the notebook, arranging them neatly in front of him. Then he went and sharpened his pencil.

He sat back down, sighed once more — a good, big sigh, one that should have cleared all the stale oxygen right out of him — and he started the first problem.

The doorbell rang.

Cody's hand froze over the paper, and his stomach went weird. *What is the matter with you?* He forced himself to write the rest of the problem out.

Voices in the front hall. And then the door sliding back be-hind him.

"Your girlfriend's here," Mickey hissed.

He closed his eyes.

"Not really," he heard someone say, very matter-of-factly.

He opened his eyes. Time to stand up. Time to act like a human being.

He heard the door slide shut. He stood up and turned. His cheerleader was standing there, waiting for him to say something. She wasn't dressed in her little uniform. Cody had a momentary twinge of regret, missing her legs.

Actually, she looked very nice: khaki pants, a white turtleneck with a red sweatshirt over it—the sweatshirt had deer and snowflakes printed on it—and her hair all pulled back. Not soft, but classy. *Just the way she wants it, probably. Unrelenting.* There were little bits of hair that had sprung loose, curling around her face. He liked those, thinking maybe she hadn't planned on their being there, softening things. He found himself looking at her shoes. They were like running shoes, except they were kind of brownish, and they looked comfortably worn. He began to feel better.

"Why are you staring at my feet?" she asked.

"Come, sit down," he said, embarrassed because his throat had so obviously needed clearing.

She came over to the table. "Where do you want me?" she asked, ice on wheels.

"Right there," he said, pointing to the chair next to him. "Right there would be nice."

"Thank you," she said civilly and dropped her purse on the floor on the other side of the chair. She pulled the chair out and slid in from the far side, not *quite* sitting in the middle of the chair—evidently having serious reservations about being that close to him.

"I'm not biting today," he said. "You can *sit* in the chair."

Not looking at him, she adjusted herself. She folded her hands together, resting them primly on the table. He groaned inside. It was going to be impossible. A freeze out. It was a thing his mother had used on him, and he never had figured out how to get around it. He picked up his math papers unhappily, meaning to put them back in the notebook. Of course, he dropped them. They fluttered down onto the floor between the two chairs.

He dived for the papers at the same time she leaned over to get them. They stopped just short of collision. And then there was a pause, and then they both sat up—without the papers. And then they both leaned over to get them again.

And then she started to laugh. It started as a giggle, but

then she put her hands over her face and *laughed.* It wasn't something he had done a lot of himself, that kind of laughing. He leaned over, finally retrieving the papers, watching her, beginning to feel a little easier.

She was laughing that way because she was nervous, too, of course. Sometimes a fight in the street would end like this—too much tension and an unexpected catalyst, then everybody suddenly thinking the whole thing was hilarious.

So, she wasn't so sure of herself after all. So, maybe he had *her* scared.

She was wiping at her eyes with her fingers. He got up and went into the kitchen and came back with the dish towel—the only remotely absorbent thing he'd been able to locate in there just then—which he handed her, being able to afford a little generosity, now.

"This is wet," she said. Damp from dinner. And then she started laughing again, holding the towel in her two hands. She leaned over and put it down carefully on the floor.

He parted his hands, standing there.

"Sit down," she said, subsiding. "I'm sorry." She sniffled. And then she sighed. "Thank you for the towel—" but that set her off again.

He sat down and waited till she was finished. When she finally had, her cheeks were ruddy, maybe because of the laughing, maybe because she was embarrassed. It made her look very cute.

It was interesting. Looking at her this close, he realized she wasn't that pretty. Her face wasn't perfect. She had nice eyes, but nothing else that was remarkable. It hadn't been this pretty, putting out the cold a moment ago—classy and hard, but not pretty. It was the life in her face just now, the flushed cheeks, the laughing eyes—it was the person inside of her showing at the window. It was a sweet face.

And suddenly, his feelings were shifting.

"Let me see your essay," she said, not looking at him, just putting out her hand.

"I don't want to," he said. Honesty. Then she did look at him, a hard look, but not really—a teasing kind of a threat. This girl couldn't protect herself for long.

He acquiesced, opened the notebook, found the paper, and handed it over grudgingly. Then he was on the defensive again.

She put it down on the table, her elbows resting on either

side of it, the fingers of her hands curled up against her temples. She took her time over the first page. She picked up the paper, carefully folding the first page back over behind the second; then she put the paper back down on the table as it had been before.

"This is really bad," she said finally, putting one hand down lightly on the paper.

"I know that," he snapped, and, taking the corner of the paper between thumb and forefinger, he snatched it back.

"Do you *mind*?" she said. "Will you give that back here, please?"

"You've read it," he pointed out.

"I need to see it. I need to know what I'm supposed to be helping you with."

"Everything," he said.

"Well, that's not my fault, is it?" She put her hand out, palm up flat, waiting for him to put the paper on it. "Come on, McClellan," she said, beckoning with her fingers. "We're too old for this kind of little game, don't you think?"

He hissed in exasperation, slapped the paper down on the table in front of her, and threw himself back into his chair. Then he got up and went over to the window.

"I know you're embarrassed about this," she said, very deliberately. "And I don't blame you. Frankly, I'm a little surprised. I wouldn't have expected this from you." Enjoying this a little, maybe.

He turned and parted his hands, a simple, sarcastic shrug. "Sorry," he said, and then he folded his arms and leaned back against the wall.

"This isn't my fault, remember?" She picked up the paper, pursing her lips and looking it over again. "Actually, it's kind of comforting that this is so bad."

"And why's that?" he asked.

"I don't know. There's a rumor going around that you're some kind of visiting Rhodes scholar, or something."

"And *what* is a Rhodes scholar?" he asked.

She laughed, surprised. "You're very strange," she said.

"So, people are talking about me?" he asked.

"All the time," she said. "You're the big mystery man. They're taking bets on your honors."

He laughed, startled into it. "Come on," he said. "Why would they do that?" He looked at her. "I never told anybody I had any honors. I never tell anybody anything. Why would they think I had honors?"

She studied him.

He folded his arms and leaned back against the wall. "I'm serious," he said. "I want to know why. What gives you the right to have any expectations about the way I write?"

She glanced down at the paper, no offense evident in her. "I don't know," she said, frowning thoughtfully. "I guess it's because you're so aggressive when you speak up in class."

"You say things in class," he pointed out.

"Not like you do." She turned the paper over on its face. "I'm not half as aggressive as you are, for one thing. And all the things you say have this—" she rolled her hands slightly— "edge to them. Like you're angry about something."

"Cynical?" he suggested wryly.

"Yes," she said. She was so innocent, so open—her face had nothing guarded or careful in it at all. Suddenly, he felt a little worried, a little uncomfortable.

"Not that that's bad. Oh, in a way, it scares me," she went on. "I don't exactly understand why." She tapped the faceless paper with a finger. "Maybe because you make me uncomfortable in my mind, sometimes. You see things a lot differently than I do. But see, I don't think that's bad. I like being uncomfortable—once in a while; it makes me think. *Some* kinds of uncomfortable do."

She turned the paper back over and smoothed it out apologetically.

"When you talk," she said slowly, "you make people understand you. I thought it was the way you used your words." She looked down at the paper. "But these words don't work."

He listened. He was astonished she'd given him that much thought.

"So," he said, his voice a little husky. "Are there other things people say?"

She looked at him curiously. "Lots of things." She was smiling to herself.

"I haven't even been there a week," he pointed out, piqued by the smile.

"That's what makes you so interesting," she said. "Nobody knows anything about you." She raised one shoulder and gave him the mock come-hither eye. "All the girls are in love with you because you're so cute." She dropped her shoulder. "All the guys think you're stuck up because you don't talk to anybody. Everybody hates the way Hunsaker fell in love with you the first

140

time you opened your mouth. And even Bruecher is obviously treating you like you're the only one in the class she can talk to.

"You've got half of the guys hating you because it seems like you're almost bored in math—and you always have the answer when Shein asks the question."

"I've done it all before," he said.

"You've taken precalc before?" she asked, skeptical.

"Yes," he said, echoing her tone.

"You can't take anything higher than precalc here," she said.

"Well, you could in my old school," he said. "So, it's no big deal."

"There's even a rumor going around that you can do logarithms in your head."

He snorted. "Anything else?" he asked.

She was studying him again. "Marty tells everybody that you're really a good guy."

"And what do you tell everybody?" he asked, watching her face carefully.

"I never say anything," she said. Her eyes were clear.

"You could've," he said. *You've had reason enough.* It was as close to an apology as he'd gotten. "Especially now. You've got lots of good material here."

"I never say anything," she repeated, very carefully, very clearly, in case he still shouldn't understand. She was stung by the suggestion.

He was still leaning against the wall, looking her over. "Well, thank you," he said finally. "I appreciate your discretion."

"It's my policy," she said, making it clear she hadn't done anything special for him. "Now, I believe we do have some work to do here? If you're tired of standing across the room."

He pushed away from the wall and slowly came back to his chair.

"I'll make a spelling list up for you, using this paper," she said, suddenly very businesslike. "And we'll work on sentence structure." She glanced over the paper again, sighing. "I just wish you'd write like you talk," she said. "This just doesn't make any sense. It doesn't start anywhere; it doesn't go anywhere. You're supposed to start at the beginning and grow to a point—"

"How can you start at the beginning of an idea?" he asked, disgusted.

"At the origin, then, all right? At the question. You explain that there needs to be discussion of the thing, because there is a question. You have to start somewhere. And then there has to be some direction. I can't believe I'm having to tell you this."

He sat down. "It's just that I've never had to do it before," he said.

"You've never written a paper before," she said, skeptical.

He smiled. "That's right," he said. "Never."

"Right," she said.

"Truth," he said.

"How do you get into college prep without ever writing a paper?" she said.

He shrugged, all innocence.

She looked him up and down, still shaking her head.

"I don't know how you get away with that," she said. "Around here, you learn to write before you learn to *crawl.*"

He shrugged again, and now *he* was smiling to *him*self.

She took a long, slow breath, narrowing her eyes at him. "I don't know," she said, half singing to herself. "You really are strange."

"Why, thank you," he said, not without satisfaction, offering her a pencil. "And now, I believe we have work to do?"

"I've got to go," she said finally. She was yawning. The clock in the kitchen had just struck midnight. The two of them had been hunched over the paper now for hours, a nice sort of weary dimness of mind progressively blunting his edges and mellowing her dignity. Cody was finally comfortable, in spite of all the circles and arrows and heavy lines that had been drawn all over his paper.

Hunsaker had been right, choosing Elise for this. She was patient, she was gentle, and she knew how to explain things to an idiot. Cody had actually learned from her, once he'd relaxed enough—things had come clear to him for the first time. It was as though he'd been trying to build a house all his life, and somebody had only just now given him a saw and a hammer to work with. It was pleasing. He was also pleased by the way the girl smelled.

She stood up and began to pull on her jacket.

"How often do we do this?" he asked.

"How often do you want to?" she asked.

Oh, don't leave, he was saying in his mind. *Stay here with me, just a little while longer.* He had to do an override on that noise before he could give her a rational answer. "You know

142

what I need," he said, finally, a bit wistfully. "As often as you can work it in."

She had the jacket on now. She shrugged, not indifferently. "Whenever," she said. "You want to do it every night?"

Something inside of him started blessing the stars, blessing Hunsaker, blessing the deep badness of his writing.

"Yeah," he said, having to shut his face down very carefully. "That would probably be wise, don't you think? If you don't mind."

"Considering how much we have to do, I think it would be wise," she agreed. "And I don't mind. As long as you stay humble." She smiled, picking up her purse. "Except not Saturday or Sunday."

"Okay."

She smiled at him. "You pick things up fast," she said. And then she added, "When you want to." She started toward the door.

"McCall," he said, quickly. It was the first time he'd called her by name.

She stopped and turned around, waiting.

And then he was embarrassed. "I wanted to ask you a favor," he said. " Another favor."

"Okay," she said.

He brought his hands together, a silent clap. "I have this assignment in my photography class. I have to shoot off a roll of film tomorrow. I'd like it to be a series of portraits. And I don't really know anybody else. I just . . . ummm," he shrugged, and he smiled at her. "If you don't have anything to do tomorrow afternoon?" But it was so unlikely, he was beginning to wish he'd never brought it up—

"What time?" she asked.

"I don't know. You know—whenever . . ."

"I have chores in the morning," she said. "And my family's going to barbecue at about five. We could do it at two or so."

Something inside of him uncoiled itself and sighed heavily.

"That would be good," he said.

"Okay," she said, and she smiled.

And he smiled. Or he tried to.

"Do you want me to come over here?" she asked.

"No," he said. "No. You tell me where you live, and I'll be there."

"It's not that far," she said. "Your aunt knows."

"She does?" he said stupidly.

"Yeah. Remember, your folks know my folks."

"Oh, yeah."

"They don't see each other that often. But they're old friends."

"That's nice," he said, wondering if it was, thinking it might be, worried that it might not be.

"So, I'll see you tomorrow at two," she said. She pushed the door open. "McClellan," she said. "Would you mind walking me to my car?"

"Not at all," he said, almost absolutely sure it wasn't a come on.

"It's just kind of late," she explained, half apology. "And there're all those trees out there."

Straightforward, simple truth. And he was wondering how she was feeling about him, now — if she wasn't minding him so much.

They walked out into the dark. She stood on the porch for a moment, her eyes closed. The night was fresh and cold and quiet. There were a thousand tiny smells here in this place, green ones, and green sounds, leaves rustling over their heads.

She opened her eyes and went on down the steps, down the path to her car.

"Nice car," he said, following along. It gleamed under the streetlight.

"It's my dad's," she said, unlocking her door. "Thanks for walking me out here."

"No trouble," he said. He meant it. He held the door for her and shut it when she was inside. Then he tapped on the window.

She rolled it halfway down. "Thanks for doing this tonight," he said. "You really helped."

"It was fun," she said.

"This is important to me," he said. And then, "I'm sorry about the way I treated you before."

"That's okay," she said. "Get back in there and go to bed. You look tired."

"Lock your door," he directed. She rolled up the window and locked the door, and then she started the engine. He stepped back up on the curb, and she pulled off into a U-turn.

He backed slowly up the walk, watching as she drove off down the street. He got to the porch, but he didn't want to go back into the house just yet. Quite a while later, he was still sitting on the steps, hugging his knees, listening to the leaves.

144

14

"He's out there, mowing your lawn," Charlotte said. Erin was standing behind her, breathing on the back of her neck while she was trying to make pancakes. "I don't think he knows *how* to mow a lawn," she told him. He kissed her under the ear. "I *think* he might be waking up the neighbors," she said, grinning to herself, pinching him off with her shoulder. He patted the top of her head.

She measured out half a cup of sugar and added it to the flour.

"Nobody should be asleep on a morning like this, anyway," Erin said cheerfully. "Let me do that." He butted her out of the way and picked up the measuring spoons. "It's my job, anyway. You don't know how to make pancakes right."

"Really," she said.

"Really," he answered.

Charlotte went to the pantry for the griddle.

"Sooo—how's it been going?" Erin asked.

"How's what been going?"

He scowled at her happily. "With Cody. Is he making you a lot of extra work?" It was a trap, obviously. He was going to make her admit she'd been wrong. Well, she'd already admitted that, so he wasn't going to make any points.

"No, as a matter of fact," she said. "Except for the laundry. I'm going to teach him how to iron. *You* could teach him."

"I'll teach him," Erin said. "You don't do that right, either."

"I'm a good teacher," she said indignantly.

"Ironing," he said. "Ironing."

She shrugged. "Who wants to be good at that?"

"I do," he said, adding the wet mixture and the dry mixture together. "Then I don't look like a slob."

"But you are one," she pointed out.

"But I don't look like one," he said. He stuck the wire whip into the batter and started mixing carefully.

"No. I'll tell you the truth," she said, plugging the griddle in. "Yesterday, he vacuumed the whole house. The day before, he vacuumed the whole upstairs. He keeps the kids' bathroom spotless. Yesterday afternoon, he helped Sawyer with his math. He hardly eats anything at all. He never asks for anything. He never leaves a mess. He hardly ever talks. He just sits there with his books for hours, studying. I've never seen anybody work like that. He's really a strange kid."

Erin turned the griddle up just *so* and dropped a pat of butter on it.

"Did you work out something with him about an allowance?" she asked, pulling silverware out of the drawer.

"Yes, I did," he said. The butter was starting to melt. He tipped the griddle, letting the butter run.

"Is it going to be enough? It's inevitable that he's going to want to go out, sooner or later, you know. And that's another thing. I think he should have a little car."

"I thought you said our kids weren't going to have their own cars until they were thirty," he said. He took a spoonful of batter and dropped it onto the griddle, a neat round blob.

"This is different," she said. "He uses every minute of the day. He can't afford the time the bus takes. He's got a little money. We should be looking for something."

"You sound like you're the kid's mother," Erin said, looking pointedly surprised.

"I am," she said. "In a manner of speaking." She made a face at him. He grinned at her and made another neat, round blob.

"Why don't you call that young heathen in, my little dear," he said, "before he wakes up the neighbors?"

Elise watched him as he fiddled with the camera. The afternoon was bright and warm and smelled like September. The aged park trees rose like columns in some summer temple, the leaves far over their heads still green, making shadow and light on Cody's cross face.

Obviously, the camera was frustrating him. It was not what she'd expected, not the kind most people she knew had—this one was more like a tall, narrow black box than any camera she'd ever seen—and it had two lenses instead of one. He had to look down into it from the top, instead of holding it up to his eye, and he had to hold it more or less down at chest level to see into it. He kept moving the camera from side to side, frowning at it and squinting, shaking his head as if the whole process made him dizzy. And just now, he was swearing softly to himself.

He glanced up and caught her watching him. He must have realized what he'd just been saying. "Sorry," he said. "It's a nasty old habit of mine." He reached around the front of the camera and turned one of the knobs.

"I suppose your friend with the letter jacket never swears," he said conversationally.

"Not very often," she agreed. But then, she was sympathetic. "It's just the way he was brought up."

Cody sniffed. He held the camera up closer to his eye and then dropped it down again.

"Are you going to start in on Steven again?" she asked.

He glanced up at her, half smiling. "No," he said.

"Good," she sighed.

"I imagine he's a fine, upstanding, decent, church-going young fella," he said, squinting down at the open top of the camera. She smiled. He'd put a lot of Western on that last word, and it had sounded too funny.

"Actually," she said, "he's really a very nice guy. You'd probably like him if you let yourself."

"Not a chance," he said.

"And why not?"

He looked up. "Because *you* do," he said, bouncing his eyebrows at her.

"Now you're making fun of me," she said.

"N-n-n-n-o-o-o-o-o," he said. "Why would I do such a thing?"

"I was just wondering that same thing," she said.

"I *got* it," he said, holding the camera very carefully. And then, more or less to himself, "Why can't Mr. Allen have thirty-fives like everybody else in the world?"

"What's a thirty-five?"

"Thirty-five millimeter," he said, taking a quick reference glance at her and then going back to the camera.

"Thirty-five millimeter what?" she asked.

"Camera," he snapped. "Hold still." He was working with the knobs on the front again.

"What is this?" she asked, pointing at the thing he had in his hands. "Some kind of antique?"

"What? The camera? No," he said. "It's just a twin lens and I can*not* get used to the viewfinder. It works like your eye; the image in here is upside-down to me."

"Are you ever going to take this picture?" she asked.

"Yes, I'm going to take this picture," he said. "Are you ever going to stop talking? You want the picture to be all mouth?"

She stared at him, totally nonplussed. He took the picture.

"McClellan," she hollered as he cranked the film, and then she laughed. He shot another one.

"The two faces of Ms. McCall," he intoned.

"*You're* nice," she said.

"As nice as Mr. Letter Jacket?"

"Oh, yeah," she said. "At least."

"Good," he said, cranking the camera again. "Wouldn't want you to feel like you were wasting your time in my poor company."

It had been kind of hard at first. Nobody had ever taken pictures of her like this, and it made her self-conscious. He wanted things perfect, and he kept apologizing about how slow he was — but then he'd take the pictures before she was ready, when she didn't expect them.

"Why do you do that?" she'd complained.

"Do what?" he asked.

"You don't let me smile," she said.

"You were smiling," he said, cranking the camera.

"Not really," she said.

"You were smiling," he said. "I don't want some little cutesy posed smile. I asked you if you'd do this because I wanted to shoot *you*. I'm not here to do graduation pictures."

"You have a terrific bedside manner," she said, glowering at him.

He smiled to himself and shot her glowering. She gritted her teeth and started to throw her hands in the air in exasperation, but it struck her that he'd shoot that too, so she pulled her hands back in immediately and composed herself.

"Just think about something else," he said. "Just talk to me." He sat down, the camera in his lap. "I wish I could let you walk around here. I'd like to just follow you, but I can't shoot that way. I can't focus fast enough yet. Not with this thing." He patted the camera. He sighed and seemed to relax a little.

"This is a beautiful place," he said softly. It was just the park, the same park she'd played in all her life. It had a wide green sward, studded with these old trees — some of them oaks and sycamores, some of them giant pine trees with heavy, hollowed skirts that made wonderful forts.

A little ravine cut through the middle of the lawn, full of irrigation water in the summer, almost empty now. The water had worn away the soil and soft rock over the years, uncovering shelves and ledges deep in the stone, now smooth with use. The grass grew down over the banks, rounding the edges, softening them, and trees grew all along, crowding close because of the water, their roots cutting through the bank and mingling their shapes with the stone.

The ravine was wider than it was deep, but when you were down inside of it, the banks were higher than your head. They'd built three heavy wooden bridges along its length for people without adventurous tendencies, or for dreamers or sweethearts. The tops of the trees arched far above them, leaning in and touching so that the place was ceilinged with trees. Another couple of weeks, and that cathedral place would be golden and scarlet with autumn. It *was* beautiful. Elise had played here since she was big enough to be out of her mother's sight, and every time she got down in the ravine, the rest of the world ceased to exist . . . only this place and its secrets, only this place and the worlds that existed inside of her own self.

Why she'd brought him here, she didn't know. She was older now, and she was too busy to pretend much. It was because he was a photographer, and there wasn't a better setting in the world than this.

She came back to herself and watched him. He was still looking around, and his face had a quiet in it she hadn't seen before. The look in his eyes, she knew; she could feel it inside of herself—he was seeing things that weren't there, listening to older times. She wondered if he'd ever read Tolkien; she was beginning to think he might like it.

When he looked at her again, she dropped her own eyes, embarrassed about watching him. She glanced up. He was studying her. When their eyes met, he didn't look away. She couldn't read his face; the quiet was still there, but it was tinged with things—a thoughtfulness, a sadness, maybe. She hoped it wasn't sadness, not the kind she thought she saw. She felt it drawing her in, and that was something she couldn't be comfortable with.

He started to say something, but he picked up the camera again instead. The quiet went out of him, the subtle colors of it dissolved into business. She couldn't come away so easily herself; there was something inside of her that was still thoughtful, and she couldn't shake the feeling. Whatever it was, he got a picture of it.

"Let's try the bridge," he said. And then he stopped, listening.

"What?" she asked. She listened. There were boys yelling,

149

but that was nothing; there were always boys yelling. "Just a bunch of kids," she said. But he had some trouble in his face, still listening.

"Here," he said, and handed her the camera. "Don't drop it."

"What do you think I am?" she asked. She cradled the camera in her arms, and followed as he climbed out of the ravine. By the time she'd climbed up over the bank, he was walking towards a little knot of boys over on the grass. He seemed casual enough, his hands in his pockets, and she followed him curiously.

As she got closer, she began to understand what was happening. There were a lot of little kids—nine-year-olds, maybe, or ten, and they were all crowded around a smaller kid on a bike. The largest of the other kids was standing in front of the bike, holding the handlebars. So. A little bully. "Little jerks," she murmured.

All the boys looked up when Cody got within a couple yards. She heard him say something, but she couldn't make out the words. The yelling stopped. Cody said something else, something else too quiet for her to hear. Whatever it was, it took the courage out of most of the boys, and they started to back off. The big one went last. She hadn't heard Cody say anything else; he was just standing there, still with his hands in his pockets. The bigger kid joined his friends and they all went running off towards the neighborhood on the other side of the park.

Cody stood there for a little longer, almost long enough for her to come up beside him. The little one with the bike was crying. Cody went over and hunkered down beside the bike. He had his hand on the handlebars, steadying himself. The child looked at Cody's hand, fear all over his face. Cody took his hand away. They started to talk.

She came up just close enough to hear what was going on. "Yes, you do," Cody was saying gently. "What's the point of saying you don't when you do?"

The little boy began to pull away. "I *don't*," he said. He had a terrific stutter.

"No, wait," Cody said. "I'm not being mean to you, man." The little boy stopped, looking at Cody solemnly, sniffling. "That's like saying you're not a boy. Or it's like telling me you don't have a bike here. You see what I mean? If something is, it is."

"I don't stutter," the little boy maintained, the consonants belying him.

150

Cody was quiet for a moment. "I know what the problem is," he said. "You think there's something wrong with that. You keep telling me you don't, because you think there's something wrong with you if you do. Huh? Am I right?" Cody was speaking very gently, and the little boy started to nod, as if he couldn't help himself.

"Listen," Cody said, shrugging. "There's nothing wrong with that. There's nothing bad about it. Doesn't mean you're stupid. It's just the way things are. You know that guy who does the television ads for the telephone? Mel Tillis? You ever see him? Well, he's a famous guy. And he stutters. And he does it right on television. And everybody thinks he's great. Those guys weren't making fun of you because you stutter, man. They make fun of you because they're stupid. They know you're afraid, so they go after you. It wouldn't matter why. It could be because your hair is brown, they don't care."

The little boy looked at him dolefully.

"Listen," Cody said. "You're a cute kid." Only half true. "You've just got to be what you are, you know? If you can change it, change it. Lying to yourself about it won't change anything. And if you don't care, don't worry about it. If they don't think you're scared, they'll leave you alone. They're just mean. If it wasn't you, they'd find somebody else. They're just stupid. Okay? Just stay out of the way for a while."

Cody stood up. The little boy sniffled. "Go on," Cody said. "I'm watching you." The little boy pushed off and got set on his pedals. Cody stood there and watched the kid ride across the grass to the sidewalk, and when he got to the sidewalk, Cody kept moving, keeping him in sight till he was well past the place where the boys had disappeared.

Elise was standing behind him when he turned around, and he almost ran into her.

"Don't drop it," he said, the first thing out of his mouth, reaching for the camera.

"I'm not going to drop it," she said, shoving it at him. "Unless you knock it out of my hands."

"Well, I didn't know you were standing there," he said. He tucked the camera into the crook of his arm and started walking back toward the ravine. About halfway there, on a little hill in the middle of a wide ring of trees, he stopped.

"Could we just sit down?" he asked.

"Sure," she said, and she did. She shoved the sleeves of her shirt up over her elbows and leaned back against the grassy hill behind her, turning her face up to the sun.

"You've got a nice tan," he remarked, putting down the camera and then himself, a few feet away from her.

"Thank you," she said, though you never could tell with him what was a compliment and what wasn't.

He sighed heavily and then he lay back into the grass.

There wasn't any breeze at all, and a sweet-smelling haze hung in the air above them. "So," she said, hugging her knees, "tell me about yourself."

"So," he echoed, "tell me about myself."

"What?" she asked, laughing.

"What do you know about me?" he asked, sounding almost sleepy.

"Nothing," she said.

He grunted. "Who's your best friend?" he asked.

"Chris Rowland," she said.

He opened one eye. "She's a cheerleader, too?" he asked.

"What is it with you?" she asked. "What's wrong with being a cheerleader?"

He closed the eye and smiled. "Don't you go to the movies?" he asked.

"McClellan," she warned.

"Priorities," he said. "Don't you think it seems kind of superficial?"

"Because you don't care about it," she said.

He opened the one eye again. "You *care* about it?" he asked, not sarcastically, just pointing out the word.

"Well," she said, irritated with him. "Not really. It's just fun, that's all."

"Fun," he echoed.

"You're allowed to have fun," she said.

He sighed again. "Okay. So—you and your friend—what was her name?"

"Chris," she said.

"Chris. You and your friend, Chris, sit down, and she says 'What about this guy?' What would you tell her?"

"Why?" she asked, grinning at him, thinking she was catching just a little glimpse behind the face.

"I just want to know," he said.

"Need a mirror?" she asked him.

"I just want to know," he said again.

"Okay," she said, settling herself and using her most parochial tone. "He's about five eleven, and he has kind of curly, dark hair, and eyes—I don't know what color. Open up; I want to see your eyes." She leaned over him. He squinted up at her. "Oh, fine," she said. "That really helps." He closed his eyes and she sat back up, sighing.

"And he's kind of—"

"Cute?" he said.

"—hard to get along with."

"Come on," he said.

"Impossible to get along with," she corrected herself. "Because you are. You are the most perverse person I have *ever* met."

He harrumphed.

"And he lives with his uncle," she went on, "who is his father's twin brother . . . "

He opened both his eyes, squinting at her again. "Where'd you get that?" he asked.

"I made it up," she said. "If it's going to get any more interesting than this, I'm going to have to start making things up."

"It's not accurate," he said, closing his eyes.

"Okay," she said. "So, he lives with his uncle who is his father's brother, not twin—"

"Not accurate," he said again.

She stopped, confused. Family relationships were muddlish sorts of things. She sat there, puzzling it out, but she couldn't see how it would work out any other way.

"You have the same last name as your uncle," she said.

"True," he said.

"And the only way you could do that is if your father was your uncle's brother. Or if your mother married somebody with the same last name."

"Or—" he said.

And then she felt a little chill. "Or if your mother wasn't married," she said.

"Accurate," he said.

"Ah," she said, embarrassed. *You're not stupid,* she told herself. *These things happen all the time.* But the truth was that she didn't know anybody it had ever happened to. Or at least, she didn't know she knew anybody. She wasn't quite sure what to do now—how she was supposed to react. How she *should* react.

"She's divorced?" she asked, sounding very stupid to herself, very unsophisticated, very naive, trying to make it work out right.

"No," he said.

She folded her hands together, fighting off the urge to blow on them and warm them up.

"I didn't think anything about it, myself," he said lazily, "until I was about four. By then, I noticed families, that usually there was a mother *and* a father. So I asked her about it."

"What did she say?" Elise asked.

"Not a word." He rolled over onto his side, leaning on his elbow, his cheek against his hand. "But she made it *very* clear that that was not an acceptable topic of conversation. And that was the most detailed discussion we ever had about it."

She knew he was looking at her; she was trying like crazy to get her balance. Somehow, she had to let him know that she accepted him without making it seem that she accepted the situation. If she did. And she thought she did — which made her, personally, very uncomfortable —

He'd said something else.

She blinked, missing it. Then he was sitting up and saying, "Well, thank you for the help —"

She grabbed at the other thing he'd said, *It's a little hard for you to handle, isn't it? Makes me from another planet. Yeah. Well.*

She put out her hand and caught his arm before he could get up, sensing that she'd hurt him.

He stopped, looking not at her face, but at her hand. In her mind, she moved the hand off him — in actuality, she made the hand stay where it was.

He sat back again, waiting.

"I'm sorry," she said, stumbling. "I didn't even hear what you said until just now. It wasn't that I wasn't answering you."

He put the camera down, and he laced his arms loosely around his knees, still waiting.

She cleared her voice, embarrassed because she had to. "It does make me uncomfortable," she said. "I'm sorry. But it's not *you*. It's the situation. It's not what I'm used to." No father. No family. No honor. And a mother who wouldn't talk about it.

"See," she said, "I think I'm probably pretty naive." He had that hard face on. Now he turned his eyes full on her. She didn't know how she'd missed it before; they were green as the grass. She wanted to reach out, touch his cheek, ease the hurt from him — because there *was* hurt there — she could see it. But she couldn't touch him. She didn't dare. There was still that dry edge.

154

"You think I'm provincial," she said.

There was a trace of a smile on him.

"There are worse things to be," she said.

He looked surprised. "Did I say you were different?"

"You smiled," she said. "You have this superior smile."

He looked totally surprised. "I didn't mean to," he said. "I was just thinking." He pulled up a blade of grass and twirled it between his fingers. "This is a strange place. It's got a lot of religion in it. Everybody seems kind of the same."

"You think so?" she said.

"That's the way it seems."

She thought about that. "It's not really that way," she said.

"It just seems like everybody goes to church. Everybody's squeaky clean. Everybody succeeds. Everything so cut and dried, right and wrong. Nobody swears."

"But that's not true," she said. "A lot of people have problems. There's a lot of stuff that goes on here. My *dad* swears sometimes." *Oh, that's just great,* she told herself. *Let's argue the validity of the place. We're normal—we sin. We're legitimate.*

"How would you know?" he asked, that smile on again.

"I don't know," she said. She *didn't* know. She kept her nose out of other people's business. She just *liked* people; she didn't have to *know* about them.

"Well," he said, pursing his lips, considering. "You can't be that innocent, I guess. I mean, you *are* a cheerleader . . ."

She made a sound of pure exasperation and knocked him over.

"The camera," he said, very acrobatic about not falling on it.

She laughed. He sat up, brushing himself off, looking very cross. "You're a pain," he said.

"Oh, McClellan," she said reproachfully.

"Oh, McCall," he echoed.

"You never call me Elise," she said.

"You never call me Cody," he said.

"You don't have a Cody face," she said. "You keep it so McClellan."

"And what does that mean?" he asked, sitting down again in his old place.

"It never moves," she said. "It's always all business."

He turned the eyes on her again, and her stomach twisted, very pleasantly. Then he smiled. There was a little touch of sarcasm, but he let the smile come through his whole face, like a window opening up, or a door in a wall.

"Cody," she cried, answering the residual irony.

He laughed, and looked away.

"Are we going to shoot anymore?" she asked.

He shrugged.

"You want to come to my house for dinner? We always barbecue on Saturdays. You could just kind of come and hang around with us tonight."

"Who's us?" he asked.

"My family." She realized two things at once: she really wanted him to come, but she was suddenly, honestly scared to death of him.

"You're sure they wouldn't mind?" he asked.

"They wouldn't mind," she said. She was sure of that. "I just hope you don't mind little kids."

"How many?" he asked, the caution in his voice put there for her sake.

"Five?" she said, making a pleading face.

"Five?" he said. "Do you keep them penned up?"

"No," she said, laughing at his mock shock.

"I'd like to come," he said, and when he smiled again, this time completely with*out* irony, his eyes had gone dark blue and clear.

Elise had a dog, a tiny collie that liked to push his nose up under your hand. She also had a forest, a personal McCall forest, all across the back of the backyard, so that you couldn't see if there might be neighbors back there. She'd promised Cody there would be children, and there were plenty of those, pretty, well-dressed, dirty-faced—thinking it was hilarious that Cody had never had barbecue before.

He hadn't had any clear expectations of what he would find in her backyard. If he'd known her father was a doctor, a pediatrician—a man with more money than Erin had—there would have been much he would have expected, mostly the wrong things. As it turned out, Dr. McCall was not so different from Elaina's father, a gentle man who loved his children and was easy with his wife, and who loved to play the guitar in the evening.

Elise's mother, a youngish, good-looking, intelligent and watchful woman, was another matter. Elaina's mother had been all warmth and food and good will, wanting nothing more than a husband for her daughter, a good man with a job, and Cody had been enough of that to win her over. He suspected that Mrs. McCall was not so simple. And Mrs. McCall kept a careful eye on him.

In all the warm evening, in the lingering light, Elise and Cody had played with the children. This was one of the things Cody had missed, since he was cut off from Elaina's family and had been too preoccupied to do much with his own cousins—Cody and Elise both of them being patient and tolerant of the silliness of the younger ones, and aware–not aware of each other.

Dr. McCall wore an apron and stood by the big black barbecue on the wide deck, wreathed in rich, salt-smelling smoke, tending the meat with spatula in hand, while his wife bustled back and forth through the French doors of the house with paper plates and salad bowls and seasonings, both of them keeping half an eye on the children's games.

They played croquet. They played badminton. They even played "kick the can." The children loved Elise; that anyone could have seen, and she was good to them, sweet with them. Later, after the food was gone, and with the dark coming on, they wanted to play "no bears are out tonight," but it wasn't to be.

"Bath," Mrs. McCall directed, pointing at each of the three youngest. "You help them," she said to Katie, the eleven-year-old. And then to Samuel, the oldest boy, "Go iron a shirt for tomorrow."

Dr. McCall was putting the barbecue in order. Cody, armed with a garbage bag, prowled the deck and the yard for stray paper plates and plastic forks; the children had been all over. He searched the neat flower beds, where the grass had been trimmed back just so, and around the children's fantastical play yard, while Mrs. McCall and Elise rounded up children, hunting around the yard to make sure none of the toys and games were left out to weather.

The children trooped up the steps of the redwood decking, their feet making pleasant booms as they climbed.

"Where do you want me to put this?" Cody asked, holding up the bag.

"Leave it on the deck," Mrs. McCall said. "Tom'll get it." And she cast an appraising eye at him, not minding the help. Elise had started clearing away the table, taking the things back

157

inside the house. And he helped her do that, back and forth between the deck and the kitchen, at every trip the kitchen seeming the warmer and the night air that much cooler.

"That's it," Dr. McCall finally announced, shutting the French doors and locking them for the night. It was dark outside now, and there was a lot of activity to be heard upstairs.

"You going to watch the movie?" he asked his wife.

"Would you like to come down?" Mrs. McCall asked Cody and her daughter. It was more than an invitation. So, downstairs they all went, descending from the studied loveliness of the upstairs rooms into the comfortable chaos that was the McCall basement, where nothing matched and everything—furniture, books, magazines—was comfortably old. Cody looked around the room in pleased amazement, immediately at ease. There was a crocheted afghan thrown over the back of the couch, a stone fireplace on one end of the room, and old floor lamps for light, so that the room was really rather dark, except for the bright showers of light from the lamps.

Dr. McCall turned on the TV, picked up the paper, sat down in his chair, feet up, and turned on his lamp, looking very satisfied. Mrs. McCall took up a place behind Samuel and the ironing board, keeping a watchful eye on the shirt.

After a while, the children, scrubbed up and glowing, and dressed for bed in what looked like their father's T-shirts, came tumbling down the stairs. The TV went off. Elise sat down on the floor by her father's chair. Katie, the eleven-year-old, made Cody come and sit at a card table and play Othello with her. She was making it plain—if her older sister should be so stupid as to give him up, Katie stood ready to take him in. She made shy eyes at him, and he treated her with every courtesy.

The three little ones wanted to be read to, demanding Cody, but getting Elise. So she put them on the couch, and read to them out of a book about Pooh.

Cody closed his eyes. Katie was taking her time over the next move. There were the comfortable drone of the story and the quiet creaking of the ironing board, and Cody abandoned himself in the peace of those sounds, and the comfortable dimness of the light, until his tough, ready fabric began to dissolve, coarseness smoothed, tight weave released.

Katie said his name at least once before he heard her again. He opened his eyes, yawning, and he made his move. "Not smart," Katie chortled, following up triumphantly with one of her own. He groaned comfortably, watching his men disappear.

"Are you sure that's fair?" he asked, and she grinned at him happily.

Samuel finished his shirt and went upstairs. His mother took his place at the ironing board, picking a little girl's ruffled dress out of the basket at her feet.

The story was over. "Upstairs," the mother said, putting the iron down, her arms out for kisses. Cody himself got a sweet kiss on the cheek from the five-year-old as young Katie looked wistfully on. And then it was time for Katie to go, too.

Drained of children, the room was very quiet.

"Now, the movie," Dr. McCall announced, folding up his paper.

Cody got up from the card table and sat down on the couch next to Elise. He put his head back and they looked at each other. "I've got to go," he said. It was a long walk, and he was finally, finally falling asleep.

"I'll take you home," she said.

"You don't need to," he protested, not unwilling to be coerced.

"You don't want to walk by the park this late," she warned.

"I assure you," he said, thickheaded and drowsy, "I can take care of myself."

"I'm taking you," she said. She stood up, offered her hand, and pulled him up off the couch.

He thanked her parents. They were very gracious, even Mrs. McCall. "We enjoyed having you," she said, putting the iron down. She seemed to mean it.

Elise, still with his hand trapped in hers, led him up the stairs. He had a nice warmth in his middle, his heart in her hand.

She let go of him at the top of the stairs. "I've got to get my purse, and the camera," she said, and then he was standing in the shadowy front hall alone, listening to the muffled sounds upstairs. He could hear the floor in the kitchen creaking as she walked through it, and then she was coming back to him down the quiet hall. He wondered how he could get these things into a picture, these sounds, this peace.

"Okay," she said, coming along, slinging her purse over her shoulder, keys in her hand. She handed him the camera, taking great care. He slung the strap over his shoulder as she opened the front door for him. He went out first and stood, getting used to the cool liquidity of the air. She pulled the front door closed behind them and let the storm door swing shut. Then they stood on the wide porch, both of them, and a wind chime in the far corner whispered in the darkness.

There was benediction in the quiet of the moment. He put a hand out for her, and she accepted it. He pulled her gently in and then he kissed her.

Too rich a taste after too long a time. The warmth in his middle spread itself all through him until he was light-headed and weak in the knees. The kindness of her parents, the mellow evening, and the sweetness of her response filled him with grace and a deep and exquisite tenderness, and he ran his hand gently, lovingly down the front of her soft sweater.

And that was the end of it.

She shoved him back so hard it hurt his ribs. He stepped back, his hand pressed over his hurt side, blinking at her stupidly. He could barely make out her face in the ambience of the house lights. Obviously, she was angry. He couldn't imagine what had gone wrong.

"I can't believe you did that," she said, her voice hot.

"What?" he asked, totally amazed.

"You keep your hands to yourself," she said, outrage in her.

He tried to say something, but for the moment, nothing coherent would take shape in his mind—he'd been taken far too off guard to be able to put words to this. "I didn't mean to do anything wrong," he managed, not eloquent, but accurate.

"*Sure*," she said.

"I'm sorry," he said.

"I suppose in New York, people who hardly know each other just generally paw each other, right?"

She sounded so hurt. That cleared his head a bit, understanding then that it was his hand at fault, not his judgment. She had mistaken the gesture.

"I didn't paw you," he said quietly.

"Oh, yeah? Well, then, what do you call it?" she asked.

He went carefully with the answer.

"I stroked you," he said.

She let her breath out, put her hands on her hips.

"It was only the way I felt," he explained, gently, worriedly. "It came out a gentle thing from me. It was a praise of you."

She folded her arms, hugging them in against her chest, and she took a few steps away.

"I wouldn't have done it otherwise," he said, suddenly afraid of losing the sweetness of the afternoon. He understood now that she was feeling used. "It wasn't for me. It was because of you." He didn't know what else he could be saying.

She had moved towards the front door, deeper into the shadow. He sighed and leaned back against the railing. He couldn't read the shadows. There was no use trying.

"Please don't do this to me, Elise," he said, pleading. It had been such a nice day, and such a simple gesture. "I was afraid you didn't want me to kiss you, after all."

"Don't do this to *you*?" she echoed.

He put his hands to the railing he was leaning against. "It's just a matter of language, I think," he offered. "Unless it's that you really don't want me."

She stayed where she was, not saying anything.

"We don't understand the same things, I guess," he said. "There was a girl back home; she used to make me feel like this." Not quite true; even with Elaina, there had been more taking than there had been here. "It was sweet between us—and she never got mad about it. How could I know you would? It's just—I never thought about it."

"*Another* girl?"

Another mistake. He wasn't doing very well.

"Someone who kept me from hurting myself at a bad time some months ago. A very good friend. The only one I had." Except for Parker. But Parker wasn't *that* kind of friend.

Still, she said nothing.

"It's okay," he said, almost whispering. "I'll walk. Thanks for the afternoon. It did me a lot of good." He did his best to smile into the place where she stood, still amazed that things should have turned so suddenly, and he started down the steps, sick inside for the loss of the moment.

"McClellan," she said.

He got to the bottom of the stairs and he stopped without turning.

"I can't believe you're that innocent," she said.

It was a strange word to use with him.

"Oh, McCall," he sighed.

"Oh, McClellan," she said, no sigh to it.

And then he was a little angry. "Do you think I'm stupid?" he asked, turning around. She had come out to the edge of the porch, out to the top of the steps, and she had her hand against the post. "Do you think I would have given up this day—you think I would have given you up—for *that*?" She stood silently

161

there by the post. "Was it such an *offence*?" He sighed. "Good night," he said, and he started down her walk.

"Cody," she said quickly, before he'd gone two steps.

"What?" he said, swinging around and putting his hands on his hips.

There was a pause. The wind chime still whispered in its dark corner. The breeze was restless in the very tops of the heavy trees.

"I hate it that there was another girl," she said.

He laughed, short and quiet. "Girl," he said, "you wear me out."

"Sorry." And she sat down on the top step.

He stood his ground.

The neighborhood was very quiet, a quiet Saturday night with no one stirring in the street. Very different here than what he'd known.

"It was not an acceptable thing," she said, a little hesitantly.

"Yes. That's what I understand—now."

She sighed and put her head against the post. "It was— no one's ever done that before. It's not a light thing." She was looking at him. "I didn't expect it like that."

"How would you have expected it?" he asked. But the question was, What did you understand by it?

"A little more underhanded," she said. "A little more planned."

He let the air out between his teeth, leaning against the railing. "That's not how I feel for you," he said. "I'd never steal from you."

"*You*'ve got a line," she said, sounding unhappy.

"No, it's not," he said. "We're just talking."

She sighed again, her head against the post. "What did you mean, language?"

He patted the railing. "How we understand each other," he said. "There are some things we did at home that must be different here. Words, things. The way the kids talk to each other sometimes. Certainly, this. I never meant to injure you."

"What did you mean, then?" she asked.

He laughed again, softly. "I'm not sure I can say," he said, realizing he was going to have to if he wanted her to believe him. "You—" he made a fist and bounced it gently on the railing. The words could get him in trouble, too. "What you are is lovely to me. Everything you are. The way you are with the children.

162

Your innocence. I wanted to climb inside of you the way you would a big coat—pulling the hood up all around my face to be safe. That's all. It was because of that feeling. A reflection of your kindness. That's all."

She sat up, resting her elbows on her knees, folding her arms over them. She didn't say anything.

"It wasn't to satisfy my hand," he said. "And I won't do it again."

"You scare me to death," she said, half-whispering.

"Why?" he asked.

"Because," she said. And no more.

He leaned back against the rail, folding his arms.

"I'd like to understand your feeling," he said. A request.

For a while, she didn't answer. That, he understood. The question hadn't been simple.

"There's a sacredness about my body," she said. "You understand what I mean by that?"

"I do," he said. He did.

"There's a holiness in it. You don't touch holy things lightly."

"No," he agreed.

She went quiet again, thinking.

"And there's more to it than that," she said.

He waited.

"It belongs to me," she said. "So far, no one else has any claim on me, not like that. That's the way it has to be. There are too many things I want to do, that I couldn't do if there was a claim on me. Like college. Like other things. I won't give *any* bit of myself up that easily. I can't be your possession, or anybody's. Not even at all. The cost is too high. Not till I'm ready to settle. And that won't be for years."

The breeze was riffling through the leaves, making them whisper; and the light from the street lamp danced across the lawn, shifting its shape. It was a new dance to him, something that had never happened on his asphalt and brownstone street.

"And then," she went on, thoughtfully, "only when I'm sure. Because I couldn't stand the hurt of giving myself to someone who wouldn't care so much about what I'd given."

"And how do you be sure of that?" he asked, smiling.

"He'll want me more than he wants anything else."

"And how do you think you're going to be so sure of that?" he asked, in his mind a ghost of a picture of his mother.

"He'll marry me," she said, simply.

163

He sniffed. "People get divorced."

"That's true," she said, sounding a little hot tempered about it, now. "But I think marriage is a little stronger commitment than baby-I-love-you-forever in the back seat of a car somewhere, don't you?"

He nodded, shrugged. "I wouldn't know."

Now he was thinking about Elaina. He'd been true to her. He might have married her; he didn't take these things so lightly, either. In the end, Elaina had sent *him* away. Now, thinking about what might have been—how she'd bought his soul with her eyes—he was glad how it had turned out. Nobody hurt but himself, and himself set free.

"Are you used to getting what you want?" she asked.

His head came up. "What?" he asked.

"Are you used to getting what you want?" she asked him again.

He laughed. "Not really. Not like you. Only what I pay for."

"You think I don't?" she asked, eyes flashing.

"I think you don't even know what I'm talking about. Believe me."

She was looking at him, trying to decide whether she should be mad about that. Evidently, she decided against it. He admired her for that.

"Still," she said. "There are things that are valuable to me. And I don't want to lose them. I don't want to lose my control over things. Over myself. My rights."

"I understand that," he said, because he did.

"I didn't mean to take offence," she said. "I didn't understand what you meant to be doing—but even if I had understood, I wouldn't have allowed it, you understand? But I wouldn't have been so harsh with you. I just didn't know what you meant. Oh, Cody—" she pleaded, "please don't be playing with me, because I can't tell, and I'll believe what you tell me. There's something about you, something I can't . . ." She shrugged, drawing her shoulders way up. And then she sighed and looked at him, her eyes soft and frightened.

He tucked his arms up tighter around himself.

"I'm not lying," he said, wearily. "But what difference does my saying that make?"

She moaned.

He took one hesitant step up. She stood up, poised to move either way.

"I don't want to hurt you," he said. "I don't want to be hurt, either."

164

She took a step down. And then another, until she was leaning against the rail next to him, shivering. He put his arm around her—"To keep you warm," he explained, before she could think anything else. And it was almost completely the truth.

"My language is the law I live by," she said.

"There's religion in it," he said.

"There's no fault in that," she said, looking up at him. "But it's more than that, even. It's what makes sense to me."

He nodded. "You don't want to try learning mine?" he asked, making it straightforward, a simple offering. "There are parts of it that are very nice."

She moved, looked away. It was something very cute. "No," she said, and then she grinned at him. "Maybe sometime—if you're around when I'm finished with what I've got to do. And if you're going to stick around the rest of your life."

"You never know," he said.

"That *is* my point."

He nodded again, hearing the smile in her voice.

"All right," he said. It was sad, maybe unbearable, but it was settled in his mind. "Then I'd better learn yours."

"And how are you going to do that?" she asked, a little braver, now. Trusting him so quickly.

"Well," he said, a little worried about that, but wanting to kiss her again in the worst way. "I've got a half an hour or so. You *are* the tutor."

As it turned out, just like everything else, she took that responsibility very seriously.

15

"Now," Charlotte said, putting the last touches on the little boys' Sunday clothes, "don't feel like you *have* to come with us." And that was nice of her, considering that she *really* wanted him to go.

"You bought me a suit," he told her. "Where else am I going to wear it?" Which meant he would go. And that was nice of him, considering he *really* didn't want to.

He'd only been to church a couple of times before, the first time with Mrs. Guicci when he was little, to the cathedral on a holy day.

All he could remember was the darkness in that cavernous place—so dark and so cavernous he'd thought the walls must keep going, all the way up to heaven. Darkness with the candles flickering dimly here and there, throwing shadows against shadows. *Statues*—stark faces peering down out of candle-lit niches. And *the crucifix.*

The crucifix was the center of those memories, a huge cross, hanging high above the altar on the shadowed wall, a nearly naked man hanging from it, his face screwed up in agony, bleeding, blood running down from his forehead, and on his hands and his side and his feet. It was a horrible thing, shadows flickering over it, so you couldn't tell if maybe it wasn't moving on its own. Cody hadn't been able to take his eyes off it, staring up there until he was so scared he could hardly breathe.

"You see what you've done?" Mr. Guicci said when they got home, Cody's face a frozen little lake with who-knows-what swimming around in the mud beneath.

But Mrs. Guicci hadn't understood.

"This isn't a Catholic child," Mr. Guicci explained to her, angrily. "He doesn't look at your symbols and understand that God is supposed to be in them. Nobody's taught him to see behind those things."

The presence of God should be self-evident, she'd argued. But she never took Cody to church with her again, and he never liked to watch TV in their house because of the little crucifix she had hanging on the wall behind—not till much time had gone by, and he couldn't see it anymore without looking.

166

The second time he'd gone to church was for the funeral. Still the dark cavern. This time, he was older, and he thought he knew where the ceiling was. But this time, the place was filled with whispers of things he couldn't understand, grief too much for him to hold—people around him in the darkness, doing things, murmuring things in the shadows, and talk of saving that was too late for Cody, having no understanding of things beyond. He had kept his eyes from the crucifix then, as if the altar and the wall behind it did not exist.

Charlotte could not have known what act of sacrifice was offered in his going with her now. He put on the white shirt and the tie—one of the kind you don't have to tie yourself—the faultless tweed suit, the argyle socks and the very serious looking shoes, and he looked at himself in the mirror, seeing a scared face.

"You look *won*derful," Charlotte had said, as he came down. "Erin, doesn't he look great?" And everyone, except Mickey of course, agreed that Cody did look truly *great*. They must have wanted him to like their church very much, considering the petting he got.

He got into the car with them, a little, cold ball sitting at the pit of his stomach.

But they didn't go to a cathedral. Their church was a simpler place, smooth walls on the outside, one clean spire. Inside were the same long pews, a stand in front for speaking, and what looked to him like a sort of altar to the side. It was a tall room, but filled with light, flooded with it, in fact—simple, bright chandeliers hanging from the exposed beams in the ceiling, large windows at the front, a touch of colored glass. A plain place, like an assembly hall, no candles, no statues, no shadows. And, as he got his courage up and looked around—no crucifix. Not anywhere. He wondered how they could call it a church.

They sat down in the pews with the people—lots of little children; it was very noisy for being a holy place. And then the meeting started. A man in a dark suit came to the stand and spoke quietly into a microphone, welcomed everyone, made a little joke, and announced a women's auxiliary meeting and a youth outing.

More like a club than anything, Cody thought, much relieved, and he began to relax.

Next came a hymn. Sawyer slipped a book out of its pew pocket and snuggled over near Cody, opening the book and offering Cody to hold half. It was a hymnal, not a breviary.

167

"I don't know this song," Cody whispered to him.

"Neither do I," Sawyer said cheerfully, but then he gave it a go. So Cody, shamed, did his best with it, too. God was in the words of the hymn. When the last of the organ sound faded like passing color at the end of the song, someone prayed. Then came another hymn with even more of God in it, and more praying, and then communion.

After that, a woman came to the stand. Cody had heard of woman priests, but he'd never seen one. "Not clergy," Charlotte whispered, leaning over so he could hear her. "Just ordinary people get invited to speak here." *Ah.* She'd said it with satisfaction.

The woman began to speak, a high, nervously careful voice, inflected as if she were talking to a roomful of small children. Cody closed his eyes and relaxed into the pew, warm with relief.

She began to tell a story.

It was a story about a child, a genius kind of child who was always getting himself in trouble. Even as he grew up, he made trouble for himself, having a philosophy and teaching people about it, stirring up trouble with the government. And the story began to get a little weird.

The man the child became went around teaching, and doing strange things no one else could do—healing people who had been blind or sick—or dead, even. Walking on water, changing the nature of things. This part of the story was not totally unfamiliar to Cody; he'd heard snatches here and there at different times over the years.

There were people who weren't comfortable with what the man was doing. *So, who would be comfortable with a person who could do such things? What else might he do, if he decided he wanted to?*

The discomfort came mainly from the fact that the man was calling himself the Son of God. *Interesting.* The leaders caught him, took him to court, wanted him executed. *For what? For healing? For words?*

"This isn't supposed to be a true story?" he whispered, leaning over to Charlotte.

She looked at him for a moment. "Yes," she whispered. "It is." He sat up again, disturbed by her answer. *Raising the dead?*

The court obliged the leaders, and the man was taken up on a hill one day. Up there, they made him lie down on a big wooden cross, and they *nailed* him to it. Put nails through his wrists and his feet and his hands, and he had to hang from the nails until he was dead. Then they stuck a sword into his side, just to make sure of it.

It was the crucifix. Worse. This time, he knew something about the person hanging there. And this time, they'd made it so he couldn't sidestep any of it—because they'd put it in words.

Cody wound his fingers together, sick inside. *What's wrong with these people?* he wondered, the horror of the image winding around his memory of the goodness of Mrs. Guicci, and Charlotte and Erin. *How could they make religion out of this? How can they talk about such a thing?* Not easily. The woman at the stand was crying, and so was Charlotte. *This is insane.*

On his other side, Tyler punched Sawyer, whispering angrily. They were fighting over Erin's pen.

The woman said his name, then, the name of the dead man, Jesus Christ, as if no one could have guessed before.

So they took him down and they put his body in a cave; and then, after three days, he came alive again. Just like that. The body was gone, and when he appeared again one or two people talked to him before they realized who he was.

He was the Son of God. He could do this thing that no one else had ever done, take his life back. *So, why?* Cody wondered. *Then why did he let them kill him in the first place?*

The woman was saying, "All this, he did for *us*," which seemed fairly arrogant and ludicrous, considering how long ago it had supposedly happened, and how many people there had been in the world.

If he hadn't done it, the woman went on, we couldn't—what we couldn't do wasn't clear to Cody. It was something like getting to heaven—we couldn't get to heaven unless Jesus Christ let himself be murdered.

And when he understood that that was what she meant, all Cody could do was stare at the woman behind the stand.

Why ever not? he wondered, completely shocked.

"If *you*," the woman said, still crying as she pointed out into the audience, "or you, or you, or *me*—if you were the only person that was ever born anywhere in the entire universe, he still would have done it. He still would have gone through it, even for just you."

Why? Cody thought again. *I would never let anyone do such a thing for me. I can't accept this. The whole thing is crazy.* He looked at his aunt. She was believing. *It makes her happy,* he suddenly realized, and it came to him with a jolt.

". . . Because he loves you," the woman was saying. "Because he loves you more than anything." She was talking now as if the man were still alive. *But, they believe he is, right?* he reminded himself. Nobody could expect him to have to die twice. At least, you wouldn't *think* so.

"How much more love could a person have," she was saying, "than to die in his friend's place? That's how important we are to him, that he should die for each person in the church, here, for each person who ever lived on the earth, for each person in the entire universe—individually, as if that person were the only person." And so she was saying that it was as if he had died a million times.

No, Cody thought. *This is wrong. No one person is worth the death of somebody else.*

But the question gnawed at him, and he didn't hear the rest of the things the woman was saying.

What about Charlotte? he was asking himself. *What if Sawyer—what if something were going to happen to him—like he was out in the street, and a car was coming he didn't see? Or if he were sick, and he were going to die if somebody didn't give him their heart or something? She'd save him, wouldn't she? Even if it killed her. She'd do that.*

But this Jesus Christ, it was the *why* of it that was bothering Cody. *What's the point?* he asked again. There was still no answer. *What did he think he was saving us from? From not being able to go to heaven? So what?* And the other question, *Why would he love people he didn't even know?*

But that was assuming the story was true. All the magic. All the strangeness. Maybe it was like all the other mythology in the world, people holding their mental ground against fear, against things they didn't understand, like death. These religious people had made up somebody who could save them. Somebody who *loved* them. Somebody to make them think they were important enough to die for.

And that was a question in itself. If Charlotte saved Sawyer, would Sawyer be happy about it? When he thought about it later, wouldn't he wonder, Why was my life any more important than hers? Wouldn't he feel angry about it the rest of his life, because it was too late for him to have any say in the choice?

But Charlotte would have thought he was worth it. Would she think Mickey was worth it? *Maybe not now,* he thought. But that was wrong—it came to him that it didn't have much to do with how worthy the person was to be saved, and everything to do with Charlotte, the saver. Nothing to do with Cody; everything to do with Guicci.

And then, suddenly, he had an ache inside of himself, an old ache like a hollow pain. There was no one left to save Cody, not from the car in the street, not at the cost of love. Erin and Charlotte had their own children. Somebody might try to warn him, but there was no one who would pay the price of pulling him out of the way in time. If the car ever did come, it would simply smash Cody to bits.

He pulled his mind away from the picture. He tried to be reasonable about it. *In the end, why should anyone bother? What have you ever done that anybody should love you like that? Love and worth. Much the same.*

And then he thought about Elise. He thought about the feeling they had had the night before, wondered how close to love it had been. The rest of the question began to fall away. The memory of the kissing spread like warmth over the top of it, not healing, but soothing, and he sighed silently.

He was remembering what she'd said, how much she wanted the things she wanted. And—knowing now that he couldn't ever have her, not *ever*—suddenly, he wanted her very much. The desire was another ache, strong and colored, but a good ache, like pleasure. *Not having,* he thought, a little amazed —is *good in its own way.*

That girl's no idiot. She knows that in the end, you only really want the things you know you can't get. By keeping herself the way she was, she'd bound him to her, made herself something in his mind that would never be satisfied. It was because of the way she saw herself—as something valuable, the kind of thing you don't give away to just anybody. The kind of thing you only give away once.

Maybe she would think she was worth Jesus Christ, he thought. *She probably would. She probably does.* And that wasn't a bad thing, really. To think so much of yourself, as long as it didn't turn you cold. But, she had taken *Cody* in—it seemed inconsistent that she should think so much of herself and still have time for him.

She loved herself. And maybe that was what gave her enough worthiness to justify *him.* At least for the moment. At least last night. He remembered her arms around him, her hands warm against his back, holding him, keeping him now from being formless.

And then he thought about his mother.

The memory of her was like an immense black hole; nothing got out, nothing was reflected. Why? Because of Cody? Because of what he'd done to her? Because there wasn't anything in him to make her love him? Nothing in him to be reflected? *Maybe.*

And if that were so, if his own mother couldn't find anything in him to love, then the rest of this argument had been nothing more than academic. She had taught him carefully to understand this one thing: essentially, he was nothing. The closer anyone got to the center of him, the less reason there would be to go any further.

But that could be wrong, couldn't it? She was wrong about her brother; she could have been wrong about me. Maybe his mother had made her own darkness. He'd never seen any love in her. Only unhappiness—wistful or bitter, it was all the same, really, pulling and pulling.

Elise was light. His mother was darkness. Elise's love for herself had warmed him. Maybe that was what was missing in his mother, that she didn't love herself. It was the truth, he realized. He knew she didn't.

Perhaps, then, perhaps it all came down to that. His father—maybe she had loved *him.* Or wanted him to love her, to make her worth it. Maybe she had *wanted* him. Maybe she thought having him would give her what she didn't have herself. She surely did get something from him. Evidently not what she'd wanted.

I *loved her,* he thought. *Why wasn't that enough?*

But his mind had stalled. The truth was, getting Cody had been worse to her than getting nothing.

From the stand a man was speaking now. People were laughing at something he'd said. The two little boys were drawing boats.

Women aren't like men, Cody thought. *Some ways, yes. Other ways, no. They aren't as maneuverable.* A man, he could get satisfaction out of a relationship just by touching the outside. Not so, a woman. They always wanted you to *stay.* Even the tough ones. Once you got inside, you had them tied up. Just like he was tied to Elise now. *Women don't move along easily once they touch, not without shredding themselves.*

If back then, his mother had been like Elise—if she'd said, *"You've got to pay my price"*—maybe Cody would have a father now. And maybe he would have a mother. But instead, she'd tried to buy somebody. And that was the thing. *You can't*

172

use what you're worth to buy, he thought. *The price is only there to show how much somebody has to pay for you.*

So, maybe his mother hadn't thought she was worth much. Evidently his father hadn't thought so either. And, if you thought about it, that made Cody not much, either.

And that's why she drinks, he realized. *Because there was nothing ever inside of her but me. And she thinks there isn't anything in the world that's going to fix that, now. And she doesn't want to try. It's not worth it. Nothing's worth it.*

The people were singing again. Sawyer was shoving his elbow into Cody's side, wanting him to hold half of the hymnal. Absently, Cody accepted it. He didn't sing, but the music pulled at him, breaking up his thought so that he couldn't follow it, leaving him with nothing but the feeling, and the cold.

All the way home in the car the family was waiting for him to say something. He knew it; he just couldn't oblige them at the moment.

"Did you mind it so much?" Charlotte asked, finally. It was such a humble way to put the question.

"It was very thought provoking," he said, finally finding words for her.

She was satisfied with that, and he could feel her attention shift away from him. She was speaking to Erin. Cody closed his eyes. Tyler jerked violently into his side, making his eyes fly open again. "Knock it off, you guys," he whispered. Tyler looked up at Cody pitifully and then leaned against him. Cody put his arm around the little boy.

"Get changed for dinner," Charlotte said, bestowing a light smack on whichever bottom might not be moving fast enough. "*Now*, Tyler."

Cody followed Tyler up the stairs, poking him gently in the back ever so often to keep him moving.

Sawyer was already in the bedroom, clothes changed, sitting at his desk, writing.

"You're fast," Cody remarked, pulling his tie off and shaking his hair out. No answer. He leaned over Sawyer, looking over his shoulder. Sawyer immediately put his hand on top of the paper. He looked up, saw it was Cody, and uncovered. He was making a list.

"What's that?" Cody asked, sitting down on his bed. He pried his left shoe off using the toe of his right shoe.

"Christmas list," Sawyer said.

"Sawyer," Cody said, leaning over to take the other shoe off. "It's only September."

"I know it. But I thought of something today, and I didn't want to forget it."

"Really," Cody said. "If it's something you want, it's not like you're going to forget what it is." He pulled off one of the argyle socks.

"There's just a lot of stuff to want," Sawyer said, shrugging, still hunched over the list.

"You already have everything in the world," Cody said. He pulled off the other sock, and then stood up and took off the suit, hanging it up very carefully. "You'd better hang up your suit," he warned Sawyer. Then he picked up Sawyer's suit and looked at it philosophically. "I'll do it," he said.

Sawyer put down his pen and studied the list.

In shirt and shorts, Cody lay down on his bed and sighed. "How many things do you *have* on that list?" he asked. He put his hands behind his head and watched Sawyer.

Sawyer scrutinized the list. "About twenty-four," he said. "It's hard to tell. I dumped some of this stuff."

"Twenty-four things?" Cody asked, incredulous. "What would you do with twenty-four more things?"

Sawyer looked at him blankly. "Use them," he said.

"Cshhh . . ." Cody hissed. He stretched his back and closed his eyes. "You're greedy, Sawyer."

"Isn't there anything you want?" Sawyer asked, sounding a bit uncomfortable. That was something you had to like about Sawyer — you could shame him.

"Hmmm . . ." Cody considered. "Well, yeah. There's something I want. There's one thing I want."

"Just one?"

Cody smiled at him sweetly. "It's expensive," he explained.

"Oh," Sawyer said, relieved. "What is it?"

"Now," Cody said, hooding his eyes. "I'm not sure I want to tell you."

"Does anybody else know?" Sawyer asked, interested.

"Not another soul in the world," Cody said, looking at Sawyer out of the corners of his eyes. "And that's the way I want it."

"I'm not going to tell anybody," Sawyer said indignantly.

Cody considered. Sawyer got up and came over to sit on the edge of Cody's bed. "We're cousins," he said simply, opening beautiful possibilities of meaning.

"Okay," Cody said, grinning to himself, enjoying the game. "It's a camera."

"Come on," Sawyer said, disappointed.

"What?" Cody asked.

"I've got one of those on my list." He was disappointed.

"Not like this one, you don't," Cody said. He reached down between the bed and the wall and pulled up his magazine. "I'll show you." There was no mistaking the page; the magazine fell open there. "Look at this. *That's* a camera."

Sawyer bent over the page. "How much does it cost?" he asked.

Cody shoved him. "What do you care?" he asked.

"I just wondered."

"You *are* greedy," Cody said.

"Well, if it's your only thing, don't you think it should be worth it?" Sawyer asked.

"Look at what it does," Cody said.

"I don't know anything about cameras," Sawyer told him.

Cody pulled the magazine away from him, turned over on his back, and held it up so that he could look at that picture. "Well, this one is beautiful," Cody said. "And I'm going to get it someday."

"Not if it costs too much," Sawyer said.

"I've still got a hundred and fifty dollars," Cody told him. "Maybe I'll get a job. Just for a while. It wouldn't take more than a month."

"You really want it," Sawyer said, almost reverently.

"Man," Cody agreed, "I ache for this." He closed the magazine and slid it back down in its place. Sawyer got up and went over to the desk and sat down, looking a little doleful.

"Whatsamatter?" Cody asked him, smiling.

"I haven't got anything that good," Sawyer said.

"Sure you do," Cody told him. "The problem is, you've already got everything."

"Are you coming?" they heard Charlotte calling from the bottom of the stairs. "Somebody needs to set the table."

"It's got to be you," Cody said to Sawyer, indicating the fact that he only had his shorts on. Sawyer grumbled, opening his drawer and stuffing the list down into it. "I'll save the silverware for you," he warned. "So you'd better get a move on."

"Cody," Charlotte said, passing the potatoes and looking very pleased with herself. She glanced up at Erin and he nodded. "We have some friends at church." She put gravy on her potatoes, doing it artistically, speaking with cheerful care. "Their son has gone to France for a couple of years—pass your brother the peas, Mickey—"

"Not me," Sawyer said with distaste. "I've had them. To *him*."

"And he left behind this little Volkswagen that he rebuilt. Don't, Tyler." She made a disgusted sound and got up to help Tyler pick up peas.

"And they said," she went on doggedly, but still pleasantly —"he wants them to sell it. They only want a couple of hundred dollars, and I think we can get them down to one hundred and fifty. And it's really quite a nice little car." She beamed at Cody, the secret out. Mickey made a sound of pure disgust, quiet enough so that she got off with just a look from her father.

"I don't know how to drive," Cody said.

"You don't know how to drive?" Sawyer echoed.

"I'm from the city, Sawyer," Cody said.

"It's not that hard to learn," Erin said.

"I could learn, too—" Sawyer suggested.

"That easy it's not," Charlotte said, sitting down at her place. "I thought you'd be excited, Cody," she said.

"Oh, I am," he said. "It's just that I've never had a car. So I don't know what it means. Yet. But thank you."

"No more bus," Charlotte said, hands out, still beaming.

"But—" Sawyer said, suddenly realizing they meant Cody should be buying the car with his own money. Which would mean no camera. Cody glared him down and he fell silent.

"What?" Charlotte asked, watching them.

"Nothing," Sawyer said.

"Well, it's just—I don't know. I—it's all the money I have left," Cody said helplessly.

"Cody," Erin said. "Don't worry about the money. It's not like you're a prisoner here. We'll buy it back from you whenever you want. But I think you'll find you don't have to do that."

Cody was aware that he was spoiling things a bit for Charlotte, and he regretted that. So he brightened up a bit, smiling, thanking them. He looked at Erin. "You're going to have to teach me to drive."

"Or Charlotte can," Erin said.

So Cody smiled at Charlotte.

"I'd love to," she said.

And with the look of a mother who meant what she was doing, she passed Sawyer the carrots.

16

"Okay, then, tonight finish up the last chapters of Moby Dick, and you have a paper due Wednesday"—Ms. Hunsaker waited out the obligatory wave of groans—"analyzing some aspect of the symbolism in the book. Now, be careful, guys. I've known people to do their master's thesis on this—forty pages at the very *least*. You don't have that much time. So be sure you—" and they all said it with her—"*limit your thesis.*"

Elise turned in her seat and grinned at Cody. What she meant was, *We're going to ace this.* But the look had meant something else to him; she'd used the private path between them, set them apart as a functional alliance. She was his friend.

"Okay," Ms. Hunsaker went on. "Be sure you're prepared. See you tomorrow."

The bell rang. Instantly the room shifted—people shoving papers into notebooks; dropping things; standing up, books in their arms. Cody took his time with it; he and Elise had plenty of time to make it to their next class. He wasn't about to rush it, their few sweet, stolen moments in the middle of the morning.

He leaned over to pull the rest of his books out from the space under his seat, bumped around by the kids on their way down the aisle. He straightened up, made a neat pile of books on his notebook, glanced up to see how Elise was doing, and froze.

Only for a moment.

Long enough to have embarrassed himself.

It made a picture in his mind—Elise standing there with her arms full of books, and Big Steve, Mr. Letter Jacket,—one hand on her shoulder and all his friends jammed up in the aisle behind him—dropping this casual, proprietary kiss on her. Quite domestic. So natural. And nothing about her to suggest that she was objecting.

In spite of himself, he took one more look at them—standing together, Steven talking—an intimate, private little laugh together.

It had taken Cody completely by surprise, both the kiss and how much it hurt him to see it. It taught him one very important thing—he had let himself get way too silly over this girl. The heat had come up in his cheeks. He picked up his books and left the room, his face burning. That was the worst of it — that it was so obvious.

He made it all the way down the hall without anybody speaking to him. And every second, he got madder. He wasn't even sure why — mad at himself, probably, for being such a fool. Mad at her, for playing him like one. All that stuff about honor. All that stuff about virtue. That was the hardest thing — that he should have been so completely taken in. And now, he was at a disadvantage with these people because of it. The whole situation was totally unacceptable.

He fooled around at his desk until Bruecher's class started, and his cheeks never did cool off. Nor did he hear much of the lecture. *That it should upset you this much — that you should care. You must be a very big fool, indeed.*

When the class was over, he stalled around — taking down the reading assignment, getting his stuff together. He didn't want that girl waiting for him. Heaven knew, she couldn't wait long, not with the walk she had to her next class. He wasn't wanting to talk to her.

And then when he looked up and found her gone — gone without so much as a *word* — he was *really* fried. Not even a *quest*ion from her. He slammed the last book down on his pile and stalked out of the room.

By the time he got to physics, he'd worked the anger down into an almost controlled mind chill. He sat there in that class, riveting himself to the lecture, feeling dangerously aggressive — right on the edge of looking for trouble. And that's the way it was for the rest of the day — his mind shut down tight as a laser, cold and intellectual, using his mother's vocabulary like a weapon. He didn't recover well from embarrassment. He never had.

He nearly got into a fight in gym. He went to the library during lunch. He caught Mrs. Shein looking at him in math more than once — the first time with respect, the second time with something more like alarm. He found that pleasing. And when he got to photography, he went ahead and developed his roll of negatives — withstood the walls of the tiny room, swore at the crimps. When the negatives were finished, he stuck them into the drying cabinet without taking one look at them.

On the way home, it started to rain.

By the time the bus finally made it to the McClellans' street, Cody was mostly just tired. He wasn't anxious for conversation, so he was relieved to see that Charlotte's car was gone. There was a semi-dry place on the driveway, meaning she hadn't been gone long. So he'd have the house to himself. A little quiet after a very bad day.

He went in through the kitchen door, shaking the rain off before he was quite inside. He dropped his books on the table. He pulled a banana off the bunch Charlotte kept on top of the refrigerator and stood by the table, looking down at his books, and wondering where he should start.

He did his math first. He was too tired to fight with anything else. He made the paper very neat, very precise — paying dogged attention to the detail.

The kitchen door swung open behind him. It scared the life out of him, and he started badly.

"Sorry," Mickey sneered, and headed for the refrigerator.

"Where's your mom?" Cody asked, not really expecting much of an answer.

She stood there with the refrigerator door open, staring at him, that stupid sneer still all over her face.

"Where is your mother?" he asked again, pronouncing it all with elaborate clarity.

"I don't kne-ewww," she said. She pulled something out of the ice box, slammed the door, and swung out of the room.

Someone should slap her nasty little face, he thought, half-heartedly reaching for his world history book. He didn't open it. He put his hand down on top of it gently and sighed. He decided he'd rather finish *Moby Dick,* and he wondered where he'd left it.

He went upstairs and looked for it in his room. Not there. He looked under the bed, between the bed and the wall, down between the two desks. Then he went down to the den and looked around, feeling back behind the sofa cushions, under the *National Geographic* magazines on the table. He even went into Erin's office, in case someone should have thought that's where it belonged. Not there.

Back to the den. *Go through everything one more time; very carefully, this time.* Frustrated. He was getting very frustrated. *It's got to be here somewhere.* He dumped everything off the telephone table.

"What are you *doing?*" Mickey was standing in the doorway.

He didn't answer. He wasn't sure it would have been wise to do so. He was putting everything back on the table, moving it piece by piece so he wouldn't miss anything.

She was still standing there when he finished, watching him with her nose all wrinkled up.

"I lost something," he said. *As if it's any of your business.*

"What?" she asked.

"Why?" he asked her.

"I might have seen it," she said. He straightened up, looking at her. He was a bit too canny to take this at face value.

"But then, I wouldn't know unless you tell me what it is," she said.

"So, what are you going to do?" he asked. "Find it before I do and chuck it out of a window?"

"I was only trying to help," she said. "You don't seem to be doing real well on your own."

"Well, I'm not," he said, sighing and taking one last look around the room. "It's a paperback book with a whale on it."

"Moby Dick?" she asked.

He looked at her sharply.

"Sawyer had it," she said.

"Sawyer?" he said. Unlikely. Or maybe not.

"You wanted to know where it was," she said, evidently offended at his tone.

"Well. Okay. So—do you know where it is?"

She looked thoughtful. "It's probably in the attic," she said.

"The *attic*?"

"If you don't want my help—"

"No, I do. I just don't—why the attic?"

"He goes up there all the time. Maybe he was reading it up there."

"You saw him take it up into the attic?"

"Isn't that what I just said?"

He narrowed his eyes at her. Her face was all innocence.

"Do you want it or not?" she asked. "Because I have stuff to do."

"I want it," he said.

"Then I've got to show you how to get up there. It's kind of hard to figure out if you don't know."

He sighed. "Okay," he said. "Show me."

She turned around and pelted up the stairs, Cody following slowly behind, uncomfortable about the whole thing.

The house was chilly because of the rain. And it was dark. He'd turned the lights off in the den before he'd left the room— nobody down there. No good wasting money. He turned the lights on when he got into the upstairs hall.

"There was a funny little hall that ran perpendicular to the main one — it went back to Charlotte's workroom and the play-room over the garage. Mickey had disappeared down that way. He felt along the wall for the light switch.

"It's just here," she said, about halfway down the hall. The walls of the hallway were all cabinets and bookshelves. Mickey was standing in front of the last of the shelves. When she saw he was coming, she gave the shelf a sharp shove. There was a metallic click, and the heavy shelf swung out slowly, blocking the hall. In a recess behind it was a door.

"This is the way to the attic?" he asked, doubtfully.

"Nifty, huh?" she said. She pulled the door open, holding it for him.

There was a narrow little passage of stairs behind, going up into the dark.

"Why don't you go up and get it for me?" he asked.

"I've got homework," she said. "Who knows where he put it?"

Cody took a step closer.

"Fine," she said. "Do what you want." She stepped around him and headed back down the hall to her own room. "Don't thank me," she said.

He didn't. He wasn't sure he should.

Cody put one hand on the wall and leaned into the recess, looking up into the dark. He could see that there was a door at the top — there was a slip of light making an outline around it. He felt for the light switch. There wasn't any. He peered up at the ceiling, looking for a light bulb. He took a step inside, and then another, and then he actually went up a couple of steps, reaching up in case there should be a chain.

And then he had the oddest feeling, as if it had suddenly gotten darker. He froze, and then he realized it *was* getting darker. He spun around, half losing his balance, to see the door swinging shut behind him. He threw himself down the stairs. The door shut. There was another click, and then a sound like a bolt sliding home.

Cody grabbed the doorknob and turned it. The door came open about an inch and a half before it hit something on the other side. There was no light on that side of the door. He let go of the knob like it was hot.

"Mickey," he said. *"Mickey."*

And then he could hear her laughing. He could hear her running down the short hall, then down the front stairs. The front door slammed. There was nothing to hear after that, except the rain on the roof and the thunder.

17

Cody's first reaction was violent. It was an old feeling, one he knew very well. He wanted to throw himself against the door until it came to pieces, pound on the walls with his fists, yell until somebody heard him and came and let him out. Embarrassment meant nothing in this place. The only thing that mattered was to get out.

But he did none of the things he wanted to do.

He'd heard the bolt go home. He knew nobody else was in the house. He knew it wasn't going to do him any good to call for help or to try and break out of here. What's more, he knew how it could be once you got started, once you gave in even the least bit; you hit that door just once with your hands—just one time, and everything inside would start to come unglued, to go wild. And after that—not remembering how to stop—to be like a crazy person, battering yourself against a solid door until you had nothing left to batter with. Insane and completely futile. He knew how that was.

He stood at the bottom of the steps in the deep darkness, closing his eyes against it, listening to the needle-drop rain just over his head. He was already shaking badly.

He tried steadying himself, making the breath come slowly, trying to keep his mental balance. He tried reason. *Charlotte won't be gone forever. It's almost dinnertime. She didn't say anything about special plans tonight. There was no note. She'll be back to make dinner. You'll be able to hear the car. She'll be back. She'll unlock the door.* A liturgy of sanity.

But all through it, the other thread—*What if there's an accident? What if she doesn't come home? It's raining. The roads are slick. What if I can't get her to find me once she comes home? What if there's a fire?*

His palms were wet. He wasn't getting enough air with the breaths he was taking. It had been a long time since he'd had to handle this kind of thing; he was rusty at it. He screwed down on the fears, shutting his mind down to minimal activity, concerning himself only with the basics.

Breathing.

He groped for the railing, his eyes still closed, and sat back on the stairwell, well away from the door, careful to touch the walls only on one side.

Try the door at the top. But he couldn't do it. As long as that other door remained an option, he could use it for mental ballast. If he made his way up these dark little stairs and found out that that door was locked too, it would send him over the edge. He couldn't risk it.

He drew a long breath. Let it out between his teeth. All slow. Very slow. His hands were still trembling violently. He was too close to the edge. Way too close.

He leaned back against the wall, bumping his head on the railing, telling himself the passage wasn't as narrow as it had seemed. Telling himself fear only made things seem worse.

He remembered when Mr. Guicci had gotten himself a key to the apartment—not that the apartment was ever locked—and one to the inside closet. It was never quite so bad after that. After Mr. Guicci had found out what was happening. A matter of waiting. Waiting, like this. Someone would come, eventually. When they missed him. After a while, Mr. Guicci had known where to look.

Or it would be Parker. If Cody hadn't shown up anywhere for a while, a few hours, maybe, one of them would come, big feet making the floor creak, coming in carefully—and then the sound of the unlocking, and the door would open. One of the two of them standing there with incredible brightness behind, like the bodies of angels in the midst of the glory of heaven.

Cody's deliverance. Cody's guardian spirit.

And that's the way it had been until Cody had finally gotten smart enough to stay out of the way when she was like that. After a while, he understood the signs. He could tell. And then, a few years later, he got to be too much for her to handle. Unless she got outside help. Which she did, every so often.

Sitting in this present darkness, Cody put his hand on his arm, rubbing it lightly over the place where the little round scars were hidden. There were memories his mind refused to touch. But coming close always made him angry. And that was good. The anger made him forget where he was. Made it seem like the panic hadn't gone into him so deep.

And every time it had happened, afterwards she'd been so sorry, so sorry. You'd have thought he'd gotten too smart for that, too. At least, after a while, after it had happened more than once. But he never did. He always believed her in the end. Like an idiot. Like some kind of weary, faithful little dog. Like it really wasn't her fault. Like there was something inside of her that did these things, and she was, herself, a prisoner — helpless and unhappy, loving him and hating what was going on.

Or it was something inside of him that set it off — something he did, something he *was* that made it happen — because he was such a hard child. Because he drove her out of her mind. That it had been his fault, he had always believed, good sense aside. So there had always been a seemingness of justice to all of it.

Until last week.

Last week, he'd stopped believing. Last week, he'd had enough. But even now, he wasn't so sure he wasn't deeply ashamed for what he'd done to her. *Harvard Law,* in the name of heaven. And now he'd left her alone, knowing she couldn't handle herself.

He bumped his head gently back against the handrail, making a little rhythm. But he had to stop that. One little sob came out of him, a surprise, and he sat up sharply, slamming his head into the railing. He took his hurt head into both his hands, cursing himself.

So little time in this place, and you act like you haven't got any sense. One week, and you don't know how to take care of yourself anymore. They make you soft here. All but Mickey. You owe her that. She reminds you what you are.

He couldn't find the wall. The cold one, inside his mind. The ice that had his little place behind it. He couldn't make a solid wall out of anger; he didn't have that much energy. He wasn't even sure the core was safe anymore. Falling into the rhythms of this place as if he belonged. Taking this family like it was some sort of drug. No good sense. Wide open. He'd never been so stupid in his life.

And you're afraid they'll trust you. Afraid you won't be able to stand up under it. What about them? What about you trusting them? You have a right to put that kind of responsibility on them? You be responsible for yourself. Nobody needs you believing in them. Nobody can tell the truth all the time.

The picture of Elise came up in his mind again. There were actual lies there, and the anger came up inside him, hot and nearly irrational. He'd been hurt this morning. He hadn't expected it — not only trusting her but trusting himself, too. He knew better.

Just what kind of fantasyland were you expecting? The girl talks about honor and you believe her?

It was all such a dangerous situation: Charlotte was a walking time bomb, good enough to him, for now, but that was based on lies, on misapprehensions, on what she wanted to believe he was. When the truth finally worked its way out, the way it always seemed to do, where would he be then? And where would Charlotte be? Not in the same place, the two of them.

It was very cold in this stairway. His head ached and his eyes burned when he closed them. He hugged himself, shivering.

Every so often, thunder rumbled. *"Like the voice of God,"* Mr. Guicci used to say. And Cody always had wondered, how could you expect anything from a person with a voice like that?

He blanked himself out, working through it all carefully, erasing everything. Thunder again. He swallowed. He was freezing.

He knew what was going to happen. Eventually, he was going to reach out and touch that other wall, touch both of them at the same time. It was a suicide thing. It would unhinge his mind, once he did that. As long as he could stay quiet, he had a chance. It was almost a game, seeing how long he could last before he couldn't stand it anymore. So he started going over math in his mind. Sets and universal sets. And then he started working through the history, trying to line things up . . .

He opened his eyes. There was just enough silty light coming through that pitiful little crack up above that he could see the wall on the other side now. Thunder. Farther away. The storm was moving off.

Please, he called to it, *if you are God—I don't care which one—Mr. Guicci's or Charlotte's or Jesus Christ. Make her come home. Make her open this door and let me out.*

He could see that wall, but his eyes were playing games with his brain. He couldn't tell how close it was. Maybe so close —he couldn't move his hand without touching it.

He forgot to breathe slowly. He could feel the air as he breathed it out, flowing over against that other wall, and then bouncing back into his face so he had to breathe it again. *It's not that close,* he told himself. *Don't be stupid.* But he was nearly hyperventilating now, and he really couldn't tell. Not without putting his hand out. Not without touching it. All it would take —one touch, and he'd know. He'd know just where it was. Know it for sure . . .

"Get your shoes off," Charlotte said. The boys were dancing all over, making a mud hole out of the kitchen floor. "Get back in here—the coats, the coats, the *coats*," she said, her hands out for the yellow slickers. Rain water all over everything.

"Take it upstairs," she said, handing Sawyer the package. She couldn't blame them for being silly. Secret sharing proliferates silliness. "Your *shoes. Look* at my kitchen."

"You *said*—" he started.

"*After* you take your shoes off." She glared at him.

He threw himself into a chair, grumbling. She took the coats back into the mud room, hanging them up on the neat porcelain hooks that lined the wall in there.

"Get the door, somebody," she yelled over her shoulder. "Tyler, how did you get a tear in this coat?" Not expecting an answer.

"Did you get the door?" she asked, coming back into the kitchen. But no. Somebody was still knocking. "Thanks a *lot*, you guys," she said, heading for the front door herself.

"He's getting it," Tyler said, behind her now.

She heard the front door open and close.

"There's still knocking," Sawyer said, standing there by the door. "But nobody's there. Weird."

The knocking was distant, muffled.

"It sounds like it's upstairs," Sawyer said. He whirled and scrambled up the stairs.

"Don't drop that sack," Charlotte warned, keeping a close eye on the package Sawyer was still carrying. "Sawyer. Take that to your room. *Now.* And then I want you setting the table, please. Don't make me tell you twice."

"But—" he said, poised at the top of the stairs and pointing back towards the workroom.

"*Get!*" she said. "I'll check on the noise." If Mickey was hammering nails into the walls again, it would be the last time.

But the noise wasn't coming from Mickey's room, she realized, getting to the top of the stairs. It was coming from farther back in the house. From her workroom?

No. From the attic.

She put a hand on the bookcase, hesitating. Very strange feeling—having something in your attic, knocking to get out. She unbolted the shelf unit. It swung open and the door behind it came open immediately.

She drew in her breath, sharply. She'd half expected some kind of ghost. She wasn't disappointed. It was Cody, standing

186

there at the bottom of the stairs in the dark, one hand out flat against the little door, as if he were expecting it to swing shut again on him.

And white faced. Totally white faced. Eyes—not wild, but *something.* Haunted. Not actually seeing her—like he was sleepwalking. And breathing as though he hadn't had air until the door opened.

"What—" she started to ask. He started. He looked down at her, and then he came down out of that place. She stepped back, put a hand out to steady him—heaven knew he looked like he needed it.

But he warded her off, slid around out of the recess, put his back against the cabinets that were the hall wall. He was shaking badly, and still breathing very hard.

"What were you doing in there?" she asked, beginning to feel the weirdness of it, and starting to tremble a bit herself.

He stared at her.

"Why was the door locked from the outside? Cody? Are you all right?"

He took one very long, very slow breath, dropping his head back against the wall. "I—" he started, his voice husky. "I'm—I have a little problem with enclosed places. Small places."

A tremor went through him. He looked her way, blinking.

"You're claustrophobic?" she asked quietly.

He nodded and then took a breath that sounded a little more like a sob.

"But how did you get in there?" she asked.

He didn't answer. But Sawyer did.

"Mickey did that to *me*, once," he said.

"What do you mean, Mickey did that to you?"

"She locked me in there once. I just went upstairs and looked at stuff until Dad got home."

A heat came up inside Charlotte. "Did Mickey do this to you?" she asked. And then she did put a hand out to touch him. He moved away from her.

"Are you going to be all right?" she asked. It was a very serious question; she wasn't sure what she should be doing for him. And she was angry. Very angry.

He nodded, a dogged-seeming gesture.

"Go lie down," she said, more sharply than she meant to. "Go lie on your bed and try to relax. Did Mickey do this? Where is she?"

"She left," he said.

187

"How long ago?" she asked.

He shrugged. And then he laughed.

"What?" she asked.

"I don't know how long," he said. He looked as if somebody had beaten him about the eyes.

"Okay, well—go on and lie down. I'm sorry, Cody. I don't know what to say about this. I wish it hadn't happened. Mickey's going to wish it never happened. Go on. You going to be all right?"

He pushed himself away from the hall, then put out a hand to steady himself. She heard Erin pulling into the driveway.

"You," she said to Sawyer. "Did I tell you to set the table?"

"But—" Sawyer said.

"Now."

She waited at the landing until she was sure Cody had made it to his room, then she went back and shut up the attic, sending the bolt home angrily. *That she could do this,* she was thinking. *That somebody I brought up should be capable of such a thing.*

"So, what do we do?" she asked, putting the wooden spoon down on the stove top and turning around to face Erin. "You let her get away with that once. You didn't even tell me about it." He dropped his eyes.

"It's gotten to the point, Erin, where I can't understand her at all. Not at *all*. I don't even *like* her anymore. That's a heck of a way to feel about your own kid."

"Well," he said, obviously choosing his words *very* carefully, "I'm not sure that telling her she can't go see *Bambi* with us tonight is going to mean much to her."

"I don't *want* to take her with us. I just don't *want* her. You understand that? That's what I'm talking about. All I need is to see that nasty little face she pulls one more time, and I'm going to slam her one. I really mean it. I've had it. I don't know who this kid is, but she's not the one I thought I was raising."

Erin shrugged—*Maybe that's what she needs. A little less tolerance. A little more reality.*

"Right," she said. "Let's start slapping our kids around."

"That's not what I mean," Erin said.

"No," she said. "But that's the way I feel."

"And what's Cody going to do while we're gone?"

"Study."

"You're going to leave the two of them here alone?" he asked.

"No," she said, irritated. *I'm not stupid, okay?* "His tutor is supposed to be over here tonight. She's supposed to get here about the same time we leave. Okay?"

"I was just asking," he said.

The kitchen door opened. She tapped the spoon against the rim of the pot, glanced over at the door.

Cody was standing there in the doorway, tousled and looking disoriented—as if he'd just awakened in a strange place.

"Hi," Erin said soberly.

"What's this?" Cody demanded. Sawyer came in from the dining room. Cody held out his hand. There was a camera in it. A very nice camera. "Is this yours?" he asked Erin. He sounded as dozy as he looked. "It was in my bed."

Erin put his own hand out for it. Cody crossed the room unevenly and gave it to him. Erin turned it over in his hands—Charlotte hadn't had a chance to tell him about it. "Not mine," he said, and he handed it back to Cody. "It's new," he added.

"It's yours, Cody," Charlotte said.

He looked over at her, blinking. "Mine," he said.

"It's a gift from your grandparents."

"My grandparents." He sounded almost angry. And then he glared at Sawyer.

"She made me tell," Sawyer said unhappily. "She's my mother."

"I made him."

Cody looked down at the camera, then up at her, his face gone closed up tight.

"There's about seventeen years of birthday presents in that," she said softly.

He turned around without a word and left the room.

Charlotte sighed. Erin was looking at her. "I'd forgotten about it," she said. "This was *not* the time."

"I told you he was going to be mad at me, Mom," Sawyer said. "She didn't take me seriously," he added, sitting down next to Erin.

"Okay," she said. She went back to the stove, gave the soup another angry stir.

"Sometimes things just don't work out," Erin said. It startled a laugh out of her.

"Sometimes?" she said.

"Sawyer," Erin said, "what is it with Mickey?"

She put the spoon down again and turned to listen. Sawyer shrugged.

"How do you feel about her?" he asked.

"I don't like her," Sawyer said.

"She's your sister," Charlotte said. Sawyer sent her a reproachful look. "You're right," she said. "It was a stupid thing for me to say."

"Is there something bothering her?" Erin asked.

"I don't know," Sawyer said. "You think she'd talk to me about it if there was?"

"She having trouble at school, you think? With her friends, maybe?"

"She has a lot of friends," Sawyer said. "They all—I don't like any of them. Like that Alison Turner. Mickey thinks she's so great; she's not great. She's conceited. All she ever talks about is her family's stuff. That's why I didn't want to invite Carl to my party last year, you remember? She's his sister and they're all like that. It's annoying. No matter what you have, their stuff is always better—and they always want to know how much your stuff cost. I've got to finish the table."

"I thought you'd finished," Charlotte said.

"I just wanted to hear what was going on," he said. "I haven't done the placemats yet."

"You haven't even done the placemats?"

"I'm doing it," he said, and disappeared into the dining room.

Charlotte sent her husband an exasperated look.

"We could trade jobs," he said.

"Very funny," she said. *Too bad the offer was so darned safe.*

"It'll work out," he said. "We'll work it all out."

She gave the soup a vehement stir and it splattered on the stove top.

"You know, Erin," she said. "I really hate it when you say that."

18

There was some question in Cody's mind about whether his tutor was actually going to show up for work anymore. There was also a question about whether he wanted her to.

He was in no position to deal with her. He was in no position to deal with himself.

He hadn't been able to eat dinner. Not even when Charlotte had brought him a tray so he wouldn't have to go down and sit with the family. He hadn't had any joy out of the sound of the fight that had gone on downstairs when Mickey finally got home.

He was afraid to touch the camera.

All he'd done for hours was lie in his bed, on a buzz. "*Relax*," she'd said. No sleep for a week. Wouldn't he like to.

He'd finally gone downstairs. Charlotte was counting on Elise being here. She didn't want him alone in the house with Mickey. Understandable. Except that he wouldn't have had the energy to break the girl's neck, if he'd wanted to do it. Which he didn't.

He was just weary.

And he was scared of Elise. He was scared she'd breeze in here as if she hadn't noticed a thing wrong. Which she might not have. It was very possible she couldn't care less whether he walked her to class or not. Whether he looked at her or not. Very possible.

His hands were still shaking.

He put his arms on the table and rested his head on them.

He could hear Charlotte giving Mickey last-minute instructions. *No TV. Stay in your room. Don't do anything — anything that will make you happy. And stay away from Cody. You know he's an emotional cripple.*

He started when she put her hands on his shoulder. "Elise just drove up," she said, her real voice mixing with the one he'd been hearing in his head, confusing him. "We're going." She patted him. He made himself hold still under her hand.

"Have fun," he said.

One more pat, then she was gone.

With Elise coming up the walk.

His stomach went very sour on him.

He felt cold all over, jumpy in his arms and legs. Just like on the bus. Way too tired.

Someone came into the room.

"Hi," she said.

"Hi," he said heavily.

She put her books down on the table, dropped her purse on the floor by her chair. She was taking her sweater off. She looked at him curiously. "Were you asleep?" she asked.

"No," he said. He folded his hands on the table in front of him.

"So," she said, sitting down. "How come you didn't wait for me this morning?" She scooted the chair a little closer to the table.

There was a pause. "You were busy," he said then, flatly.

Another pause. "Oh, yeah?" she said. He didn't know whether she was looking at him or not.

"Yeah," he said. "Or that's the way it looked."

She made a little noise in her throat.

"So," she said. "You left because you were mad."

"Well," he said, his head beginning to ache now, way in the back. He dropped his cheek on his hand, and then ran his fingers up into his hair. "I wouldn't say mad, I'd say, more disappointed."

"You sound mad now," she said.

He laughed. As if he had the energy for anger. "Believe me," he said. "I really couldn't care less."

"Oh, really," she said.

"Kiss anybody you want, Miss Holiday Spirit," he said, sitting back into his chair and looking at her dully, his head half-cocked to the side and his arms folded. The hands were shaking again, and he didn't need her to see that. "And so will I."

"So you're mad that Steven kissed me," she said.

"Not mad," he said.

"Disap*point*ed," she said.

He shrugged.

She looked exasperated. "It wasn't that big a thing," she said, doing her own shrug. But her voice had gone higher. She was more upset than she seemed.

"And neither was the other night on the porch," he said.

She turned her face away from him.

192

"Steven," she said after a moment—and going very, very carefully—"is one of my oldest friends. We grew up together. He lives next door to me. What do you want me to tell him? *'Hey. Don't treat me like a cousin anymore. I belong to McClellan, who moved in here four days ago.'*"

"Did you tell him about the other night?" Cody asked.

Another pause. "No," she said.

"Why not?" he asked her, his voice very detached from the question.

Silence.

"I'm not going to hurt him because of you," she said.

"But you can hurt me because of him," he said.

"He's my *friend*," she said. "I don't *belong* to you."

And that probably should have meant something to him. But his mind wasn't working right, and he was suddenly, suddenly flooded with a very hot, very unreasonable anger.

"So," he said, his voice gone deadly and cold, "this is part of your sacred, holy rules. You get to do what you want, and everybody else just waits your pleasure. Everybody else keeps hands off, and you go around dispensing your *affections* like some kind of generous little philanthropist. So what you gave me was charity. How thoughtful! For the new kid on the block. The Jefferson High welcoming committee. Just to get me acclimated. All you cheerleaders do that? What a great bunch of girls. They assign you to me?"

She made a sound between her teeth and brought hard fists up against her face. He couldn't let it go.

"The funny thing about this," his voice still quiet and cold and dead, "is that you actually hurt me. That's something. Nobody's been able to do that for a long, long time. You should feel good about that. There've been social workers who wished they could get half that far into me. You're very good. Congratulations."

She pressed her palms against her mouth. Crying. She stood up and picked up her things and left the room. "Congratulations yourself," she said to him from behind. And then the dining room door shut.

He dropped his face in his hand.

He pushed away from the table and stood up and sat down and stood up and went over to the window.

Congratulations yourself. You grew up just like your mother.

He caught his hand back just centimeters, milliseconds away from slamming it into the wall. It wasn't his wall. He would have broken something if he'd hit it that hard. He had to stop himself twice.

And his head had began to throb, and his stomach was heaving.

He threw himself back flat against the wall, and slid down it till he was sitting on his heels.

Control.

His breathing had gotten away from him again.

He put two fingers across his wrist, across the place his mother had touched, and he thought about the knife sitting in Erin's desk. *She was right, all along,* he was thinking. And he groaned with it.

Elise stood in the front hall, her sweater over her arm, her purse dangling from her hand. She was breathing as though she'd run a mile, trying to stop the weeping. Embarrassed. Hating him. Hating him as absolutely as she had ever hated anybody in her life.

But not wanting to leave.

She heard television. Someone was watching television, just down the hall. That girl cousin of his was. She wandered down there towards the sound.

He hadn't been absolutely wrong.

He *was* absolutely the nastiest human being she'd ever had anything to do with.

The room was dark, except for the TV. So Elise went in quietly and sat down. She pulled up her purse and dug through it for some tissue. There was only one other person in the room. The girl. That's what Elise had expected. The twelve-year-old with the nasty mouth.

The girl turned around and gave her a sour look.

Try me, Elise looked back at her. *Tonight, I could take your face off, I don't care whose kid you are.*

Elise's stomach had been in knots all day. She hadn't understood why Steven had done that this morning. It wasn't the usual thing. Maybe because he'd sensed something. She should have told him. She should have talked to him about it.

Cody.

Chris had told her about math today. *"Arrogant,"* Chris had said. *"He's like a genius, but he's totally hostile."* That he was a dangerous person with dangerous weapons was now obvious. She shut her eyes and wished it was still Saturday night. There'd been such a sweetness to him; he'd seemed so vulnerable. And maybe that was the most dangerous thing of all.

Elise took a deep breath and blew it out slowly. For that, she got another sour look from the floor.

"I can't believe you're watching this garbage," Elise hissed at her, a little surprised at herself for it.

"Did somebody ask you your opinion?" the girl asked. She got up off the floor and stalked out of the room. She was going to talk to Cody, of course. And that put Elise in a very bad position.

"You want to get your girlfriend out of here?" the girl was saying. Surprise—her voice carried very well. Elise got up and went to the door of the den, looking for a chance to slip out, listening for the other voice.

"Your *girl*friend is in here bugging me," the girl said, her voice a little louder. "Cody, you better answer me."

There was no answer. None Elise could hear.

"*Cody,*" the girl said, not so sure of herself now. "You better answer me. I know you're not asleep." Another pause. "Your girlfriend is bugging me."

Then he said something. "I don't believe I understand." Ice. Total ice.

"Well, ex*cuse* me," the girl said, confidence returned. "I'm not *stupid*. If you're going to have a fight with your girlfriend, please just keep it in *one* room, okay? Because I don't need her in here bugging me."

"She's not my girlfriend," he said. He sounded weary. "Not any more than you're my cousin."

"Oh, *that* makes sense," the girl sneered. "Unfortunately, I *am* your cousin." It was so ugly. The girl was so ugly with him.

"Oh, really," he said.

"Yes, *really.*"

"You know, you really are a stupid, nastly little girl." It hadn't come out like an insult—more like a conclusion. Elise closed her eyes and leaned against the door frame, wishing herself somewhere else.

"You know, you are a *stupid* boy."

"What are you so scared of?" he asked her, his voice so low Elise could hardly hear him. "You scared of losing something? You think your mother's going to forget you because of me? You scared there won't be enough food to go around, and you'll end up hungry?"

"Nobody asked you to come here," she said.

"You don't know, do you?" he asked.

"What?"

"You're spoiled. And you don't know it."

"*Spoiled?*" The girl laughed. "*That's* a joke."

"You don't see it," he said, almost like he was talking to himself.

"And you're so wise," she said.

"It's incredible that anybody could be so naive," he said.

"I'm *not* naive."

"No?" He laughed. "When was the last time you ever needed anything?"

"*All* the time, buster."

"Okay, let's just say—let's just say dinnertime comes, and you're hungry, but your mother is too . . . *busy* to get you anything to eat. Okay? So you have to fix yourself something."

"I do it all the time."

"And let's say you open up the cupboards, and there's nothing there."

"Then you get some money and you go buy yourself something," she said.

"There's no money," he said. "There's no money and there's no food."

"So, you go tell your mother." She was still sneering. And he was right. You could hear that she didn't have any idea what he was talking about.

"And it's cold, and your last pair of pants you can't wear anymore because the seat's gone out of them. And you don't have even a shirt that has elbows in it."

"So you go tell your mother," she said again.

"And she hits you across the mouth," he said.

"This is stupid."

"And then you pull one of your cute little fits with her, and she gets good and sick of you, so she hauls you off by your hair and throws you into a closet and slams the door and locks it. And then she leaves."

"My mother never would," she said.

"And she doesn't come back. You're in there an hour. And then two hours. And let's say, she doesn't come back all night. Let's just say, you just sit in there all night—"

"I wouldn't just sit there."

"And what would you do?" he asked, bored with her.

"I'd kick and I'd scream till somebody came and got me."

There was a silence then.

196

"You always think there's going to be somebody, don't you?" he asked.

"Anyway, my mother wouldn't do those things."

"And then she finally comes back. And after a while, she opens up the door, and there you are—filthy, because there's no bathroom in there, see—and hungry and thirsty, and with your hands bleeding from beating on the door. And you can hardly stand up—"

"You're sick," the girl said.

"And she looks at you and she says, 'Well, well, well, I thought you'd be dead.' "

"You're *really* sick."

Elise leaned heavily on the door frame.

"Nobody's mother would say that," the girl said. But her voice had changed.

It was very quiet. "Is that what you think?" he asked.

Another silence.

"Mothers aren't like that," she said.

"Ah—" he said. "But you're wrong." Elise put her forehead against the wood. "You wouldn't pitch a fit very often if that's what you got for it, would you? Not if you knew your mother could do that to you. You probably—" he lingered over the words—"wouldn't think quite so much about Reeboks then."

"But you're right," he went on, his tone shifting. "Your mother would never do that. She probably feels like it. But she'd never do it. You just don't get your Reeboks. I feel so sorry for you."

"So, I'm supposed to think you're so deprived?" she said. "I'm supposed to think that's the way it was for you at home, right? Well, I don't believe you. I said mothers aren't like that, and I meant it. Nobody's like that."

"Oh," he said. "You're wrong, girl. *You're* like that."

"I am not."

Silence.

"It's not the same thing," she said, sounding scared. "That was just a joke."

Elise pushed away from the wall, wondering what they were talking about.

And then the girl spoke again, her voice very low, very intense—not at all like a child. "I really hate you," she said, and then she pounded her way up the steps, sobbing and sounding very *much* like a child.

A door slammed upstairs, and the house went silent.

Elise realized she was shaking. She leaned back against the wall and hugged herself. There was a darkness here she wasn't used to. She was way out of her league.

She took a long breath and then pushed away from the wall. Still hugging herself, she went out into the hall, softly across the hard floor—put her hand out against the frame of the dining-room door and eased herself into the opening.

He was across the room, a smudge across the bottom of the wall on the other side. Deep in the shadows. Staring at the floor.

She didn't know what to do next. So she did nothing. She waited. He finally lifted his eyes and saw her there, but there was no reaction at all. His eyes were like dark holes in his face, bored down into the hollows over his cheekbones. He looked like death. The hair on her arms rose.

She cleared her throat. "Was that your mother you were talking about?" she asked, knowing he could cut her to ribbons for the question.

"Yes," he said, dully civil. "It was."

"Was it the truth?" she asked.

"Yes," he said, same voice. "It was."

She felt the tears hot in her eyes.

"Everything?" she asked. *Everything,* she answered herself, looking into his face. He turned it away from her. Her knees had gone weak.

"How could she be like that to you?" she whispered.

He laughed—a short, ugly sound.

"She wasn't what you'd call a nice lady," he said.

"Is she dead?"

The question surprised him. He considered it. "To me," he said.

"I'm sorry," she said.

Another laugh.

"Really," he said. "Sorry for what? Sorry you let me touch you? Sorry you got yourself associated with me? Sorry you had to hear this?"

"Sorry for everything," she said, on the edge of hating him again.

"Ah," he said, like that certainly explained everything.

"So, you were right about this morning," she said. "I'm sorry about this morning. I didn't mean to hurt you."

"Well," he said bitterly. "It's surprisingly easy to do these days."

"I'm apologizing," she said.

198

"You weren't a minute ago. You feel sorry for me now."

She didn't answer him.

"Let's see—what else can I get as long as we're making penance."

"You have to make everything so hard?" she snapped.

He fixed her again with those hollow eyes.

"It was the way I was brought up," he said.

She turned around in exasperation and slapped the door hard with her open hand. It was a violent thing to have done, and her palm stung. She held it against her and glared at him.

"You don't have to make it so hard," she said, her voice level again.

He didn't answer. He seemed to pull back inside of himself.

She took a step towards him. His head came up and he looked at her, a little wary now, as if he were some wild thing she had cornered. She came closer, slowly. His eyes held her off.

She stopped. "Your mother's not my fault," she said.

He didn't say anything.

"You were right to be mad. And everything you said was true. I should have told Steven. But I was scared to. I don't want to hurt anybody. Up to and including you. But I'm going to tell him. Because it's going to happen again."

"Not with me," he said.

She looked at him for a long time. "Then I guess I won't have to worry about it," she said. "Because it won't happen again."

He took in a sharp little breath, and the places around his eyes all tightened up. He moved one hand, putting it over the other wrist.

"Cody," a voice said behind her. Cody and Elise both jumped.

It was the girl again, messed up and red eyed. *Don't start,* Elise said with her own face.

The girl ignored her. "None of those things were true," the girl said.

"I think they were all true," Elise told her.

The girl's mouth trembled. She looked away. And then back again. "I'm not like that," she said. And then she made a little sob. "I'm really not. I just didn't want you here. I'm really sorry. You can stay. I'm not like what you said." And then, tearfully, from the soul, "How could your mother do that to you if she loved you?"

Elise looked down at him. He hadn't said a word. He stared

at his cousin for a long time where she stood across the room, weeping against the butt of the door. Then he looked up at Elise, and away.

"Cody," she said.

He put one of his wrists gently over the other, and then his face began to fall apart. He screwed it up, trying to hold on—she could feel the pulling of it inside herself, watching him. He put his forehead down on his knees before it all came completely undone, and then he began to weep.

19

Whether he'd been asleep, and for how long, and what kind of sleeping it had been, Cody couldn't quite tell. He suspected that he had been; the room kept shifting its center on him, sliding up to the side so he couldn't tell if he was lying on his back or on his side, or on which side—but everything seemed pleasantly round and simple, and that made it so he could exist without thinking anything in particular and everything all together, all at the same time.

Voices woke him. Right under his window.

And he was in bed. He remembered, now—the girls had made him go to bed. Because Elise had said he was too, too tired to argue any more, and he had wished that she would stay with him and hold him a while—which was not to be.

A car door slammed, and then Mickey's voice, "He had a mental *breakdown*." It came up through the cool night air, clear as light. As if she was telling the neighborhood. And someone shushed her. Charlotte's voice. And Elise's.

"Working him too hard," somebody said. *Me?*

And then Mickey again, which was nice, because she was the loudest and took the least work—telling them everything.

All about closets. Which was sad. Because now Erin was going to have to know some of it. The words kept spinning him off to other thoughts—not even awake enough to worry about getting back to sleep.

But then a little fear came. *What if,* it whispered, *what if they think I'm going to be violent with the kids because my mother was violent with me? They don't know. They don't know how hard I've tried to be different than she is. They don't know I'd rather die than hurt a child. What if they send me away now?*

Charlotte's voice, " . . . poor boy." And that meant him.

He yawned and pulled the quilt up over his shoulder.

Another car door slammed and the voices moved away. They turned the front light off, and the room went completely dark. *It's all right,* the voice inside his head was saying. *A long time till morning, and it's all right.* The floor swung gently up the other way, and the bed in the middle felt so sure about everything.

Once in the night, he woke again—not very much—not enough to know if he was in a dream or not. Someone had been stroking his hair. Not Elise. But gentle, and he couldn't imagine where it had come from.

When he opened his eyes again, the room was streaming with light, and Sawyer was telling him he was late for breakfast.

Breakfast was a bit of an ordeal. Nobody said anything, but everybody was very kind and very patient. No arguments about anything through the whole meal. Everyone very careful. Supportive. It was humiliating.

He was relieved to get on the bus, except that he couldn't figure out how to go to school today without running into Elise. Not that he didn't want to see her. Just that he didn't know what he was going to say to her. He had the deepest of convictions that she wouldn't have betrayed him to anybody else; it was the only reason he'd found the courage to go to school at all.

He was standing at his locker, pulling down the morning's books, when somebody came up and bumped him from behind. He looked around, surprised, and there was Elise, bright and cheerful—as he never was in the morning—and with a friend. His cheeks went hot, and he turned around to get the last book.

"I was afraid of that," Elise said, and she bumped him again. "You're embarrassed, aren't you? Come on. Comeon-

comeoncomeoncomeon—" she wheedled, bumping at him over and over. "Be my friend? Pleeeeeeeeease?"

He did a little side-step turn to get away from her. "Knock it off?" he said, not unpleasantly, kind of looking around to make sure nobody in this ant hill of a hall was watching them.

"Tell me you're okay," she said.

He gave her a significant look and glanced at her friend, then turned around and closed down his locker.

"This is Chris. My best friend. You remember me talking about my best friend? Notice we do *not* have on matching clothes. This is Cody. He's a pain in the behind. We had a fight last night, but I think he's better now. He hates having friends around after he's lost a fight." He tucked his books under his arm and started down the hall. They followed after him, none of them in any great hurry.

"Well," Chris said. "Nice to meet you, anyway." He glanced at her again.

"Hi," he said. She was a pleasant enough looking girl. But she was grinning at him, which made him uncomfortable. Maybe Elise had been talking about him. Probably she had. *Something nice, maybe? Dream on.*

"I'm in your math class," Chris added. And he remembered that she was. A little heavier than Elise, she was—solid-looking, pretty, but tougher than Elise, a little irony around the eyes. That look about her eyes made him feel a little bit better.

"You have nice eyes," he said to her. She glanced at Elise and laughed.

"Sorry," he said, also glancing at Elise. "So—" Chris's hair was a little darker than Elise's, and she had it pulled back in a thick pony tail. "You're a cheerleader, too?"

"You want to make something of it?" she asked, still grinning.

"They told me they got you a car," Elise said, bouncing the conversation around.

"Yeah," he said. "That little blue Volkswagen up by the garage."

"Did you drive it today?"

He smiled. "No."

"Let's break it in this afternoon, then," Elise said.

He stopped and leaned back against the hall radiator. "Can't," he said.

"Can't?" she asked.

"Elise," he said. "I don't know how to drive."

202

"You *what?*" the girls said together.

He shifted around, glancing up and down the hall. "Would you stop, please?" he said. They were embarrassing him.

"Because it's a standard?" Chris asked.

"Because it's a car," he said.

"You are *so* weird," Elise said.

"You do *not* drive in the city," he said. "Not in my part of the city."

"Really," Chris said.

"Honest," he said.

"You're going to have to teach him," Chris said to Elise.

"*I* can't teach him how to drive a standard shift," Elise said.

"Sure you can," Chris said, giving her a little bump.

"My uncle will teach me," he said.

"No," Chris said. "No fun."

"Did it ever occur to you that a person might not *want* a girl around when he's learning to drive? That it might make him uncomfortable? That it might even humiliate him?"

"This is something we *have* to do," Chris said.

"This girl is *not* a good influence on you," he told Elise.

"So, when should we do it?" Elise asked Chris, as if he hadn't said a word.

"Saturday morning?" Chris said.

"That's good," Elise said.

"But—" he started.

"Gotta go," Chris said. "See you in math."

"Excuse me?" he said, but she was gone.

"Come on," Elise said. "We're going to be late."

"Wait, wait, wait," he said, catching her sleeve. There was something he wanted to say to her, or to ask her—or to hear her say to him. She settled in beside him, leaning back on the register, not quite looking at him. And then he couldn't figure out exactly what it was he'd wanted to say.

"What?" she said, still not quite looking.

"I don't know," he said.

She pushed herself away from the radiator. "For this, we're going to be late?"

He looked at her reproachfully, and she settled beside him again.

"Okay," she said. "What is it you want? You want something."

He did a little private laugh, because he knew very well what it was he wanted, and he knew very well he wasn't going to get it. That is — if you took things at their simplest. She flicked a little playful warning at him with her eyes.

He sighed.

"So, you're trying to tell me you don't want me coming around anymore," she said. He understood that this was a tease. Or he thought it probably was. He would have been something more than surprised if he'd thought she had any question in her mind about his feelings, at least where she was concerned. He thought he'd made that only too ridiculously plain.

"No," he said, anyway. Playing the tease for straight.

"Then what?" She was a little nervous, too, maybe. "Will you relax?" she said.

He sighed again.

"Do you need help on the paper?" she asked.

"Do you *need* to ask that?"

"No." She looked away. Then she looked at him. "Kind of a scary thing between us, huh?" she said. So, she knew what he was on about. And maybe that was making her nervous, too.

He shrugged. "What are we supposed to do now, Elise?" He was willing to look her in the face, but she wasn't giving him that.

And then she seemed to decide something, and she did look at him, a long, sober moment. She leaned over finally and kissed him on the cheek, a light, feathery thing that brought him up away from the wall. But she was gone by then, moving away from him.

"We're going to be late," she said, again.

"This isn't fair," he said, catching up to her.

She grinned at him. "Who ever said anything was going to be fair?"

It was not a bad day, after all. He was generally feeling a little better, in fact — not quite so tired anymore, a little more even in his thinking. It was his chemistry, he guessed — one big blow up and all the toxins rearranged. So maybe there'd been something good about it. Cleared the air in his head. It was an ordinary day — no flights of brilliance, no looks of concern, nothing spectacular. Just doing it. And having Elise for a friend. And eating lunch with the Happy Nerds.

And as the day had gone, so the week went. Things were better at home because Mickey had finally subsided somewhat. Or at least she wasn't fixed on him anymore. And he felt better because he'd done the family a proper thank you about the camera.

The camera was a miracle, beautiful and expensive and real —far and away the most beautiful thing he'd ever been close to having. He hadn't wanted it at first; it had seemed wrong, too big a gift from maybe nonexistent grandparents, and coming at the worst possible moment.

Now that he was gentler, he let himself look at it, hold it, and he told himself it was his own. Really his own. He worked his head off for the family because of it, as much as Charlotte would allow. It was getting to the point where she didn't want him to do anything but take care of his own life; she'd get cross with him for getting out the vacuum. She was treating him as if he was some kind of saint.

He was very apprehensive about Charlotte. She was being so careful with him, so impressed with him. The story about his mother had only made things worse; now, he was a battered child who had to have things made up to him. It was as if he couldn't do any wrong in his aunt's eyes. He was bitterly afraid of what would happen when she finally woke up and started seeing things a little more the way they were.

It was a constant presence with him, that worry. A shadow over his shoulder. And the more he was troubled by it, the more careful she got with him.

In other parts of his life, he was actually doing quite well. He'd ranked top of the class in the last math exam. And Elise had come over every night to help with the paper. He hadn't so much as touched her once since the bad night—only because he'd made his own mind up not to push things. And maybe because he wasn't so sure he understood how she felt about anything. It was definitely not because he didn't need her.

He loved the photography class. At first, it had been confusing—all the chemicals and the procedures and the timing. But once he'd begun to see the patterns coming through, things had started to make sense. And the more he did, the more he loved it.

Mr. Allen had liked Cody's first assignment. "You're really picking this up, aren't you?" he'd said. But the prints weren't good enough for Cody. The first ones had been way too flat, way too gray. And then he'd gone too dark. And then he realized he didn't like what he'd done with the composition.

Towards the end of the week, Mr. Allen called him up to the desk at the end of class. "So," he said. "You don't mind doing this stuff." And when Cody gave him a little shake of the head, he went on, "You take this very seriously, don't you?" He picked up one of the final prints and squinted at it. "We have an opening on the staff," he said. He looked up at Cody. "We don't usually invite first-year students into staff positions, but we need somebody, and I think you can do it. It would mean some after-school hours."

"Which staff?" Cody asked.

"The photography staff. Yearbook. Newspaper."

"The photography staff," Cody echoed.

"Are we not communicating?" Allen asked him.

"No. I think we are. I just—I think I'd like that. Thank you. I mean, yes. I'd like to do that. That's what you're asking?"

"Yes," Mr. Allen said.

"Yes," Cody said.

"You're sure," Allen said.

"I think—*yes.* I'm sure."

"It takes a lot of time," Mr. Allen warned. "You don't want your grades to suffer."

"This is what I want to do," Cody said. "This is all I really want to do."

"Well, okay then. Good enough." Mr. Allen stood up and stuck out his hand. "Welcome aboard."

That night, Cody slept well for the first time. And he slept all night with his hand on the camera. And the next morning, he put his best prints in an envelope and mailed them off to John, in New York.

It had been three days of almost normal life. And then came Friday. Right in the middle of physics, Cody was pulled out of class, called down to the office. It was like waking up. It was a visitation of his mortality, gravity reasserting itself. And he was badly out of practice with the feeling.

"We've got a mistake here," the counselor said, smiling tightly up at him from her place behind the desk. "This school has no records on you."

"Really," he said, spinning a lie in his mind, but feeling very uncomfortable about it. "Maybe I wasn't there long enough for them to have gotten them. Did you spell the name right?"

She spelled his name for him.

"That's the right spelling," he said, a picture of puzzlement.

Then she mentioned the name of the school. He echoed her, allowing quite a bit of surprise to show on his face. "I don't think that's the right school," he said.

"It's the school you gave me," she said. "The address fits."

"May I see?" he asked, putting his hand out for the file. Reluctantly, she gave him the file. And then he let her see his sudden understanding.

"I did give you the wrong school," he said. "That's the *other* school." He laughed. "I must have been nervous."

And she could understand that—first-day jitters. She certainly understood. And if he would just tell her the name of the right school, and make sure she had the right residential address . . .

And that's what he gave her. Finally. The right school. The right address.

And when he walked out of that office, he knew his days were numbered.

20

It was a high September day, cloudless and brittle-skied. A haze darkened the blue air where it dipped down over the tops of the trees and houses, and there was a crispness in the air that belied the strength of the sun, a thinness that said the tomatoes should be in, and the screens off the windows.

Cody had a green smell in his head, and green stains on his shoes. He'd put the lawn mower away just before the girls had pulled up to his curb and honked for him. The rest of the family was out in the garden, digging potatoes.

"Let's go," Elise hollered, jumping out of Chris's car. "I'll drive the bug—you go with Chris."

"Just so you know," he said, strolling down the lawn to the car, wiping his hands on the legs of his pants, "I'm not totally ignorant about all this. My uncle taught me this morning—ninety-five percent of what I have to know about cars."

"Oh, really," Elise said.

He tossed her his keys. "Yes. He did."

She put one hand on her hip. The sun shone down on her head and made little glints of color in her hair. "Like what?"

"He told me all about gasoline."

"Like, what did he say?" she said, sassing at him.

"That it costs money, and I'm not allowed to use any. And he told me about drive-in movies."

"Oh-oh. What did he tell you about that?" Chris asked, leaning out of her window in the shade of one of those big old sycamores.

"That I'm never, never to go to one, as they are all dens of iniquitous abandonment," he said, solemnly.

"Get *in*," Chris said, pulling her head back inside.

"I'd really like to go to one," he added wistfully.

"You'd better watch him, Elise," Chris warned. Elise laughed and trotted up the driveway to his little car. He climbed in next to Chris.

"Seat belt," she told him.

"Yes, ma'am," he said, reaching back over his shoulder for it. "As I said, I'm not completely ignorant."

"That you aren't," Chris said, as if it were an understatement. She checked her mirror, and pulled out into the street.

"That was a pregnant sort of a thing to say," he said, squinting up at the tops of the trees.

"Oh yeah?" she said.

"Wasn't it?" he asked. "You said it like it had to mean something."

"They may say a lot of things about you, McClellan," she said. "But *no*body would call you ignorant."

"And that's not supposed to get up my curiosity?" he asked.

She grinned at him. "What do you care?" she asked.

"I don't know," he said. "It's interesting to me. Don't you like to know what people say about you?"

"No," she said. "I always feel bad, after."

He nodded. "Should I feel bad?" he asked her.

She laughed. "Not really," she said. "Okay. Nobody does as well as you do in math without wearing glasses and carrying a calculator. There are guys in our class who fit that description, and what you do in there makes *them* look normal."

"Oh, thanks," he said. "You were right. I shouldn't have heard. We could've started out with a simple 'Good morning, how are you?' "

She laughed and gave him a sidelong glance. "Fine," she said. "Sorry."

He looked out of the window again. "I'm not that smart," he said, serious. "I've had the material before."

"Where? MIT?"

"Come on," he said.

"What are you going to do when you grow up? Invent space travel?"

"Is this hostility?" he asked.

"No," she said. "I really want to know."

He smiled out of his window. "I'm going to be a photographer," he said.

"Like, you're going to take portraits of brides?" she said, sounding a little disappointed.

"Like, I'm going to take portraits of starving children in the Third World."

That she didn't seem to mind.

"You like that," he said.

"It sounds more like you," she agreed. And then she got casual. "So. You kind of like Elise?" *Ah. The reason I'm in this particular car this morning.*

"She's a nice girl," he said, his face turned away from her, grinning to himself.

"That's it?" she asked, taking a quick look at him.

"She's been nice to me," he said.

She sniffed.

"I'm not answering this the way you want me to," he said.

"Don't you think it sounds a little cold?" she asked.

"Oh, not really," he said innocently. "If you asked her the same thing about me, she'd probably give you basically the same answers. Except the nice part." He was fishing, now.

And she laughed. It was the kind of reaction he'd hoped for, a laugh that said—*If you only knew.*

"I'm missing something here," he said, blanking out his face.

She glanced at him again. "I doubt it."

"You wouldn't think I was such a genius if you could see my writing," he said.

"Lise says you're so smart, it's scary."

He laughed. "She didn't say that."

"I promise. Ver *Betum.*"

"Well," he said. "That was nice of her." Chris gave him a sour look.

"She'd kill me if she knew I was telling you this. But she really likes you. I've never seen her so interested in anybody. I'd hate to see her hurt." Her voice had dropped with that last bit; he took it as a warning.

"You think I'm going to hurt her?" he asked. "I don't think I'm really in a position with her to do that. She's just nice to me, that's all. She's a nice person, taking care of a new kid."

"Is that what you really think?" she asked him.

He ducked his head. "I don't know," he said. "She keeps to herself."

"Well, take my word for it," she said. "She likes you enough that it's got her scared."

"Really."

"Yes. Really. She doesn't scare easy."

This wasn't really telling him much. That Elise was interested in him, yes. But he didn't understand why she was, and that made him nervous.

"If I actually do have an advantage with her," he said, "I promise, I would never play on it." He said it quietly, so she'd know it was different from his other answers.

"I hope not," she said. "It wouldn't be that hard for you to do."

He didn't answer. She was making him uncomfortable.

"Listen," Chris said. "She's out a lot. She's always in the middle of everything. You'd think she knows how to take care of herself. But she doesn't. She only knows how to take care of other people. The only real boyfriend she's ever had is Steven. And he treats her like she's something made out of spun glass. No bumps. No bruises. So she's not tough. And she doesn't know how to be careful. She never really had to learn.

"But along you come, and suddenly everything's different. I don't know what it is—but it's different with you. She's not hooked on Steven. They're old friends. She knows she could get into trouble with you; she can't read you at all, which is no surprise, considering nobody else can, either—and she doesn't know which way you'll jump. But she's hooked on you. She's a very gentle girl."

"I know," he said.

And now he was *very* uncomfortable.

"What do you want me to do?" he asked.

"Tell me if you care," she said. "Because, if you don't, you tell me, and I'll take care of her. This isn't a game. Not where Elise's welfare is concerned."

"So. You want me on or off."

"I want to know if you care."

He sighed, and he watched a lady pushing a stroller down the sidewalk.

"It matters to me," he said. "More than I'd like to say."

She nodded. "Good," she said. "I didn't want to have to do that."

"But I can't be the only one responsible," he said to her. "Elise is a big girl. She's not the only one who can end up hurt."

She took a quick glance at him.

"She's not the only one made out of glass, either," he murmured. "Just do one thing for me."

"What?" she asked him.

"Just remember, I told you—I'm not that smart."

"Don't hurt her," Chris said.

He made a hiss. "You think I intend to?" he asked. "Is there somebody out there talking to her this way about me? I'm not going to hurt her—not meaning to. Okay? And not because I'm afraid of her friends. Because of her. Okay? Is that what you want from me?"

She had a little color in her cheeks. "I just wanted to make sure you weren't playing any games with this."

"Games?" He laughed. "I really don't have time for that. But I can't give you a personal guarantee."

"I'm her friend," Chris said, something between another warning and an apology.

"So am I," he said. "If there's room."

"This is the stick," Elise told him.

They were sitting in this tiny car in the middle of a huge, empty parking lot.

"This is my uncle's church," he said, peering up at the spire.

"I know," Elise said. "It's mine, too."

"I never saw you there," he said.

"Same religion, different meeting time," she said. "Are you listening to me?"

"I'm listening," he sighed. And he tried very hard to do what he was told. The whole thing turned out to be a terrifically humiliating experience.

"*Gas*," she kept yelling at him. "Shift. *Shift!*" And then, "*Brakes?*" and his little car jerking flatuently around the parking lot. Humiliating.

"That's it," Chris said finally, sitting in the back, leaning up through the front seats. "That's better."

"Better," he said. "Better than what?"

"Better than awful," she said. "I've got a date this afternoon. Get me out of here."

He offered to drive her over to her car.

"It's my father's car," she said. "Just let me get out here and I'll walk over there, thank you. I think we're plenty close enough as it is."

Elise got out, pulled her seat down so Chris could climb over it — Chris out, Elise back in. Chris closed the door for Elise, then leaned her crossed arms on the window sill. "You be good now, children," she said, meaning Cody should be good and forget everything she'd told him and not get her in trouble. He only grinned at her, making no promises.

"I don't like him," Chris said to Elise, pushing herself off. "See you."

Elise smiled, watching Chris on the way to her car. "She doesn't mean that," Elise said.

"Maybe she does, and maybe she's the wiser of the two of you," he said. He practiced putting his car in gear.

"That was good," she said. She patted his hand. She was being cute.

On second thought, he pulled the car back out of gear, turned his hand over so that hers fell into it. And then he laced his fingers through hers, and he smiled at her. "Thanks for the help," he said. He thought he knew what he was seeing in her face. She hadn't pulled her hand away. There was a feeling inside of him, a complicated feeling, and he moved to her, hesitantly, not at all sure of himself.

She was very sweet with him. Very reserved. He kept her hand as he kissed her, making no other movement, not aware of anything in that moment but what they were doing. It was like drinking peace.

When they parted, he sighed, sliding way down in his seat, his palms hard against the steering wheel. A laugh came up inside him, different than the usual one — happy.

"What is it?" she asked.

He smiled to himself. "I like the way you make me feel," he said. And he smiled at her again. She put her hand on his arm, light as anything. And then she brought a kiss to him, and it was wonderful.

"I don't know what to do about you," she said, eye to eye with him a moment later, no more than five inches from his face. Then she sat back in her own seat.

"I know," he said. "Isn't it great?" *So, schmooz. So, fine. You are playing games. You are what you are, and you know what you know; and you know you don't know how to handle —or not handle—a girl like this. But that's okay, right? As long as you got what you want. It's all right because all that's really at risk here is her.*

"I won't lie to you," she said, going serious on him. "I never will."

He looked at her, scared of the promise and incapable of making one to her. "Sometimes it's hard to tell the truth," he said.

"I promise—" she started to say, but he put two fingers gently against her mouth and stopped her.

"You never know what's going to happen," he said. "I'll do the best I can for you. I'm really stupid about most things. I'm not very good at other people." It was meant to be a warning. By the look on her face, he thought she hadn't taken it that way at all, and that scared him, too. So it was with Elise, just like it was with Charlotte. They all felt sorry for him. Womanly pity. Everybody wanted to mother him. They weren't going to like it at all when they found out what they'd had their hands on all this time.

The problem is that I wasn't lying. I'm just as hooked on her. What am I supposed to do? I like her. I need her. Is that so bad?

Knowing what you know, yes.

The simple touch of her hand surprised him. His hunger for it had surprised him.

It's more than that. I like her. I really do. It's the truth. She's important to me.

Remember that, then. And remember this—you can't risk her without risking yourself. Not and be a human being.

"We'll be friends," he said with a touch of desperation. "And when we go away to college, we'll write. And we'll dance at each other's weddings. And maybe it'll be the same one. Eh? You never know."

She laughed. "You never know," she said.

He messed up her hair. "You're so cute," he said. "Want to go to a movie, tonight?"

Her face got serious again. Very serious.

"You have a date," he guessed. "I shouldn't have—"

She put her whole hand over his mouth. "You don't mean a drive-in?" she said, her eyes wide.

No, he let his eyes say. Lots of horror. He pulled her hand away from his mouth. "How could you *think* such a thing?"

And then she got a wicked look about her. "Darn!" she said. *Darn!*

He took both of her hands. "You don't really know me yet, Elise," he said. "You've really got to remember that. There are some things I'm just not prepared to tell you, yet. There're lots of things you don't know. But I'd really never hurt you. Not meaning to. I just don't want you trusting me too far, okay? Please? I'm very serious. I don't think I could live with it, if you trusted me the way you want me to trust you. And you've got to remember—I'm not used to playing by your rules. I take responsibility for myself, but I'm not used to the rules."

She took a good, long look into his face. "Okay," she said. "Okay." She settled in her own seat and sobered up.

He smiled. "Thank you," he said. And he dropped a kiss on her cheek. "Now. I'm starving. Are you starving? Let's go get something to eat. And I'll drive."

"Absolutely not," she said. "Out of the car."

So he got out, and she got out, and they both came around the front bumper, each on the way to the other side. He caught her around the waist as she passed him, not wanting to wear out his welcome, but willing to take what advantage of it he could—while he still had it.

She didn't seem to mind at all.

21

"This is Thayne," Mr. Allen said, pointing to a lanky kid. The kid was squinting at a negative he was holding up against the safelights. He gave them a glance through the gloom of the darkroom, across the long, black trough they used for a sink, and did a little wave. "He's your boss." Mr. Allen dropped three cannisters of film into Cody's hand and pushed open the developing room door. "He's only a junior, but he's a lot like you — he's got a gift for this. Believe me, he knows what he's doing. You can probably learn more from him than you could from me."

As it turned out, that was the truth.

"This is really all I do," Thayne explained later, showing Cody the finer points of turning out a test strip. "The thing you want to keep in mind here is that good, solid separations between the exposures are going to save you time and paper later on."

A whole line of trays sat side by side in the trough — first, the developer, then the stop bath, then the fixer, then the wash. Thayne pulled the strip he'd just done out of the stop, let it drain, and then dropped it in the fixer. He didn't even use the tongs. Very impressive.

"What do you mean — that's *all* you do? Should you need more than this?" Cody said, nearly intoxicated with the smell of the fixer.

"Now, look here — you see what I mean? Look at this. Now look at yours. You're not paying attention, McClellan — look at that. You jerked the cover sheet. How're you going to tell anything by that?"

"Okay," Cody said. He started over.

"What I mean is — I don't do anything else. I don't draw. I don't play music. I don't *want* to do anything else. I don't even take women out."

"Women?" Cody said, smiling. The enlarger fired.

"That's what I said."

"Your art just takes up too much of your time," Cody said. The enlarger kicked out, and Cody pulled the cover sheet back a touch. "That's very noble."

"Further. You've got to move it back further, or how are you going to see anything? Yeah. That's right. Now you'll be able to tell what you're doing."

Cody flipped on the enlarger again.

"It has nothing to do with nobility," Thayne said, moving around the end of the trough, over to his own work station.

"Oh yeah?" Cody said. The enlarger kicked out again. Cody moved the cover sheet back once more, gauging the distance carefully. "How many times should I do this?"

"I'd give it five exposures, anyway—"

"Okay," Cody said, reaching for the enlarger timer.

"No. The truth of it is really humiliating. I just can't talk to girls, that's all. I don't have any sisters, for one thing. And anyway, I've got a face like a pizza. And look at me—Ichabod Crane. Who wants to go out with a pizza on a stick?"

"Done," Cody said happily. He pulled the little strip out of the easel and took it over to the trough. "Get the timer for me?" he asked Thayne, and then he slipped the strip into the first tray, holding just the very corner with the tongs. Finally, he put the tongs down, and he picked up the paper and ran his fingers lightly over the surface, warming the chemical. "Girls are funny," he said, thoughtfully. "You never know."

Thayne grunted. "You never want to pull anything before it's spent at least a full minute in the developer," he said, catching Cody almost in the act of an early pull. "You pull it too early, it won't tell you anything. You don't have time to get true blacks that way. Have a little courage. Be patient. You don't get true blacks, you sure won't get true whites."

"Ah," Cody said. And he looked at Thayne's back, and he smiled to himself.

Thayne dropped him off at home after the lab work. Cody hadn't quite worked up the courage to take his driver's license tests yet. And even if he had, he wasn't sure he was ready to go outside the neighborhood—yet. Every day, he thought it might be fun to take a little drive. Somewhere safe. The school parking lot was not quite the perfect environment—yet.

He found the letter waiting for him on the kitchen table—a big manilla envelope, addressed to him, postmarked New York. He dropped his books on the table beside it, sat down, and took it in his hands.

John had sent him something.

Sawyer slammed into the kitchen from the hallway. "Hiya," he said, on his way to the back door. Then he noticed the envelope and hovered at Cody's elbow a moment.

Cody slid the prints out of the envelope. His prints—back to him.

"Somebody drew all over your pictures," Sawyer hissed.

Cody looked up from the letter that had come with the prints. "What?" he asked.

"Somebody took a pen and drew all over your pictures," Sawyer said, offended.

"John did," Cody said.

"Who's John?" Sawyer asked him.

"He's the photographer I met on the bus," Cody said. "He's my friend."

"Your friend drew all over your pictures?"

"Yeah, look. He's showing me things. Like right here—see, there should be a little place right here that's lighter than the rest, see? Just right here, right along the top of her cheek. He's teaching me. He *remembers* me."

"He wrecked the pictures," Sawyer pointed out.

"The pictures were no good in the first place," Cody said.

"They didn't look no good to me," Sawyer said, pushing off from the table, back on course for the outside.

Cody held up the prints, looking them over. Then he put them down, picked up the letter again, and read it to himself.

Your exposure is too soft. Part of that may be in the negative; a little bit harder negative will get you truer blacks. But your contrast problems are partly in the printing. Don't be afraid to leave the paper in the chemical; don't pull it the second you see the blacks begin to come up. You want a good, crisp contrast, and that's going to take a little courage. You gotta let it sit until it really takes.

And you've got to keep in mind what we talked about before—it's all an illusion. You have to use the light the same way the eye would. No highlights—no depth. If you sacrifice one, you lose the other. Don't be afraid to let the shadows go very dark. Take a look around you. Shadows are darker than you think. If you don't let them go as black as they need to be, you lose perspective on your grays. Let them go; then your highlights are going to be hotter.

Your composition is pretty good. I would have expected that. You've done well for your first few prints. Keep working. Send me anything you want.

So, how's it going? I guess you got where you meant to go. Was it any better than the place you left? Take care of yourself. Let me know if I can help.

It was signed *John*. No last name. So, John thought they were friends. Cody went over the letter again, and then he picked up the prints and studied them closely, humming pleasure to himself.

The back door opened. "Are you ready?" Charlotte asked, a lot of irritation in her voice.

Cody looked up, surprised and a little muddled.

"Your license?" she said. "We're going *today*. Did you forget?"

He had forgotten. His stomach went funny on him.

"Are you mad?" he asked.

She was slamming around the kitchen. "No," she said. "Not at you. Are you ready? You've been reading that manual every night for the last two weeks—you *ought* to be ready."

"Yes, ma'am," he said. He put the prints away. "Did something happen?"

"I'm sorry. I'm *sorry*," she said, mad at herself. "It's just—" she started, caught herself—stood still, a little fight going on in her face. Sawyer came in through the back door. She pulled a drawer open, finally, looking for something.

"He shot it once more after you left," Sawyer announced, coming in through the back door.

"While you were back there?" Charlotte demanded, fire in her eyes.

"Yes'm," Sawyer said.

"*Swell*," Charlotte said, and slammed the drawer.

"The kid next door has a BB gun," Sawyer explained. He must have caught the puzzled look on Cody's face.

"And he uses *our* fence," Charlotte said, opening and slamming another drawer, "to hang his target on. Which means that when he gets carried away and shoots at *our* birds, he shoots into *our* yard. Besides the fact that he's a nasty little backtalking—" She stopped herself with an effort.

"I wish I had a BB gun," Sawyer sighed.

"What is it? Built into the male genetics or something?" Charlotte snapped. "You can forget it. The only reason for anybody to have a gun is if they have to protect themselves—which you don't—or if they're going to kill something—which I hope you never will."

"Mo-om," Sawyer said. "You can't kill anything with a BB gun."

"You have a cousin who's blind in one eye because of a BB gun."

"That was an accident," Sawyer said.

"So is the kid who lives next door," she spat. "Like an eight-year-old never makes mistakes. Like there aren't people *living* over here. Like he has the right to kill our birds."

"Maybe he doesn't know any better," Sawyer offered.

"How many times have I told him?" Charlotte asked — rhetorical question.

"Why don't you talk to his mother?" Cody asked her.

"*Right*," Charlotte said, shouldering her purse, and fishing in it for her keys. "I *have*. And you know what response I get? 'Boys will be boys. That's just the way boys are when you live in the country.' See? No responsibility there. Never mind it bothers the neighbors. It's only *me*, after all — consider the source.

"And then you know what I hear? From *other* people, mind you. She thinks I'm *terribly* intolerant. *Intolerant*." She took a deep breath, and closed her eyes. She let the breath go. She opened her eyes and looked at Cody. "You ready? 'Cause let's go."

"Yes, ma'am," he said. "If I could just go up and get my manual—"

"I'll be in the car," she said. "And *you*—" she turned on Sawyer. "You'd just better make sure you get your work done before we get back. Get it?"

"Mother. *I* didn't say you were intolerant."

"Well, you'd better get upstairs before you find out how intolerant I *am*."

"Man," Sawyer said, and he shoved Cody's chair back under the table.

Chris fell in beside him in the halls. It was just before sixth period.

"I saw you drive in this morning," she said.

Cody smiled.

"You didn't run into anything. That was very good." She smiled at him. But there was something in her tone, something he picked up and couldn't read. "You going out tomorrow night?"

"Elise has a game," he said. She stopped at the head of the stairs.

"Aren't you going to the game?" she asked.

"No," he said.

"She'd probably like it if you did," she said.

"I've got to be in the lab." She nodded, her lips pursed. She wasn't satisfied with the answer.

"You could take her out after," Chris said.

"She's coming over after." He was going carefully, not sure where the traps lay.

"To tutor," she said.

"Ostensibly," he said, going for a little comradery. It didn't go.

"That must be nice for you. You just sit at home until she comes to you." Hostility, then.

"I've done something wrong," he said. "You're telling me, I'm doing something wrong." The bell rang. She glanced at her watch. "If you don't tell me, Chris—how'm I supposed to know what you're on about?"

She gave him a long, unreadable look.

"Girls like to be asked out," she said, finally. "You know? Like, on purpose. Like, it's something you *thought* about."

"They do?"

"Yes. They *need* that."

Yes. Need—we understand that concept. So girls' needs are acceptable.

She looked down at her watch again. "I've got to go."

"Are you going to be seeing her?" he asked. *Did she send you to tell me this?*

"If I ever get to class."

He nodded. "I envy you," he said.

She turned a slight grin to the side. "You want me to tell her you said that?"

"Whatever's right," he said. She didn't hook on the slight turn in the words.

"Okay," she said, flipping him what was left of the grin. "See you."

He was tempted to pull the print at forty-five seconds.

"No," Thayne said, his elbows on the rim of the trough, watching in the red glow of the safelights. "If you've got it wrong, fix it at the exposure, not in the developing."

"I know," Cody said, agreeing. "I think this is going to be okay."

"Private lessons?" A girl's voice floated out of the shadowy place over by the Omega enlargers, tucked away on the far wall.

"What's it to you?" Thayne asked, good naturedly.

"Okay? Look." Cody pulled the print over, straightened it out so they could see the subject straight up. "Right along there." He pulled the print. Thayne shook his head. "Fifteen seconds more," he said, but Cody finished draining it and dropped it in the stop, face down.

"Fifteen seconds, next time," he said. He pulled it out of the stop, drained it, put it in the fixer. Thayne slid along next to him.

"He was right. There's the highlight. See? Right along the edges of the cheek, there. So the negative's okay. This one, anyway. *Look* at that," he said, pulling the print closer. Pleased.

Thayne took the print out of his hand, drained it, held it up for a moment so he could get a good look at it. "Very nice," he murmured.

"Those are beautiful highlights," Cody said, rubbing his hands together, very satisfied. He rubbed his hands on the towel he had over his shoulder. "Now," he said.

"Beautiful," Thayne murmured.

"Is that staff work?" the girl's voice came again, a light flashing on behind it in the dark. "Because you guys have newspaper to do tonight."

"Don't worry about it, Jeannie," Thayne said, making it half song–half sigh, as if he'd said the same thing too many times before. He sighed and dropped the print back down into the chemical.

Cody went to get the spec sheet on the newspaper shots. When he came back, Thayne was still hanging over the fixer tray, looking at Cody's picture.

"What's wrong?" Cody asked him.

"Nothing," Thayne said.

"You just can't get over my highlights," Cody said, grinning. "Well, neither can I."

"Can't get over this face," Thayne murmured.

Cody put the assignment sheet down at his station and went over to lean next to Thayne, both of them looking down at the print. *Funny,* he thought. *There is a face there.* Elise's. He hadn't seen it that way for awhile.

"Not stupid looking the way some of them are," Thayne said, barely a whisper.

"*What* are you *doing?*" Jeannie asked, coming out of the shadows, carrying her own piece of paper. She stopped by the fixer tray on the way to the other end. Holding her paper up and away, she leaned over to see what it was they were looking at.

"*Oh,*" she said, and put her nose in the air and went on down to the developer.

"You think she's pretty, Thayne?" Cody asked.

"You think I'm blind?" Thayne said.

"I'm serious. I want to know. I don't see her anymore, myself."

Jeannie looked up quickly. "You broke up?" she said.

"Broke up?" Cody echoed.

"You said you're not seeing her anymore." She was doing a heavy agitation on her paper.

"No. I said I don't *see* her anymore. I'm too used to her to *see* her. She's just my friend."

Jeannie sniffed.

Thayne sighed. "They say she's got it for you," he said. "What would it be like?"

"Get out of here," Cody said. "She hasn't got the hots for me. We're friends."

"Everybody knows you're going together," Jeannie said. "Big secret."

"*Going* together? *Going* together? What is that? Everybody in this school has to be a big expert on everything? No, we're not *going* together. She's nice. She's just nice."

"Is she?" Thayne asked. "What do you talk about? What's she like?"

Jeannie sniffed again.

"Melville. I don't know. Stuff. She's nice. She's just a genuinely nice person."

"She's a soshe. She fits with them."

"With who?"

"With the soshes." Jeannie had moved through the stop and now she was sharing the fix tray with them. "Her own little set. They have their own rules, their own little dress code — guaranteed *better* than anybody else. Football players, student government — the *pop*ular ones. The shallow-minded ones." She gave him a venomous look. "You ought to know. You're one of them."

Cody's mouth fell open.

"*Really*," he said.

"You're trying to tell me you're not?" she asked.

"I'm not," he said, feeling the first prickles of social outrage.

"You're a liar, then," she said.

"Jeannie," Thayne said, dreamily, still picture gazing. "Lay off."

"This girl is the only friend I've *got*, okay?" Cody said. "What makes you think I'm one of *them*?"

"You can't be serious," she said, sneering.

"Fine," he said. "Tell me."

"Look at the way you're dressed. Look at the classes you take. Look at who you hang out with."

"Yeah," he said. "Look who I hang out with." He spread his hands, taking in the room and the two of them.

"You're not hanging out here," she said. "You work here."

"I don't hang out," he said.

"You hang out with the brains at lunch, and with the soshes the rest of the time.

"Like *her*."

"She's my *friend*."

"Yeah. You're just a bunch of miniature Yuppies." She turned her back on him, going back to her station.

And Cody was wondering what his problem was—that he should be upset because he was pulling this whole middle-class act off so well.

"My word, Jeannie," Thayne said. He used the prongs to pull Cody's photo out of the fixer and then he dropped it in the wash. Cody leaned back against his station, his arms folded, looking into the shadows where Jeannie was working. It was really bothering him, what she thought.

"You don't know how wrong you are—" he started. But it was too ridiculous. He turned around and picked up the spec sheet. "Where're the proofs?" he asked.

"*I've* got them," Jeannie said. It was another challenge.

"Do you mind if *I* look at them?" Cody's patience was running thin.

Thayne sighed. "Give him the sheets," he said. She emerged from the shadow and handed the proofs to Thayne. "*You* give them to him."

"What is her *problem*?" Cody said.

Thayne sighed again. "It's just the way she is," he said. "It's the journalist in her. Don't let it bother you." He went over and reached into the wash to touch Elise's picture. "Anyway," he said, lapsing into his dream again. "If I had what you have, I wouldn't care what *any*body said to me."

A few days later, Cody was getting some things out of his locker just before lunch. Somebody came up and bumped him from behind. It was actually more of a shove. He was turning around, expecting Elise—or more likely Chris—when he caught another shove. With this one, he had to use his hands to keep his face out of the metal door of the locker.

And the old instincts kicked in hard.

He sidestepped and turned, nothing in his face but the anger in his eyes.

"*Hey*," the Turk said, standing there in his letter sweater with a couple of his friends. Just out of reach. No books in his hands, face insolent. "How ya doin'?"

Cody gave him the eye. Then he deliberately turned his back, getting his books, but never off balance, and listening.

"So. You going to lunch?"

Cody wondered what he was supposed to be reading in the voice. *Does he think I'm stupid?*

"That's where I'm going," Cody said, keeping everything out of his own voice. Unmoved. Unconcerned. Face on cold. He slammed his locker shut and spun the lock.

"Well, listen," the Turk said, falling in beside him, friends behind, "I think we should have a little talk. And I think this is probably a good time." He put his hand on Cody's shoulder. A mistake.

Cody didn't react. Not yet. He was reading the guys behind.

"I think there's something you just might not be aware of, my man," the Turk said. He was arrogant and patronizing, assuming—what, that Cody was going to be impressed with the Turk's reputation? "We don't want any little misunderstandings. We don't want anybody unhappy, do we? You know Steve Hewlette? He and McCall—they're kind of like the school mascot couple, you know what I mean? I mean, they've been together—you understand—for, I don't know . . . since they were babies. We all like that. We think that's just . . . warm, you know? We'd hate to see anything upset that. It'd upset *every*body. I mean, it's definitely tradition, you know? And this is their senior year."

"Your concern is touching," Cody said. He felt the tension in Turk's hand.

"Well," Turk said, maintaining the stupid cheerfulness, "we've all been friends a long time."

"You want to get your hand off my shoulder?" Cody said, cold—no obvious threats.

"Pardon me?" Turk said, transparent sarcasm.

Cody stopped dead, and turned halfway to the back. "Get your hand off me," he said.

Turk moved his hand off, as if he'd only just realized how un*pleasant* the touch had been. "Well," he said to his friends. "If the guy's not going to take a little friendly advice, maybe we just need to explain things a little differently, eh? Later, my man."

The Turk's friends brushed by Cody, giving him the look. Cody made no move. No fighting in the halls. Not now.

After that, he understood some things. He wasn't the only animal here. The violence in this place was just less honest, more of an undercurrent. In a way, that was a comfort. He wasn't so alone. Ironic that the Turk would have made him feel more at home.

But it scared him for Elise, who didn't understand those things, and *wouldn't*.

And it made him go very privately to Erin's desk, and dig the knife out of the drawer. He didn't mean to carry it. But he put it in the glove compartment of his little car, just in case.

He didn't tell anybody any part of it. He wasn't sure any of his people would believe him if he tried. And it might raise too many questions about him, too many things he wasn't interested in bringing to light just now. It was all going to hit the fan soon enough. He wanted as much unclouded time as he could get—to give them a Cody they knew to offset the Cody they were going to find out about.

And that was enough to keep him good for now. That and wanting very badly to keep all the things he finally had.

22

Hunsaker finally gave Cody his first grade. It was along about the fourth paper he'd done, an analysis of sonnet form. And she gave him a *B*, which was not good enough. But she'd written under it, in her small, neat, half-printed script, *You keep this up and I'll give you your A.*

He passed the paper up to Elise. She looked it over, read the end, picked up her pen as if she intended to add her own note, and then put the pen back down without writing. She turned around and looked at him. There was pride in the look. They smiled at each other, and warmth welled up inside of him. She handed the paper back. He took care not to touch her hand, taking the paper from it. She looked at him again; her face was saying something different now, something more private than pride. And he wished fervently that they were alone.

Ms. Hunsaker started her lecture. Elise let go of him. As she did, he caught something out of the corner of his eye—somebody watching, a shared grin. People *watch*ing. He faced front, his cheeks gone hot, nursing a sore mixture of offended privacy and pleasure.

Hunsaker was announcing another paper, due Friday. *This one had better be right.* He watched Elise's profile, privately, from behind the hand on which he leaned his cheek. *It will be. As everything else finally is.*

Cody went through all of his negatives, all his proof sheets, the stuff that was his life—shots of the house, an interior of Sawyer's window, one of the kitchen table with the books on it and the fireplace behind—and a million portraits: Sawyer, Charlotte, Erin, the baby—and Elise, so much of Elise.

Then he spent a lot of time in the lab with them, making sure the composition was right, that the blacks were black and the whites were white. He wanted them perfect.

There was one shot he'd taken with Mr. Allen's infrared filter—the sun going down, an intense gathering of heat, a small stud of brilliance embedded in a rounded, broiling mass of layered clouds—the sky after thunder, the sky before darkness.

That one he printed on—very carefully, thinking as he did it—*"A portrait of God."*

And when they were all as perfect as he could make them, he bundled them up and sent them to John. *Be pleased,* he said in his heart but didn't write. *See me in these.*

"Two of you have perfect scores," Mrs. Bruecher announced. "Only two out of thirty college-bound students had enough command of the material to master this test. I will admit," she said, peering at them over her glasses and moving heavily across the room, "this test was not a simple one. Still, anyone who invested any thought or energy in his or her study should have been able to make a good showing. The mean score in this class was personally disappointing to me."

The mean score had been an eighty-two. And so, there was the *C.*

She put a paper down on Danielle Forrester's desk. "Congratulations, Miss Forrester," Mrs. Bruecher said flatly, crossing the room again to drop the second paper on Cody's desk. "Congratulations, Mr. McClellan."

She handed out the rest of the tests in significant silence.

Danielle leaned over her desk, sending eye signals to Cody. *Success,* she said. *But they'll all hate us good.* They smiled at each other across the room, and then Bruecher officially started the class.

Cody hadn't been particularly surprised by his grade. He'd worked his head off to get it, and he'd felt good while taking the test. No magic or brilliance involved.

But Danielle was right: they were both catching some malevolent looks. And they both had the sense to lie low for the rest of the lecture.

"Does she really help you?" Charlotte asked him, standing in the doorway as he set his books out neatly on the dining room table. The question was half tease.

"She's going to get me an *A* in English," he said. "And we kiss. And that helps me a lot." He grinned at her, and she glared back at him, scandalized—but not really.

And then she was the mother. "You watch your step," she said. "Her parents trust us."

He didn't mind the warning at all. What he minded was the way she did it—as if it were just cursory. As if she certainly knew him well enough to know she really didn't need to say anything. That, he didn't like. Being left alone with the responsibility, he didn't like.

And then Elise was there, and that's all in the world he had to think about.

She was going over his rough draft; he was studying the planes the shadows made on her face, and wondering how she ever had time to get her own work done.

"You know," he said vaguely, "there's a dance after the game this week."

"There's always a dance after the game," she said, but she was looking at him out of the corners of her eyes.

"Mr. Allen—Thayne was going to shoot it for the newspaper, but he has to go to his grandmother's. So Mr. Allen, he thought maybe I could give it a go."

"You mean, shoot the dance?"

"Yeah."

"That's great," she said.

"I thought, maybe," he went on, considering how nice it might be to put out his hand and touch her face, "you wouldn't mind doing it with me."

"Going to the dance with you?"

"Well. Shooting it with me. Going with me. Yes."

She didn't smile at him. She smiled down at his paper, her cheek against her hand. "Like a date?" she asked.

"Well, kind of," he said. "Maybe like a date. Kind of."

She tilted her head slightly.

"Okay," she said, and then she let a tiny slip of a grin come his way. "I'll kind of go with you."

"All right," he said. "All right." And then he went quiet, and so did she. He sighed, and she took up his paper again, reading, ignoring him.

He couldn't get over the sweet curve of her cheek, the soft, fluted border of shadow around her eye.

She glanced at him.

"What?" she asked.

"What?" he echoed.

"What are you looking at?" she asked.

"You," he said.

She squirmed a bit, embarrassed, but he could tell she was pleased to have him look.

He smiled to himself, and raised his eyebrows at her, playing.

"*Cody,*" she said, and colored up, becoming quite pretty.

"I was looking," he said, "at the play of the light on your face."

"Oh, really," she said.

He nodded.

"All you see is light," she said, her eyes laughing at him.

"All I see is shadow," he corrected her.

"You take that camera everywhere," she said. "I don't think I ever cared about anything as much as you care about that. What do you see in it?" she asked, meaning more than one thing.

He put his elbows on the table and rested his chin in his hands. "That's a complex question," he said. "Do you really want an answer?"

She put his paper down. She hadn't been asking before, but she was now.

"I don't know," he said. "It's kind of complicated. There's a lot of . . . feeling I do, looking through it. And then there's science. You know, you don't see what's really there. You just see the way light reflects off things. It depends on the light. It depends on the atmosphere, and your eyes, and sometimes what your brain expects to see."

She was doing that little search of hers, that little poking around behind his eyes. Looking for his soul, maybe. *Someday, let's hope you find it.*

"Okay, you see that?" he asked, pointing at the chandelier hanging over their heads. "That's our light source. It's how I see your face." He leaned forward and touched her face with his hand, drawing one finger tip gently across her cheek, just over the line of shadow. "Here, there's the highlight," he said. And then, so softly, with the back of his finger, "And this, the shadow."

She closed her eyes.

It was very strong when he kissed her, the thing that Charlotte had said to watch. He wasn't good with the responsibility; he couldn't hear it, and he kissed her again, drowning in it.

She drew away from him, her eyes a little surprised, holding him off and begging him on, and he sat back in his seat and did as Charlotte had asked. But something had happened. His heart was pounding in his ears, and he wasn't sure he wanted to stay in his chair.

"Are you okay?" Elise asked, and that helped. That she should be worrying about him shamed the part of him that was thinking only of himself. *The part that's really me. The part that still has to be dealt with.*

"I'm okay," he said. "Sorry." But he wasn't. Not really. And neither was she, he could see that—just a little out of her depth, she thought. She was like Charlotte in this, too—she trusted him, and she wasn't afraid. It suddenly scared him badly.

This isn't right. She's touching somebody, but it's not me. She doesn't know who I am. She only knows who she wants me to be. And if she knew, she'd quit. And she's going to know. And I can't stand what's going to happen then.

"Can I talk to you, Elise?" Poised on the very edge of annihilation.

"Cody, we need to work," she said. And that was true. They did need to work.

"There are some things I need to tell you." His arms had gone cold and his head a little dizzy. He was going to tell her everything, because he couldn't stand knowing what she didn't know. Because what she was giving him, he wanted, and he wanted to have the right to have it.

But she didn't understand. And he knew what she was thinking—she was thinking he was going to ask her hard questions, about *them*, about the relationship—she was afraid he was going to make her promise things.

"Not now," she said to him, sternly—sidestepping, but with that cute little beg. "Cody, *please? Please??*"

Well.

Relief and an unhappy guilt.

He'd only had so much courage.

It all came apart on one of the first days of October, when the nights had finally gone cold and the mornings were frost. Cody settled himself in homeroom, tucking the books he didn't need under his seat, smoothing the paper Ms. Hunsaker would call for the moment she walked into the room, just being alive without thinking too much about it.

All around him, people were doing the same things, rustling and talking and settling in for the day. The air smelled of first-day furnace, and Cody was remembering the way the radiators in his old school used to knock on mornings like this.

"We're going to have a test," somebody in the back said.

Everybody groaned.

"How do you know?" someone else asked.

"The Turk always knows," somebody on the other side of the room said.

"Yeah, he does. How come you always know?"

The room had gotten quiet, and everybody was looking back at Turk.

"It's not going to be that bad," he said, sounding as if he really did know. "And you won't have to worry about the curve, because I have a feeling the New York Whiz is going to end up sitting this one out."

Cody chilled.

"What are you talking about?" Danielle said.

"McClellan," Turk said. "His school records came in yesterday."

Cody sat very still. He hadn't expected it to hit him quite this way.

"So?" Marty said.

"So. I think you'd be surprised to find out some of the stuff in there."

"Blow off," Marty said, and he turned around front. Elise was looking at Cody; he could feel it, but he couldn't look back.

"Well, let's see," Turk went on. "They talked about vandalism. And they talked about arson. And the police were mentioned—oh, I think quite often, weren't they, McClellan? And he has a cumulative grade point average of about zero point zip. That accurate, McClellan?"

Cody didn't answer. He'd gone deadly cold inside, and he wasn't answering anybody.

"He's a runaway," Turk said. "From an inner city school. And his mother's a wino."

"Shut up," somebody in the back said.

"I'm serious. This is the truth. I give him ten minutes before he's out of here," Turk said.

The door opened, and Hunsaker came in, her arms full of test papers. She paused just inside the room, sensing something, then came on slowly, surveying the faces.

"We've got a test this morning," she said, dropping the stack of papers onto her desk.

There were no moans.

Ms. Hunsaker became very careful.

She picked up the top section of papers, cradling them in the crook of her arm, and made her way across the room, meaning to hand out the tests row by row, all the time watching, testing the air for what was up.

Cody felt Elise looking at him again. He was caught between the cold inside of him and the heat he knew showed high in his cheeks. Ms. Hunsaker was standing in front of Marty, now, counting out tests, but with her eyes on Elise. The entire front row was sitting still, tests untouched, watching.

Ms. Hunsaker had followed Elise's eyes. "Cody," she said quietly, but it was loud in the room, "are you all right?"

The question was so ludicrous, so unexpected, it pulled a laugh out of him. "Sure," he said, bitterly, but he couldn't meet her look.

Marty handed the papers back over his shoulder. Cody took his and passed the rest along. He put the paper down on his desk, making no move to read it, to pick up his pen.

"You only have forty minutes," Ms. Hunsaker said, glancing at the first row uneasily. Nobody had touched the test. "*What?*" she said suddenly. "*What* is the problem?"

The door hissed open.

Cody wasn't surprised to see his counselor's round face there, dark and angry. The atmosphere in the room was stifling; they all understood by this that Turk hadn't been messing around.

Ms. Hunsaker went to the door, exchanged a word, began to disappear through it, faded back momentarily to say, "You're on your honor" and fix them with a serious look before she let the door close behind her.

"Seven minutes, twenty-six seconds," Turk said.

"On our honor," someone in the back said. It was Steven's voice, and there was disgust in it.

There was a ghost of a headache at Cody's temples, and he'd gone definitely light-headed. It was different than before. He didn't know how to deal with it anymore. He picked up his pen, but he couldn't focus his mind on the paper.

The door opened again. "Cody," Ms. Hunsaker said. "Could you step out here for a moment?"

He put his pen down and took a ragged breath. The worst was standing up. Standing up and walking out in front of everybody. He wondered when he'd lost his arrogance. Ms. Hunsaker held the door open for him, let him pass her. It was cooler in the hall.

The counselor was out there, her weight on her back leg, her arms crossed over her broad bosom, with what he assumed to be his folder sticking out from under one of her arms. She didn't look pleased.

"Cody —" Ms. Hunsaker said, sounding as if she wasn't quite sure how to proceed.

"Young man," the counselor cut in, turning the angry eyes directly on him. "You lied to me." She was puffed up with indignation and outrage. He didn't really blame her for that.

He met her eyes. "Yes, ma'am," he said. He hadn't expected his voice to be so clear. The answer sounded cheeky; it hadn't been meant that way.

Her eyes narrowed. She was taking this very personally. "Looking through these records, that doesn't really surprise me. Just explain to me what you thought that was going to accomplish." She was having trouble with the fact that he was meeting her look.

"You wouldn't have given me the classes I needed if I hadn't," he said. Truth. Simple.

"You don't know that," she said.

"I think it's the truth," he said.

"I suspect he's right," Ms. Hunsaker said quietly. She caught the hard edge of the counselor's look.

The woman lifted one finger. "You played me for a fool," she said. "That won't happen again. The fact that you got these classes—through whatever means—does *not* mean you're going to keep them. We have a program here tailor-made for kids like you."

The headache bloomed, burning the backs of his eyes.

"You're not going to take him out of my class," Hunsaker said, as if she was thinking maybe she hadn't heard right.

"He doesn't belong in your class," the counselor spat.

"He's pulling an *A* in my class," Hunsaker said. "What's the point in taking him out?"

"He doesn't belong in your class," the woman said again, unfolding her arms, holding out the file and giving it a shake. "Take a moment to look through this—"

"I don't need to look through that," Hunsaker said, eyes beginning to flash. Cody was looking at her, not quite believing what she was doing. Guardian angels, light around the edges of the door—

"You can't hope to handle this boy in a class like that—"

"We're doing just fine," Hunsaker said. "At least, we were before you disrupted this class—*look*," she went on, intercepting an offended protest, "I understand your feeling. Nobody likes to be made to look ridiculous. And there's no excuse for McClellan's misrepresenting the truth. So, fine. If school policy makes provision for discipline in a case like this, then fine. But I see no reason to take a child out of a class he's doing well in because the records would indicate that he *shouldn't* be doing that well."

"*I* don't believe he could be doing all that well."

"What you believe is not material. *I* am the teacher. I'm perfectly capable of assessing my students' progress. I won't let you take him out of this class. It's *my* class. If you want to take this to Dr. Hammond, then fine, we'll take it to Dr. Hammond. But I think you'll find she backs me up."

The counselor's face was burning. "We'll have to see," she said stiffly. And then to Cody, a parting shot: "We're not through with this."

They watched her make her dignified way back down the corridor; Cody, with his back against the lockers, pain in his head, shivered.

"So it finally caught up with you," Hunsaker said.

He nodded. He'd been holding his breath. He let it go now, tipping his head back and closing his eyes. "Yes," he said. And then he looked at her. "Thank you," he said.

She shrugged. "I only told her the truth."

"I'm not pulling an *A*."

"You will be."

Cody sighed.

"Hard, isn't it?" she said. "When everybody else has got the control."

He looked at her again, surprised. "Yes," he said. And then quietly, but through his teeth, "I hate it."

"I'm not that much older than you," she said. "It's not as if I don't know that." She looked at him. "From what she said, the records are bad."

"I know. Why do you think I left? There was no way out of that."

She nodded. "And hey—what was going on in there?" She tilted her head at the classroom door. "*Some*thing was up."

He nodded.

"You going to tell me?"

"You should know—Tourquey has some kind of direct line to the office." It wasn't a comfortable thing to say, but he owed her, now. Even more than before.

"So—"

"He knows a lot of things."

"Like about your records."

"Among other things, yes."

"About the test?"

234

He didn't answer.

"*Really. Very interesting.* And I suppose he told everybody everything." Her eyes *did* flash. "About you. And about the test. Which explains a lot." She pursed her lips, and her eyes narrowed. "We'd better get back to work."

And then Cody realized he was going to have to walk back into that room.

She was watching him. "Don't underestimate them," she said. "There are some good kids in there."

And the better they are, the worse it is.

"You look so miserable," she laughed. "Come on. You knew you were going to catch it sooner or later. It could've been worse. Just forget it. They will. Nobody's going to care. Not if you don't."

He gave her a reproachful look.

"Okay," she said. "So maybe I'm a *little* older than you. The point is, you still have to finish that test."

She pulled open the door and held it for him. And when they walked back into the room, she laughed.

At the end of class, it was still very quiet. Hunsaker collected the tests, and Cody saw her almost trash them. But she changed her mind and sat down at the desk with the papers in front of her.

"Leave your essays on my desk on your way out," she said, and then she sat back, preoccupied, chewing on her thumb.

The bell rang. Cody was better now; he'd had half an hour to get himself at least the appearance of balance. He had his books together—most everybody did, as Hunsaker called in the tests before the bell, but Elise was still fooling with hers when Cody stood up to go.

"Cody," she said, quickly, looking uncomfortable—for the first time, awkward.

"See you," he said. He knew what she wanted.

"*Cody,*" she said. "I need to talk to you."

"*Oh,*" he said, one finger up as if he'd just remembered something—but transparent, carefully transparent, "I'm not going to be able to take you tonight. Allen thinks I'd better just concentrate on the assignment. So, another time." So she wouldn't have to do it herself. So he wouldn't have to hear it.

"Cody," she said, again, unhappy, reaching for him.

"It's okay," he said, totally casual now—a little shrug of the shoulder, the face, it didn't matter.

They had an audience by then.

"So, you're not going to let me say anything," she said. There was maybe a little anger there, but more of something else.

He looked her straight in the eye, a hot, bitter, self-righteous look. "No," he said. Finished the look. Left the room.

It was a hard day after that. They were all watching him, which was understandable, if nearly unbearable. He didn't say a word all day, didn't leave himself open, didn't look a soul straight in the eye — on the outside again, peering in — a stranger to the things he'd begun to like taking for granted.

He was running, lying low, and he knew it, and he cursed himself for a coward; if he could have found another way of dealing with it short of actually running away, or doing some kind of violence, he would have done it — would have done it gratefully. But he only had what he knew, and that was not much.

He couldn't face lunch, so he went to ground in the library. But they flushed him out of there before fifth period, and gym was the last place on earth he wanted to be.

When Cody showed up at the door of the photography lab an hour before his time, Mr. Allen didn't blink an eye.

"Why don't you develop this stuff?" he said, tossing Cody two rolls of thirty-five millimeter film, and giving him a push towards the darkroom.

Cody had the sense to understand that this was an act of kindness, and he embraced it with his whole soul. He spent a long time over the film, his eyes closed in the otherwise perfect blackness of the little room, trying not to see behind his eyelids the old images, the nightmare ones that were suddenly real again.

When he finished the film and couldn't think of any other good reason to stay in the dark, he opened the film room door. The dim safelights were almost too much for his eyes by then. He carried the wet films to the drying cabinet and clipped each one carefully to a hanger.

Mr. Allen was standing behind him.

"This came for you," he said, apologetically, and he handed Cody an office slip. "Why don't you just leave your books in the back and I'll watch them for you."

Cody held the little slip in his hand, his stomach gone clammy and his head tired. "I may not be back," he said. "I'd better take them."

"Well, okay," Mr. Allen said, and he put his hand on Cody's shoulder. "But just remember — we need you here."

236

He hadn't expected that, the kindness. It made things harder. Made his eyes sting. "Thanks," he said after a minute. And Allen gave him a pat, and then went back to his class.

They didn't keep him waiting long in the office.

"Miss Ellis will see you now," one of the front desk ladies said, almost the moment he'd sat down.

He'd been psyching himself all the way down from the lab. *She can't hurt you. They can't hurt you.* And it had done him a little good—brought him barely over the line, given him a little bit of a feeling of control.

He came up slowly on the office door, hearing voices. One of them, he began to understand, was his aunt's. And then he was there, standing in the doorway, one hand casually against the wall—holding him upright. The voices stopped, and the two women looked up at him.

It was all in Charlotte's face.

The world had come to an end.

23

For the moment, they were frozen in their places, Miss Ellis with her hands folded in prim self-righteousness, Charlotte with Cody's damning school folder spread open under her hand.

Then Miss Ellis raised an eyebrow. "Come in," she said, sterilely civil. "You may sit down."

Cody took a step inside the little office, but he was not going to sit down.

"Have you seen these?" Charlotte asked him, tapping the folder with the tip of her middle finger.

"No," he said.

She sat back, her lips tight. Her face was cold, except for two hot, flushed places over her cheeks. And her eyes had gone totally to coal; when she fixed them on him, they did him great harm.

"You'd better look at them," she said, her voice obviously controlled.

Miss Ellis closed the folder and held it out to him. It was distasteful to him, taking something from her hand, but he put his books down on the chair behind him and put his own hand out for the folder. He leaned back against the wall, knowing he looked much easier than he felt, and flipped the folder open. There were a number of computer forms in there, and several sheets of handwritten material.

The top section of papers was a collection of entries, all the grade school stuff, all the junior high—for each teacher, a long entry. Behind those was a high school report, a cumulative profile put together by the school psychologist. The last included a lot of personal material about his mother.

He scanned through it all—except the parts about his mother. It was very bad. Worse even than he'd expected. Turk hadn't mentioned half of it.

He closed the folder and put it back on the desk, his face held carefully, carefully empty.

Ellis opened the folder, going to the back pages. She began to read out loud, picking out single words.

"Violently antisocial." She glanced at Charlotte. "Gang mentality. Possible psychosis. Dangerous. Violent. Known to carry weapons—switch blade, zip gun—known to have been involved in violent gang activity. Known to have been involved in heavy vandalism. Numerous counts of suspected arson. Suspected of several violent acts, among them assault, battery, other felonies, possibly manslaughter. Recommendation: extreme caution. Police involvement."

Very, very bad. Almost funny.

Charlotte was looking at him.

"Manslaughter?" she asked, her eyes burning narrow and her voice on the edge.

"You have to ask me that?" he said, his own voice gone broken. She was pulling it all out of his soul.

"Evidently," she said.

He blinked and looked away from her, breathing out heavily. He'd expected this—but not honestly, not in the heart of him.

"Why didn't you tell me these things?" she asked.

"Why should I have told you these things?" he asked. "How did I know that these things were in here?"

"You lied to me," she said.

She might as well have spit on him.

He pulled himself in. Suddenly, he remembered a lot of things, a lot of cold hard things.

"I never lied to you," he said. He said it straight across, voice hoarse, but steady, adult. He was past appealing to her. He wasn't her child anymore. She didn't deserve that. Not now.

"You lied to *me*," Miss Ellis reminded him.

He turned a look on her — *Who are you?* — held it to chill out — then turned back to Charlotte. "I told you that I was going to be lying in here, from the beginning. I told you I'd been in trouble. I told you I'd been in fights. I told you I had no grades. Where was the lie in that?"

"You didn't tell me everything. You didn't tell me *this*." She picked up the folder and let it drop onto the desk.

"I didn't tell you," he repeated softly, deliberately, "every-thing."

"When did you say anything about fires?"

"You're right," he said, still quiet. "You're right, I didn't. I'll tell you, now. Everything. I was in fifth grade. You want to look at it? You just open the file — it'll be there. Fifth grade. Sternberg — you find that? College man, fresh on the inner city. Crusader, going to turn the bad kid around. Gonna look good on his record, isn't it? To turn around the kid nobody else could reach. Except he can't do it, because he's a fraud. Kid's not stupid. And that makes the guy mad, and the guy gives up the act and gives in to hating the kid."

Ellis had a sour look on. Charlotte's jaw was tight, teeth clenched, everything tight.

"So one day, the guy's finally had it. The truth comes out. In front of the whole class, the guy begins to lose it, and he yells: '*You're stupid. You* can't *do it. You're retarded.*' This he says in front of all the *peers*. Not pleasant. Not kind. The kid is em-barrassed. Understandable. The embarrassed kid is angry. And he sets fire to the guy's wastebasket on the way out to recess. Nobody could ever prove who'd done it. But the guy knew, and it made the record. And every year they read it. What does it say? Mentally retarded, right? Firestarter. And all those years after that, there *was* somebody setting fires. Not me. Never again after the wastebasket. But the arsonist never got caught. And so it went on my record."

Ice across Charlotte's fire. *Believe me or not. I never cared before you. I don't care now.*

"The test scores back Mr. Sternberg up," Miss Ellis said.

"What?" Charlotte said. It was an interruption; she was irritated by it.

"The I.Q. The Iowa."

Tests he'd trashed on purpose. Very satisfying at the time.

"*Aunt* Charlotte," he said, shutting the counselor out— speaking carefully, always quietly, but with a bitter edge. "The records are inaccurate. There was no gang for me. I didn't *fit.*"

"Did you ever do vandalism?" Miss Ellis asked, cutting into it.

"Yes," he said, looking at Charlotte.

"Did you carry a weapon?" Miss Ellis continued to ask. Cross examination.

"Yes," he said. It was ridiculous, the fat woman and her smug questions. He nearly smiled.

"A zip gun?"

"*What* is a zip gun?" Charlotte murmured.

"No."

"A knife then?"

"Yes."

"A switchblade knife." She said the last with satisfaction.

"Yes."

"Do you still carry it?"

He didn't answer.

Charlotte stared at him.

"Not in school," he said.

Charlotte made a small, unhappy noise and leaned her forehead against her hand.

"Then the records are actually *quite* accurate," Miss Ellis said, carrying her point.

"No," he said, looking at her, and not hiding a shade of the disgust he felt.

"At the very least," she said to Charlotte, "I recommend pulling him out of his present classes and putting him in the reclamation program."

"No," he said.

"The classes in which you are presently enrolled are beyond your ability," the woman said, patiently, reasonably.

"I lead my precalculus class," he said.

"The precalculus course is a top level college preparatory class. There is no way you could be leading it."

"I'm leading it."

"You want to explain to me, please, how a child with this record could reasonably expect to do as much as *pass* a course like that?"

240

"I do the work," he said, getting very weary of her.

"You do," she said, smiling to herself. "And how do you manage that without having had any of the preparatory training?"

"I've had the training," he said.

"Really. Perhaps they left that out of your record."

"He does the work," Charlotte said, dully.

"I'd assume there was cheating involved, Mrs. McClellan." The outrage came up on him, a beam of hot clarity.

"How could he be cheating and still lead the class?" Charlotte said, sounding tired of the whole thing.

"I've had the material before," he said. But his edge had slipped. Charlotte had just surprised him.

"When?" Ellis asked.

He looked at Charlotte, and he leaned back against the wall, considering. "There was a kid I knew," he said, going slowly, watching Charlotte's face. "His father was a surgeon, a famous one. They had *money*." He tore the word. *Money*. "He was crazy to get into med school. He was scared his father would kick him out if he didn't. But he couldn't cut the math. He just didn't have it. So he paid me to do it for him. So I did it. All the way through."

"You took his tests for him?" Miss Ellis asked. *Come on,* she was saying.

"It took some work," he said, allowing himself a tiny smile. It had taken some brilliant work.

"That was cheating," Charlotte said.

"It was a *job*," he said.

"It was cheating," Charlotte said again.

"You cheat when you let somebody else do the work for you. *He* was cheating. *I*," he finished, "was doing a job."

"The point is," Ellis said, "you don't belong in that class."

"The point is," Charlotte overrode her, "you didn't tell me the *truth*."

"I *did* tell you the truth. Everything that mattered. You didn't want to hear it. You saw what you wanted to see."

"The *truth*," she said, "is what I wanted."

"You want it now?" he asked, and he scoured himself for what he still remembered of his mother, all of it—the voice, the vocabulary, all the viciousness, and he fixed his eyes on Ellis's satisfied round face. "Did this woman tell you," pointing at Charlotte, "that her oldest son was involved in a shoplifting incident at a local Seven-Eleven? Within the last month."

Charlotte gasped.

241

"And did she explain to you that the same child is obsessed with guns? It's an unhealthy fixation—a proclivity to violence, perhaps bordering on psychosis."

"What are you doing?" Charlotte said.

"And did she tell you that she, herself, is considered by her neighbors to be an intolerant, antisocial reactivist? She interferes with other people's children; she disturbs the social fabric of the area." He turned to Charlotte, surprised. "You didn't tell her these things? I can't understand why you wouldn't have told her these things. I thought you were an honest woman."

"You're insolent," Ellis said.

Charlotte was breathing very hard.

"There's truth in it all, isn't there?" he asked her.

"We're having a little meeting this afternoon," Ellis was saying. "All of the teachers involved, and the administration. We're going to be deciding how to proceed with this boy. You're welcome to attend. You probably should be there."

Cody turned and picked up his books. He straightened up, nailing Miss Ellis with a look. "That's fine," he said coolly. "You go ahead and make your decisions. But understand this—this is *my* life you're talking about. And if you think I'm going to let you mess with it, lady, you're very wrong."

He turned around and left the room. Charlotte called after him, but he was gone. He found himself standing in the main hall, just standing there, out of breath and shaking, and maybe a little crazy. The bell rang. Maybe the last bell. It didn't matter which bell.

There was no way he was going back to the lab. He couldn't have done any intelligent work.

He didn't even stop at his locker—there was precious little reason to take work home at this point.

And precious little reason to go home. And nowhere else to go.

Except the car, at least, was his. His money. His car. He'd go get into it and see how far a tank of gas could take him.

24

"McClellan!"

Somebody called from behind him, from the edge of the parking lot. It must have been the last bell, because there were kids coming into the lot from all over. Cody turned around, walking the last little bit to his car half backwards.

"Wait up." It was Elise's Steven calling him.

Cody was not inclined to wait for him.

"Will you stop?" Steven trotted after him. Stopped when he got a couple of yards away. "I got to talk to you." Turk and a couple of guys coming up at his back.

"I thought you had a football game," Cody said, coldly.

"Yeah, well—we got to talk."

"Do we," Cody said, turned around, kept moving.

"McClellan," Steven said sharply.

Cody stopped, faced him, face set.

"I know what you were thinking this morning. But you were wrong."

"Was I."

"Yeah, you were."

Cody laughed, looking his contempt. "You keep nice company, don't you?" he said, lifting his chin at Turk and the others.

"That's not the point," Steven said. "The point is, you hammered Elise this morning." He was angry; now Cody could see it. Righteous. Mad.

"Yeah, well," Cody said bitterly, feeling the irony. "That's too bad."

"At least, you could have listened to her."

"I don't think I needed to do that," Cody said.

"That's the point. That's just what you needed to do. You were wrong about her, man. She's a good girl."

"She's still a good girl," Cody said, biting off the words. "You have her back intact, if that's what's eating you—" He started towards the car again.

"You're stupider than you look," Steven spat.

"Really," Cody said, turning back for the third time, this time the last time. He'd finally taken enough.

"Yeah, really. You think that girl would dump you because of that trash this morning? You're crazy. She *likes* you, man. She doesn't listen to stuff like that. She was trying to tell you. That was garbage to her, *man*. She was trying to tell you that everything's still fine, but you might as well have slapped her in the face. You're a fool. And if you ever hurt her like that again, I'll kill you."

"And get kicked off the team?" Cody said, mock worry.

"You're a jerk."

"Come tell me about it."

And Steven did. He crossed the space between them, and he shoved Cody — something he shouldn't have done. Cody moved into it.

"A teacher," somebody hissed.

Steven pulled himself up short, and he and Cody glared at each other.

"Another time," Steven promised, turning away.

"Name the place," Cody said, but he didn't like the timing. The whole interchange hadn't been good for him, off balance from the beginning.

He turned around, unlocked the car, and slid into the seat. He shoved the keys into the ignition, and then he finally heard what Steven had been telling him. *It didn't matter to her.* He sat there, his hand on the keys a little shaky with reaction, going back over what had happened. Thinking about what Steven had said.

He closed his eyes and went dead inside.

Is there anything in your life that you haven't trashed?

He turned the keys and gunned the engine, let it settle, and then — pulled back carefully out of the parking space, and out into the driveway into the street. If he'd had another kind of car, he'd have been tempted to do another kind of driving. He was gentler with the little bug than he wanted to be with himself.

So Steven had taken away the purity of his wounds. He couldn't even be legitimately hurt. Charlotte and the family, Elise, his mother — more guilt than he knew how to handle. He was driving around the streets aimlessly, tired, tired to death of everything.

And it grew inside him, to wonder if he had the courage to step out of it, once and for all. Not a decision. But part of one. Trying to figure out a way that wouldn't hurt anybody else, not make a mess for anybody. A rest. An end to it. Absolutely serious about it, for the first time in his life.

There was a white Thunderbird in his rearview mirror. It had been there for a while. Following him. Special order factory paint. Arrogant. He squinted into the mirror. Turk's car. Turk and friends. Following him with a reason.

Cody made another turn.

He took another look in the mirror, expecting to see Steven with them. But he wasn't there. It made pain inside of him—pain for Elise, and for Cody—that Steven had no more honor than to send his friends out to take care of his enemy for him. It was an unexpected grief.

He'd made his way into a quiet little residential area—tiny brick houses, all in a line; old trees, bright little gardens; cars parked all along the curb. Turk followed him there.

Cody chose his place, pulling up so he was double parked, making it a little awkward for them, a little public. He leaned over the passenger seat, flipping open the glove box. He had his hand on the knife when he made the decision to leave it where it was. *If you take it now, somebody's going to die.* "It's going to happen anyway," he muttered, leaving the knife where it was. He put the camera down on the floor, out of sight, and closed the glove box.

When he sat up, he knew he wasn't even going to fight.

Whatever else happened, he was out of it. He didn't care what they did.

He opened the door of his car as the Thunderbird pulled up behind him. He pulled himself out of the seat, keeping his movements easy and slow. There was an old lady on her hands and knees, working a flower bed, the leaves of a maple tree, scarlet-rimmed, dancing in the air over her head. She looked up at him and smiled. All he could hear was the pulsing of his heart.

The doors of the white car opened. He locked his car, thinking about the camera, and then he went around the front of his car to the street side and waited for them.

There were four of them.

He watched them coming. He was calm now, and almost quiet inside. Three of them came on, no mistake about what they had in their faces; they'd worked themselves up to this. But the last one was hanging back. "I don't like this," he was saying.

When they got close, Cody said, very quietly, "You got a problem?"

Turk slammed his fist into Cody's gut, just below the stomach. Not totally unexpected, but it had come quicker than Cody'd thought—no talk first, no prelude. The pain immobilized him, doubled him over; that did surprise him—he hadn't been set for it, not quite ready. And the raw violence of it shocked him.

From the first moment, he realized that Turk didn't know fighting; there was no ritual to this—it was hate, undiluted violence, no control. Ignorance. Very, very dangerous. And Cody knew then, he could be a dead man in ten minutes, easy, without them ever meaning to take it that far.

It was only what he'd been thinking he wanted. They were handing it to him, no responsibility, no worries.

But he didn't want it anymore.

He heard the old lady shout from her yard.

They straightened him up and he saw Turk move. The knee came up like a pike between Cody's legs and he was bent over again, sick to his stomach, almost out of his head with the pain. A fist came up under him, and they knocked him over with it. He almost didn't catch himself with his hands; he almost hit the asphalt full on his face.

He heard shouting, yelling, but it was all far away from him by then. He could feel it when they kicked at his side, but there was nothing significant about it.

And then it was quiet. Quiet for a long time.

He heard somebody crying.

It was a sad sound. He thought it might be the lady with the trowel, and he was sorry about that. Or it could have been Elise, because of what he'd said to her. It never crossed his mind until he knew for sure—it might be Cody, crying. But that's who it was.

The sun was on his face, too bright to stand. Everything very quiet. And then one voice talking: " . . . some damage," it said. "We'll look at the pictures."

And then he had to worry about the camera—if they'd taken that, too.

Something stung his face. He reacted to it, jerking away, striking at the place.

"We've got company," somebody warned, and they held his wrists. No more martyrdom—but he couldn't break the hold they had on him.

"What's his first name?" the voice was asking. "Cody. Cody, listen. You're all right, Cody." Over and over. Soothing. "You're all right now, okay? Nobody's going to hurt you now, okay? Come on, Cody. Let go. This is a safe place for you, Cody. Come on."

His mind was coming up out of the dark.

"That's right," she said, almost crooning. "Just relax. Just relax."

He sighed. It came out a sob. He relaxed his hands.

"That's good," she said, and put his arms down, gently. He didn't know where he was. But he knew he was hurt. He tried to open his eyes.

"You're going to have to wait just a minute, honey," she said. "Let me get you a little bit cleaned off here. This is going to sting." It was the truth. "Shhh," she said when he moved.

His head was throbbing.

"Where am I?" he tried to say, knowing he wasn't outside anymore. But his face wasn't moving the way it should, and he slurred the words.

"Holy Cross," she said, understanding him. "Your aunt's here."

He groaned.

"Let's try opening those eyes again, Cody. Can you do that?"

He tried. There was something clouding his eyes, and he couldn't see out of them properly, couldn't clear them; there was only the whiteness of the room, only the blurred light. He tried to blink, meant to rub his eyes, but she caught his hands on the way there.

"I can't see," he said

"Your eyes are swollen," she told him. "We don't want to touch them for a while. Understand? Just rest. This is going to sting again."

"Don't," he said. But she went ahead anyway.

"We've got to get you stitched up here, kiddo," she said, and she stung him again.

Tears were coming out of his eyes. They burned. He was too tired to fight them. He relaxed enough to let the dizziness float him for a while, until it made him sick to his stomach.

"Sit up, now," she said, helping. "If you can."

"No skull damage," the doctor was saying. "We've been very, very lucky. We've got some bruising through here, so we'll have to be careful with those ribs. But there's no serious internal damage. If it had gone on much longer, or if he'd been any less healthy a kid than he is, we could have had some real problems. As it is . . ." and it went on, at some points becoming distressingly embarrassing.

" . . . mostly severe bruising." The doctor finished. "You can bet he's going to be sore for a while."

Cody got his eyes open enough to see something of the room; Charlotte was standing next to the doctor.

"You can come in," the doctor said, and there were two policemen coming through the door. Cody had an instant fight or flight that nearly made him faint.

"They only need a statement," the nurse was saying, her hand on the small of his back. He'd been shaking anyway, shivering all over. It was worse, now. They only wanted to know who'd done it. He couldn't tell them; there were rules about that. His teeth were chattering.

And so they finally left, and the doctor left, and Cody would have thrown up if there'd been anything in his stomach.

"What happened?" Charlotte asked him, sitting across the room, watching it all, sounding tired but still angry. The shivering got worse. The nurse was wrapping his ribs, and the room was cold.

"Get him into some sweat pants when you get home," the nurse said. "This should heal up in no time if you keep him quiet."

"My classmates don't like me much," he said, going for wry. His lips were too swollen. The talking hurt, and the words didn't sound like much.

"This kind of thing doesn't just happen, Cody," Charlotte said. "You must have done something to bring this on."

He looked at her. She flinched, looking back at him. He couldn't answer her. He just sat there with the tears coming down his lumpy face.

"Oh, Cody," she said. "You're asking me to believe you just stood there, and somebody just *did* this to you. You didn't have anything to do with it. You didn't even defend yourself."

The nurse, still busy, spoke. "He didn't hit anybody, Mrs. McClellan," she said. "If he had, we could see it on his hands. If he'd had a weapon, he wouldn't be looking like this—unless they'd picked up somebody else, looking worse."

Charlotte blinked at him. "He doesn't need to hit anybody to start something," she said. "He just needs to open his mouth." Her jaw tightened, and she glanced away from him. "Why did you let this happen?" she asked. "Couldn't you have stopped it?"

She was crying, his aunt.

"You didn't want me to fight," he said.

She looked away, her hand over her mouth, and she sat there silently for several minutes. "I'll be back," she said to the nurse, and she got up and she left.

"Okay," the nurse said. "Lie back here. As long as she's gone, we might as well get down to business."

He stared at the ceiling, trying not to think about what she was doing, lying quietly.

"You're doing fine," she said. "You're a good, reasonable patient. But I'm thinking maybe you let them beat more than your face. Aren't you angry? If somebody tried to do this to me, I'd have a good piece of 'em before it was over. If somebody gave my kid this kind of beating—" She pressed her lips together, hard. "The police just wanted to know who did this."

He sighed again.

"Why would you let them do this to you?" she asked him. "I really want to know."

"I had to," he said.

"Why?" She cut a piece of sterile gauze, and began to fold it.

"My reputation. It's bad. If I'd hit anybody, they would have put me away." His chest and his arms had gone heavy. His eyes were still burning, the tears running down his face into his ears. There was a place on his cheek that was throbbing.

After a while, Charlotte came back in and sat down.

"Mr. Allen is going to find somebody else to shoot that dance tonight," she said. "He said to tell you he hopes you feel okay. He was sorry. 'Next time,' he said."

The sound that came out of him had started off to be a laugh.

"You need some rest," the nurse said to him. And then to Charlotte, "More than his body needs a rest, if things are going to mend." And she handed Charlotte a small stack of prescription forms. "Talk to the doctor before you leave."

Cody sat on his side of the car, silent, his forehead against the glass of his window, staring out through it absently as she drove him home. He hadn't really expected to go back there again, back to the house. It made a little well of pain inside him, thinking about it.

They'd given him a couple of pills at the hospital. He was a little fuzzy brained because of them, and very slow.

She was driving through an area he didn't know. It disoriented him. And then she stopped the car, and he was totally confused. She'd pulled up in front of a little park he'd never seen before.

He swallowed, and sat quietly, shifting his head to find a cooler place on the glass. He closed his eyes and drifted.

"I owe you an apology," Charlotte finally said. Her voice was husky.

He shifted again against the window, a little dull surprise getting through. He didn't have the energy to figure out what she was saying.

"Erin was right about me. I wasn't being fair to you. This is my fault. This whole thing."

"Not the whole thing," he said, tried to say through his hurt lips. After it came out, it didn't seem like the right thing to have said.

"I didn't—" she sighed. "Maybe I could take only just so much of you at one time," she said. "Maybe . . . I'm just not . . ."

"It's all right," he said, because he had to say something, because she was asking him to do too much.

"It's *not* all right," she said. "How could it be all right?" She took in a sharp breath. He turned his head to look at her. She was staring out of the windshield.

"You've been really a good kid," she said brokenly. "I really do care about you. I know it must not seem like it." She glanced at him, caught him watching her, couldn't maintain the contact. "I don't know. I just—when I saw those records, I guess I just felt conned. Like you'd been running a con on me all these weeks."

"I'm not that good," he said. The slurring was worse now, with the pills.

"I just got mad, that's all. And it scared me. But I should have been better than that. I should have stood up for you."

"You don't know me," he said.

She was quiet. Then she touched the wheel with the tip of one finger.

"By now, I should know you better than I do, you're right."

And maybe that was true.

"I'm just a kid," he said. "I'm stupid, and I make mistakes. I don't know . . . obviously, I could be better."

"There was nobody on your side," she said.

"Mr. Allen," he offered. "Ms. Hunsaker."

But that didn't seem to make her feel any better. He was thinking he should be enjoying this more, that his pride should like it. But his head still hurt, and he didn't like it that she was feeling so bad.

"How did you know where I was?" he asked, making an effort to be lucid.

"They called me from the hospital. They must have run your plates or something."

"I thought you were supposed to be at a meeting."

"I didn't go. I went home."

"Oh," he said. There were some kids in the park, playing with a big black dog. "How come?"

She didn't answer for a while. The black dog was jumping in and out of an irrigation ditch that ran through the lawn. It was almost dark.

"I was afraid you'd go home and get your stuff and leave," she said.

"You thought I'd hurt the kids."

"No," she said, quickly, absolutely. "I never thought that."

"That's good," he said. He was all collapsed against the door.

The dog was gone.

"You really have a knife?" she said.

"Yeah," he sighed. "I do."

She moaned.

"It's okay," he said. "I cut cheese with it."

"Oh, Cody," she said.

"Erin keeps it for me," he said.

"He does?"

"Well, he did."

"He did?"

"Yeah." *Shouldn't that make it better?*

She was straight arming the steering wheel. "He didn't tell me," she said.

"He didn't think you'd like it."

She pulled a breath in between her teeth.

"He didn't, huh?"

"He makes mistakes, too, he said."

"He did. Well, he's right about that. Did he know about all of this?"

"About—"

"About what was in the records?"

"*I* didn't know what was in the records. I mean, not specifically." Interesting, the way that last word came out.

"So, he didn't know."

"He didn't know anything."

"That's good," she said grimly. She shook her head. "See, I get mad at him, too. Just because you love somebody doesn't mean you don't get mad at him."

"You haven't been mad at me before this," he said.

She looked at him.

"You never yell at me."

"I don't?"

He started to shake his head. But he changed his mind. "No," he said. "You never do. But you yell at Sawyer a lot."

"So, I guess that makes you feel like a guest, huh?" she said, after a minute.

"Kind of."

"That's not what we want, is it?"

"I don't know," he said.

"You need a mom, huh?" she said, more to herself than to him. "Or a friend, at least. Maybe you need me to butt out."

It was dark now.

"For sure, you need to go home," she said, and she started the car. But she didn't put it in gear. "Will you stay with us still?" she asked him. "Can we give it another chance? There aren't any more little surprises, are there? You don't have any, like, crimes or little kids around I don't know about?"

"No," he said. "No little kids. No crimes. Just spray paint and bricks. But I gave that up."

"Okay," she said. "So—we start over? We both start over?"

"Fine," he said. His voice was almost gone. "Yes. Okay?"

"And that knife?"

"I'll give it back to Erin."

"Is that the best you can do?"

"Yes, ma'am," he said, going adrift again. "Please."

"Okay," she said, took a breath, blew it out and up so that it made the hair over her forehead bounce. And then she backed the car out into the street. "La'chaim," she said, and headed homeward.

Just after supper, Elise went out to fetch her father the evening paper. The sun had only then gone down, and the whole sky full of clouds was lit up from underneath, billowing crimson and vermillion with green sky behind. The color took her by surprise, and she stood, holding the screen door, watching it.

It had not been an easy day.

The color began to ebb out, the clouds at the top going shadowed and dark. She let the door swing shut and bounced down the porch steps, hand lightly on the rail, her mind elsewhere and her spirit coveting a kind of color that wasn't so fragile.

The paper was halfway down the walk. As she bent over to pick it up, she realized there was somebody standing on the sidewalk—watching her, she thought. She straightened up, the paper in her hand, and half turned, glancing back over her shoulder.

He *was* watching—a boy, somebody Steven's size, but not Steven. She smiled politely, an apology for having looked at him at all, and maybe a reproach for his watching. Then she did a double take—his face. His eyes were swollen shut, everything else on it dark and bruised and horrible to look at.

It scared her. She started up the walk, deeply ashamed that she'd stared at him.

Then she stopped, her heart beating very hard. She turned slowly and looked at him again. Recognized the shirt and the hair—

"Cody?" she said. Not real. *What if it's not him? What if it is him?*

The boy didn't move. And by his silence, she knew him, and she came to him. "What *happened*? Did you wreck the car?" Her heart was slamming.

"My aunt gave me five minutes to talk to you," he said. He sounded very dozy, and he could hardly move his mouth. Hard to understand. "I'm supposed to be home in bed."

"What—"

He held up his hand, and when she stopped, he dropped it back down by his side. "I just wanted to tell you. I'm sorry about this morning. I'm sorry I misunderstood. I didn't mean to hurt you." He paused, closing his poor eyes. "I never mean that."

"I didn't mean to hurt you, either," she said, unhappy to be standing here apart like this, hungry to understand him, to put a hand on him at least. "I was mad at you," she added, because she had to.

"I know. I'm sorry about tonight. About the dance."

"What happened?" she asked him again. "Aren't you going to tell me what happened?"

"No," he said. "I've got to go." He turned around and sort of lurched away. She saw the McClellans' car by the curb. Cody's aunt got out and helped him get in.

"Call tomorrow," Mrs. McClellan told her, calling softly across the sidewalk. "I'll explain it. I've got to get him home now."

"Where's the paper?" her dad asked from the front door.

"Okay," she called to Mrs. McClellan, and then, over her shoulder. "I'm coming, Dad." The McClellans did a U-turn and drove off down the street. Elise stood there watching them, feeling as if she'd just lost her soul.

25

It was a timid knock. He wasn't sure he'd heard it at first, then it came again, dragging him up out of his sleep. He rolled off his side onto his back, groaning. Everything had stiffened up.

"Come in," he croaked.

The door came open slowly, and Mickey came creeping in.

"What time is it?" he asked her. *What day is it?*

"Seven-thirty," she said. "We just got through with dinner." It had seemed later.

"Same day?" he asked.

"Same day as what?"

"As before."

She screwed up her face and looked at him. "As before what?"

"Is it Friday?"

"Yeah, it's Friday." *Idiot.*

"So whatcha need?" he said, ignoring her tone, trying not to move any incidental parts of his face.

"Were you asleep?" she asked, looking a little uncomfortable.

He made a sound deep in his throat, trying to clear it. "Kind of," he said in a half whisper. His eyes kept closing on him.

"Elise called," she said. "We're all invited over there tomorrow for the last barbecue."

"Mmmm," he said. Not interesting.

"I wanted to ask you—" she said. "Can I ask you something?"

"Sure," he said. The word came out of him like air out of a cushion, and he groaned softly as he tried to come up on his side. He was trying to be polite, trying to give her his attention. She perched herself on Sawyer's chair, drawing her feet up, just out of his easy line of sight.

"You look so gross," she said, curling one hand up under her chin. "I never saw anything like that before. I hate looking at you." Not that she wasn't looking.

"Well, thanks," he sighed. "What do you want to ask?"

Then she got awkward, and her question wouldn't come out. "Why," she said, finally settling on a tack, "would somebody want to beat you up?"

"They don't like me," he said, with something like a sleepy laugh. "Very simple."

"That's what I thought." She started fiddling with the things on Sawyer's desk. "Don't you hate it when people don't like you?"

"When they do stuff like this, I hate it," he said. "Otherwise, I don't really care."

"You don't?"

"No."

She put her hands in her lap.

"Do you?" he asked, going for the obvious.

"Why don't they like you?" she asked him.

"I don't know," he said. "They don't know me. Sometimes that's all it takes. Or maybe I have something they want. It doesn't take much for people like that."

"Don't you wish they'd like you?"

"Those guys? Guys like that?" He shook his head gently. "Not especially."

"Just so they'd leave you alone." It was finally coming through his muddled brain; she was here for a reason. She'd come for something. Philosophy, maybe. Not his strong suit. So he answered carefully.

"If I had to be *like* them to get them to leave me alone— *huh-uh.* Not worth it. If they don't like what I am, fine. They don't have to like it."

"But then, what if you don't have any friends?"

"Does that matter?"

"To some people," she said.

"You only got to please yourself and your God, Mickey," he said. "If you don't please yourself, it doesn't matter how many friends you think you have. You don't have any."

She was chewing on her bottom lip. "What if you hate being the goat?"

"I don't know," he said, sighing. "Maybe after a while, you just get used to it."

"Are you used to it?"

"Am I?" He laughed. "No."

"So, what if you can't?" she said. "What if you *have* to have friends?"

"Friends are like family, Mickey. They take you for what you are. You don't *buy* them. If you have to buy them, they're not worth what you've paid."

"They beat you up," she said, a little desperation in it.

"They always do," he said, "one way or another. And they do it to each other. You're never safe with them, no matter where you stand."

"So, what do you do?" she asked.

"I don't know," he said, because he didn't. "But sooner or later, you've got to just *be* what you are. Or else eventually you're gonna die inside. You can always try to be better—you can cooperate with people. You can try to get along. But to make yourself be *different* . . . it doesn't go, you know? It doesn't make you happy."

She slid off the chair. "Nothing does that," she said.

"Being loved could do that," he said, with a little twist in his heart.

"That's what we've been talking about," she said.

"No we weren't," he said. "That's a whole different thing."

Charlotte was calling Mickey, looking for her downstairs.

"It's not like you have a lot of answers, you know," she said.

And then he did smile. "Well, you're right about that."

She sighed and gave him a mildly disgusted look. Charlotte was calling again. "I'm not supposed to be in here," Mickey said, and then she was gone.

The last thing he'd expected to be doing next evening was going to anybody's barbecue. And the last thing he was expecting to see in Elise's backyard was Steven's face. But that's the way it happened, and that was what he saw.

Elise's mother had met them all out in front, walked them through the house and out onto the deck. There was a volleyball net set up in back, and there were a dozen kids running around it. Sawyer and Tyler were down there like a shot, and Mickey only a minute after them.

Cody, limping along behind everybody else, didn't actually see Steven until Elise had very gently installed him in a chaise lounge on the deck. She stood there by the chair, smiling down at him—maybe a little nervously, which made sense, considering—and that's when he saw Steven down on the lawn, going up for a ball, right into the net. It was a bit of an unpleasant shock.

Cody took one long, disbelieving look at Steven, then he turned the same look on Elise. But she wouldn't go guilty for him. So now he was cross and sullen besides being cross and sore, and he settled himself into the lounge. He wouldn't look at her, and he wouldn't talk to her.

"Fine," she said, and she vaulted over the deck rail down onto the lawn.

"*Elise*," her mother said, giving her the don't-do-it-again eye. And then Mrs. McCall sat down to begin a comfortable complaint about the stresses of child rearing, Charlotte as sympathetic audience.

Nobody paid any attention to Cody after that. Not for a long time. There was the murmured conversation of the women as they passed between the deck and the kitchen, and the brighter, louder laughter of the men, all blended in a wash of the wild children's voices.

After a while, Cody stopped scowling at the volleyball game. The pills wouldn't let him focus himself on anything too long, and he began to drift. It was a hazy afternoon. The tops of the trees in the yard, a forest of massive, fragmented umbrellas, were laced with tiny, shifting shafts of dusty light, leaves just turning with the cold nights, a touch of color here and there, just enough to keep you from being sure what it was you were seeing.

Cody squinted into the light, dreaming leaves, until his eyes ceased to focus and he fell into what were only the textures of the time—smells and sounds and colors, lulled by the dancing of those needle shafts of light.

". . . have to go?" someone was saying close by.

"I've got practice." Even closer. Cody came swimming up out of his dream and pulled himself straighter in his chair, hand going to the corner of his mouth. The simple shift of his weight had made him dizzy.

He opened his eyes and found Steven, squatting down by the foot of the lounge, closer than Cody had expected anybody to be, almost too close for focus. He got an adrenaline rush from that, but his body had no patience with it.

Steven crinkled up his own face, grimacing at Cody's. "Looks bad," he said.

"Thanks," Cody said flatly; there was that slight slur. He hated the disadvantage.

"Look," Steven said, his voice low, private, "I think we understand each other pretty well. I'd just as soon you'd never come here in the first place, and I think you know why." His eyes travelled over Cody's face. "But none of my *friends* would ever do a thing like this—not to anybody." He grinned. "Not even to you."

He took something out of his pocket and tossed it into Cody's lap. And then he sobered. "I'm pretty sure I know who did this," he said, getting up. "They're going to pay for it."

And then he was gone.

Cody felt around in his lap until he found Steven's gift. He held it up where he could see it—a pair of mirrored shades. He held them for a moment, going very thoughtful inside. And then he did a little private smile, tapping the glasses against the palm of one hand. He pulled the ear pieces out and studied them, wondering if he could get the things on without ripping his face up.

"That's a good idea," Charlotte said, her voice carrying across the deck. "Why didn't I think of that?"

He glanced over at her, but it wasn't Cody she was talking to.

He slid the glasses on, carefully, shifting them around until they fit into the least sore places.

"Okay," Dr. McCall sang, sitting down on the deck steps with a guitar in his lap. "Who wants a song?"

"I do! I do!" the kids shouted as they jostled each other, racing from the net to the steps and settling around the doctor's feet.

"The Fox Song," one of the kids yelled.

"The Bells."

"Swing Low."

The doctor started to play.

"That's not the one I said," a small girl hollered, offended.

"Will you guys knock it off, please?" the doctor said, glaring at them over the guitar. "Are we going to sing here, or what?"

"We're going to *sing*," Tyler shouted happily.

The doctor started a song, and the children followed him, roaring in the choruses. Cody closed his eyes behind the shades, let himself slip again, adrift in the silver voice of the guitar, and the little silvery colors that were the children—all of it woven peacefully around with the salty smoke of charred hamburgers and gray charcoal.

26

Cody wore the shades to school his first morning back at school. The swelling was down, but the bruises were ugly, and the abrasions looked almost worse. He *felt* worse, stiff and sore, and his stitches itched. And off balance, not sure where he stood with anybody, embarrassed—not sure how to proceed. He got to school early, more comfortable with empty halls than with the thought of company.

By the time Marty came in, Cody was safe at his own desk, shades on, doing some reading.

"Let me see it," Marty said, dropping his books on the desk.

Cody looked up at him, startled.

"Your face—" Marty got one knee onto his own seat and leaned down to get a good look at Cody. He flinched, even before Cody took the glasses off for him. "I didn't think it was going to be that bad."

"That's not half of it," Cody said, working the shades back on. "So, how did you hear?"

"My dad went out on the call."

"Your dad."

"My dad's a cop. He was out there when they picked you up. He's the one who called your mother."

"He also took the statements," Marty said, looking at Cody curiously. "I never would have stopped my car in the first place. I would have driven straight into the garage at the city building."

"Where the cops hang out," Cody guessed.

"You got it."

Cody could just see himself doing that.

"He said you wouldn't tell them who did it."

Cody didn't answer.

"You should have told him. I could tell him — it's not that hard to figure out. Those guys don't deserve that kind of courtesy."

Cody shrugged.

"You got guts, Cody," Marty said, and he sat down and started stowing his books away.

Cody went back to his book, waiting for Elise to come in. He wasn't comfortable about her; he wasn't sure what she was thinking, now — it wasn't as if they'd had a lot of chance to talk. The room was filling up. The story had evidently gotten around; the first thing anybody looked for when they came in was Cody's face.

As kingfishers catch fire — he was reading, keeping to himself — *dragonflies draw flames; As tumbled over rim in roundy wells/Stones ring; like each tucked string tells, each hung bell's* —

There was the sudden, explosive sound of a big book slammed flat against the floor. Cody jumped. Everybody jumped.

Turk was standing next to Cody's desk, smirking. He'd dropped the book there — no accident, of course. Making a point.

Cody considered, quietly working out the costs, the ramifications, of a reaction. He was too angry to let the thing go; it was a deep anger — he wanted Tourquey very badly. But that was a shame to him: from here on out, it would be too easy — Cody knew the difference between them, knew what he could do to a coward like this. Revenge was too cheap a shot.

So he pulled back, holding a hard line on himself. Ending the thing was as far as he was going to go. Now, out of simple courtesy, he did what he would have done for anybody who'd really dropped a book — he bent over and picked it up.

"That's very *good*," Turk said.

The room had gone silent.

You want to die, Cody said to him silently.

"You're really not so bad a guy, huh? That's a nasty looking accident you had there, my man. We wouldn't want that to happen to you again." Another smirk, and the Turk swaggered down to his seat.

They were all waiting.

Marty was waiting.

"I wouldn't worry about that," Cody said quietly, the line slipping.

I'm no saint.

Turk's books went down hard on his desk. "I don't think I heard you?" he said.

"Shut up, Tourquey," somebody said. Steven, just coming in the door. "Sit down. Keep your mouth shut." Nothing passed between Cody and Steven, not a look. Steven just went back to his seat and sat down.

Elise still hadn't come in.

"You better watch yourself, McClellan, my man," Tourquey hissed a heartbeat after. There was bravado in it, to make up for what Steven had just done. He was backed up into it now.

Cody took his time, turning around carefully in his seat, mindful of the ribs—one arm along the back of the chair. He wasn't going to let Steven run interference for him. And now he had a clear view of the Turk; nobody got in the way.

"It's over, Tourquey," Cody said, still quietly. Not going to threats. Not going for theatrics. "It was the first time. It was the last time."

Said gently, it was still a slap in the face. Tourquey glanced around the room and found no way out. Everyone waiting.

"You're a dead man, McClellan," he spat finally. And maybe he thought he meant it.

"That's true," Cody said. He took off the glasses so they could all see his face, and he spoke very softly. "It's been that way a long time." He had Tourquey's eyes now. "I haven't got a lot left to lose." He held Turk's eyes just a moment longer. Then he put the glasses back on and turned back into his own place.

For a moment, nobody moved.

And then somebody started it, "ooooooooOOOOOoooo—" Tension broken. It was hilarious bedlam, definitely swinging around on Cody's side. It made him very uncomfortable.

"You want to tell me what's going on?" Ms. Hunsaker said, standing in the doorway with a bunch of papers on her arm. She

261

started across to her desk, and then she caught sight of Cody. At first, she was amused—seeing only the glasses. Then she saw the rest, and they all watched the color drain out of her face. The laughter faded unevenly. She took a quick, canny look around the room, the end of it resting on Cody.

"Well, okay," she said into the silence. "I have your papers."

They pulled him out of class again, right in the middle of the lecture. Ms. Hunsaker took the pass from the runner and then handed it to Cody. She gave him a little smile with it, just for himself. *Good luck. You'll be okay.* All the way down to the office, he was wondering if she'd made him a promise.

The ladies in the office sent him straight back to counseling, this time to a different office. They were nice about it. He slipped past Miss Ellis's door, trying not to be as nervous as he was.

He found the right office. The door was standing open, and he could see the woman at the desk—short, curly gray hair; thin face; businesslike, nothing soft. She was studying a student folder.

He didn't want to go in.

She looked up and saw him standing there, gave him a professional smile. "Come in, Mr. McClellan," she said, not unkindly. "Please sit down."

He did as he was told. Poised at the very edge of the chair.

She was studying his face. No flinch, no grimace in hers.

"I'd like you to take the glasses off," she said. "If you can."

He took them off.

"Thank you," she said. "I don't feel like I'm communicating unless I can see your whole face." She pulled a single sheet out of the folder, closed the cover, and set the bulk of it to the side. The paper she placed where she could see it, and then she folded her hands on the desk, and looked at him. It had been his folder.

"You would like to know what happened in the meeting Friday," she said.

She waited for him to answer. "Yes, ma'am," he said, embarrassed. Very nervous now.

"You know that Miss Ellis was fairly adamant that you should be removed from your present program."

"Yes, ma'am."

"As it turns out, there's very little support for that in any quarter." She was looking straight across at Cody, no patronizing—one adult to another, as though she believed he had dignity.

"There are some things you need to understand before we go on." He lifted his chin. "What you did with Miss Ellis is inexcusable."

He bit back his argument. "Yes, ma'am," he said again, and saw a certain wry amusement in her eyes.

She touched the piece of paper lying in front of her. "I'm going to tell you some of the things that were said at that meeting. I think you have a right to that."

He waited.

"There are no complaints about your behavior here. The general feeling is that you deport yourself as an educated person should, that you take your work seriously, that you are disciplined. Several teachers mentioned that you are aggressive in your thinking—not at all shy about your opinions, and suggest that you have a tendency towards—shall we say—ideological perversity. That you're an iconoclast. You know the word?"

He shook his head.

"It means that you have little reverence for what most people view as the acceptable status quo. It means you're thinking, actually. That can be very wearing for a teacher with thirty-five other students to worry about. But it can also be refreshing, depending on the teacher. I think they were all a little shocked by the severity of the report—but you have to remember, these people are professional teachers; they understand how these reports are sometimes built. Miss Ellis explained to them that you're a runaway. I think that impressed them—that your presence here is strictly of your own doing. Generally, I think I can tell you, they like you very much. They were disinclined to give the report much credence."

She picked up the paper. "You might like to know—your strongest supporter was Mrs. Bruecher."

Surprising, yes.

"Miss Ellis had suggested that your grades were the result of cheating. Mrs. Bruecher made it clear she didn't agree." There was a thoughtful pause. "I'm going to tell you what she said, because I think she was right. But I want you to be careful about how you listen to this. I want you to understand it the way she meant it."

He nodded slightly.

"In her view, you're a child trapped in the weakness of an adult system—she feels that you've been dealing with it as well

263

as you know how, with the tools you've had. Further, she felt that you shouldn't suffer any more for that at this point, and that was generally agreed. As far as this school is concerned, you'll be judged only on present merits."

He sighed and bit his bottom lip. And then he sat back into the chair, and closed his eyes.

"It's been hard, I know," she said, the voice a little softer. "That does not, however, excuse you from lying." Softness gone. "Lying is immoral, Cody. Do you understand that?"

He understood that it was a legitimate question.

"Yes, I do," he said.

"As strange as this world has gotten to be, there's still a remarkable amount of trust going on in it. You made an enemy out of Miss Ellis because you won her over, and then you betrayed her. She has a right to be angry. You sacrificed her dignity for your second chance."

He dropped his eyes. What she was saying was true—he'd known it all along. Still, given the chance to play it all again, he'd have done it the same way. He wasn't proud of that, but he understood it, and he accepted it. This woman wouldn't. Still, he thought she was trying to be fair—

"They're going to push you hard after this. You know that. You're a curiosity for them, a challenge."

What's new?

"Evidently, you're very bright. You know that, too."

"No, ma'am," he said. "I only suspected."

She bent down a sudden smile, aiming it at the paper she still had under her hand. But she recovered from that. "From this point on," she said, "I'll be your counselor. It's too bad it wasn't that way from the beginning. I think we might have understood one another. At any rate, if you should have any problems—family, school, whatever—you're welcome here. Believe me, McClellan, we want to see you succeed, and we'll do everything we can to help you to that end. I don't suspect we're all that different from your old schools in that regard. I think you'll realize the difference is in you, if you'll give it some thought."

She handed him his pass.

"One more thing, McClellan," she said as he stood up. "There will be no excuses made here for you because of all this. You pull your weight. You stay out of trouble."

"I never intended to make trouble here," he said.

She smiled. "I know," she said.

And then he smiled at her.

"Thank you," he said.

"You're late to class," she told him, making it just dry enough that he could feel comfortable about coming back.

"I gotta *talk* to you," Marty said, catching him out in the hall outside the locker room. *"Now."*

"What?" Cody asked, following Marty into the locker room. It was empty; everybody else was already out on the floor. "You're late," Cody said. "Coach is going to kill you for being late."

"No, he won't. Anyway, I'm not going to be that late. I just have to get changed." He was on the way to his locker, way in the back. He sat down on the bench and took off his shoes.

"They really beat the daylights out of you," Marty said, watching Cody ease himself down the aisle.

"It's not the first time somebody's done that," Cody said, thinking about sitting down.

"I know," Marty said, peeling off his socks.

No surprise, there—locker room intimacy, not as if you could hide your scars. The whole thing made Cody tired. "Maybe I shouldn't have come today," he said, pulling a face as he settled on the bench.

"Maybe you shouldn't have," Marty agreed.

Cody looked at him. Marty threw him an inscrutable look and threw his shoes and socks into the locker.

"What?" Cody asked. *What now?*

"Have you seen Elise today?" Marty asked him, starting on his shirt.

"She isn't here today," Cody said.

"Oh, she's here."

"Oh, yeah?" A little dread coming on. Weariness of it.

"Have you seen that report on you?"

"I've seen it."

"Then you know what's in it."

"Basically. Marty, is there a point to this?"

Marty sat down in his shorts, his pants all wadded up in his hands, looking at Cody through those stupid glasses. "Tourquey's girlfriend broke up with him Saturday because of what he did to you."

"So?"

"So. She hadn't really seen the whole report, she just got a glance at it Friday. She got hold of it this morning and read it. And she made a copy of it."

Cody pulled his breath in between his teeth.

"She gave it to Elise this morning in the parking lot."

Cody let the breath go, a soft moan.

"I don't know," Marty said. "Maybe it'd be better if everybody could just read it and get it straight."

Cody sighed.

"There are a lot of stories going around. They get worse all the time. I've already heard three versions about what happened this morning. You come off kind of a dangerous guy, you know? I don't think Tourquey would have pushed it this morning if he'd known then what he's heard since."

"So, what're they saying?"

"You don't want to know. Forget it. Two days, and nobody'll remember a thing. But they'll probably leave you alone after this. What was in that report, anyway?"

"Everything," Cody said, wearily. "You name it. Every bad thing in the world. Not very much of it's true."

"I figured," Marty said. "You should have seen some of the stuff they wrote about me before they figured out I was weird because I was smart."

"Oh, yeah?" Cody said, a little smile.

"You know it," Marty said. He got up and pulled on his gym shirt.

"So," Cody said softly. "What do I do now?"

"It'll be all right," Marty said. "They may be scared of you, but I think they really like you in their own strange ways."

"Elise," Cody moaned.

"*That* is a problem. But you know women. You'll figure it out."

"Yeah," Cody said, sighing. "Don't believe everything you hear."

The closer it got to lunch, the harder things became. He'd completely lost his anonymity. It was as if he had some kind of disease—people moving out of his way, staring at him. He was agonizing inside, wondering where Elise was and what she was thinking.

I thought we were friends, he thought. *I really thought we were. But maybe this was just too much. Maybe you shouldn't ask that much of anybody.*

He was tempted to go sit in the library, even though he'd promised Charlotte he would eat. But Marty and some of the other guys caught him and dragged him into lunch with them.

"Hey, bad man," one of the regulars called as Cody and Marty put their trays down at the table. "How ya doin'?"

Cody smiled and eased himself down into the chair. There was a collective grimace. Cody sighed and picked up his fork.

There wasn't a person in the lunch room that wasn't keeping at least half an eye on everything Cody was doing.

"Tell me something," Marty said, his voice up and carrying, "They say you've been in a lot of trouble."

Cody looked at him, puzzled. "Not really," he said.

"Have you ever been arrested?" Marty was getting louder.

"Marty, what are you doing?" Cody asked him. He looked around. Everybody at the table was watching.

"Just answer the question," Marty said. "Have you ever been arrested for anything?"

"*No,*" Cody said. He tried to spear a bit of spinach with the fork.

"Have you been in a lot of fights?" Marty asked. They could hear him all the way to the back.

"I've been in a few," Cody said unhappily.

"You could hurt somebody if you wanted to, couldn't you, Cody?"

"*Marty—*"

"Answer the question."

"I suppose so."

"Have you ever hurt anybody in a fight?"

Cody folded his hands into his lap. His head was starting to hurt again, and he couldn't get his breath right. He asked, in misery, in undertone, staring into his spinach, "Why are you doing this?"

"You probably even know how to kill a person, if you had to?" Marty asked.

Cody started to get up from the table, but Marty caught his wrist and pinned him with it. The kid was stronger than he looked.

"Will you answer?" Marty asked.

Cody stared at him, breathing hard.

"Just answer," Marty said.

"I've seen it done," Cody said, and he could feel tears on his face.

"Would you ever kill anybody, yourself?" Marty asked, no heart showing.

"*No.*"

"Has any kid ever messed you up like this before?"

"Not for a long time."

"Could you have stopped what happened to you on Friday?"

Cody nodded, helplessly. "I think so," he said.

"If you'd wanted to, could you have hurt them?"

Cody stared at Marty. "I could have crippled them, okay? Is that what you want? Then, yes. Yes, I could have stopped them."

"So there was more than one."

Cody didn't answer.

"And you didn't stop them."

"No. I didn't." Dogged answer.

Why? The question hung in the air, unasked.

"Are you going to get revenge?"

Cody looked at him. "I wasn't thinking about it," he said. "Could you be done?"

"So, see guys," Marty went on, ostensibly talking to his table but knowing how big the audience was, "McClellan knows how to take care of himself. If he'd wanted to, he could've handled those guys. No matter how many there were. But he didn't. He'd rather get hurt himself than hurt somebody else. He's just a civilized kind of guy."

And he turned around and smacked Cody on the shoulder. Cody gasped.

"Oh, sorry," Marty said, and suddenly the room wasn't silent anymore.

Cody was sitting there with his hands in his lap, going hard for balance.

"Good work," somebody down table said.

"That was bad, Marty," Cody said. He understood it, now, but he wasn't happy.

"Somebody had to do something," Marty said, taking a mouthful of applesauce. "It was getting out of hand. Eat your lunch."

"I'm not hungry."

"Don't be a jerk," Marty said serenely. "Eat your lunch."

"You're not a real comfortable person to sit next to, Marty," Cody said. But he picked up his fork again and poked at the spinach.

"What happened to *you*?" Jeannie cried. She dropped her books on a desk and came up and took Cody's face between her hands.

"Please?" he said, detaching her from his person.

"You know what happened to him," Thayne said reasonably, leaning out of the darkroom door. "We've got work to do back here."

"You should have whacked 'em a good one," Jeannie said, following Cody back into the dark.

"Let's forget it, okay?" he said.

"I'd take off the sunglasses back here," Thayne said.

Cody pulled them off and hung them from the neck of his sweatshirt by one earpiece.

"That looks very cool," Thayne said pleasantly, handing Cody a proof sheet, "but they're going to fall in the chemical the first time you lean over."

Cody pulled the shades off his shirt and put them on his enlarger stand.

"The crops are all marked," Thayne went on. "Make sure you keep the exposures clean."

"What a bunch of cowards," Jeannie muttered, off in her dark corner.

"Does your face hurt?" Thayne asked.

"Yeah, it hurts," Cody said, holding the proof sheet up under the enlarger light so he could see it. "I wish people would stop reminding me."

"Sorry," Thayne said. "We're journalists."

"I didn't mean you," Cody said.

"Yes, you did," Thayne said. "I only wish I could've been there. I could've shot the whole thing."

"That would have been helpful," Cody said, juggling the negatives and the holder.

"You're quite the romantic figure this afternoon," Thayne said, squinting at his own proof sheet. "And Lady Elise? Is she soothing your wounds?"

"Not really," Cody said. He slid the holder into the enlarger head.

Thayne sighed.

Cody started working with the f-ring, trying to guess on the exposure. "I don't know why you think you can't talk to girls," he said, dropping his voice. "You talk to Jeannie all the time."

"Jeannie," Thayne said, taking a furtive look over his shoulder, "is not a girl."

"Sure she is," Cody said. "What do you think girls are?"

Thayne pursed his lips, studying his negative. "Elise McCall," he said, "is a girl."

"No more than Jeannie," Cody told him. "And Elise isn't that easy to get along with, either."

Thayne flipped off the enlarger and pulled a piece of paper out of the safe. "You think Jeannie's all right looking?" he asked.

"Yeah," Cody said, with maybe a few mental equivocations. "She's not bad."

"What are you guys whispering about?" Jeannie asked, leaning over the trough, agitating the print she had in the developer.

"You," Thayne said.

"Could I get in here, too?" Cody asked her, his print in his hand. She moved her print over without a single rude word. "Thanks," he said, a little surprised.

"Mr. Allen wants you to shoot the game on Friday," Thayne said. "And I'm going to be at my grandmother's during homecoming, so he wants you to do that, too."

"Me?" Jeannie asked.

"McClellan."

"*Me?*" Cody asked.

"It's not that big a deal. You just shoot a couple of rolls of our guys at the game—like, you have to find out which ones are our guys, okay? Touchdowns, if possible."

"How do you tell a touchdown?" Cody asked.

Thayne turned around and looked at him. "It helps to know something about the game."

"I'll teach you, if you want," Jeannie said.

"I'll ask my uncle," Cody said. "Thanks."

"At the dance, you just shoot a couple of clutches, and a couple of shots of the homecoming queen—*kitsch* like that."

"I don't know," Cody said, doubtfully.

"It's no big deal. It's no different than what you were going to be doing last week. Look, it's a month off. You can take the dance Friday, if you want. Warm up with it."

"I was going to do that dance," Jeannie said.

"Fine. He'll take the couple of dances after that, then. Okay, McClellan? So you get warmed up."

"You should give homecoming to me," Jeannie grumbled, draining her print over the stop bath. "That's the *only* way I'll ever go to one."

Thayne looked at her, thoughtfully.

"Okay," Cody said. "I don't suppose an assignment like this could be said to have any, like, anthropological value to it?"

"Sure it does," Jeannie said. "Think of it as a study of the roots of modern social primitivism."

"I like that," Thayne said, showing some respect. "I like that very much."

27

"Well, hi," Charlotte said, wiping the heels of her hands on her pants. She was working on a little flower bed by the back door. Cody almost stepped on her, getting out of the car. "How'd it go today, buddy?"

"It was awful," he said, and he slammed the car door.

"Talk to me," she said. She had a little rake shaped like a claw, and she was combing it through the empty dirt. There was a little pile of weeds beside her on the driveway.

Cody took his books inside and then came back out and did his best to sit on the back steps. He put his feet out in front of him and gingerly leaned back against the steps.

"Somebody gave Elise a copy of the records," he said.

She looked up at him. "I know," she said.

"You *know*? How could you *know*? How is it that everybody in this town knows *everything*?"

"Everybody always knows everything," she said. "People talk. They always do. Wasn't it that way in New York? You know it was, eh? Well—in this case, since I am your guardian, and since Rosalee McCall is Elise's mother, and also a very good old friend of mine—it only naturally follows . . ." she let it trail off and gave the ground another good combing.

"Elise never showed up at home room," he said. "But she was at school."

"Rosalee called the school about those records—so they know somebody made a copy, and they probably know who it was. Nasty little wench. I'd like to know where she gets off doing a thing like that."

"She used to feed her boyfriend preview copies of his tests, too," he said.

Charlotte stood up, slapping her hands on her thighs. "I hope they hang her from the highest yardarm. Come on. I've got to start the chicken."

He struggled up off the step and followed her into the house. She hung the claw on a little hook inside the porch and then took her shoes off in the mud room. He drifted along in her wake, waiting for her to tell him the rest of it.

"The whole thing was a little tough for Elise to take, as you may imagine," she said. She went over to the sink and ran the water, rinsing her hands off. "Sit down." He did. The ritual milk and cookies came, this time with some fruit yogurt on the side. "Milk for bones?" she said, poking him in the shoulder.

"So, what did her mother say?"

"The question is, what will her *father* say?"

"I was never out of line with her," he said. "Not after the first time."

That got a raised eyebrow out of his aunt.

"I didn't *know*," he said doggedly. "Now I do."

She wrung out the dishrag and brushed a counter top with it.

"I had a good, long talk with Rose," she said. "I told her what I think about it. I told her Tom could talk to Erin. I don't know what they're going to decide. I don't know what I'd do in her place. I don't know what Elise is going to want to do."

"What did she say about Elise?"

"That she was upset. She really likes you, honey," Charlotte said. "But you gotta know, this is going to be like culture shock for her. You know what it did to me. Young girls can have a very romantic view of life; that may be in your favor. I just don't know. Is that the only thing that went bad on you today?"

"No," he said. He sighed. "It was just a hard, hard day."

"I shouldn't have let you go," she said. "I think maybe you'd better go on upstairs and go to bed for a while."

"I have work," he said, but he wasn't really arguing.

"Fine. There will *always* be that. Finish the milk and get upstairs, okay? We need to baby you a little bit for the next couple of days. Just till you get better. Now, go," she shooed him away from the table. "No books," she warned.

"No books," he agreed.

He stopped in the doorway and looked back at her. "I think I love Elise," he said softly. "What'll I do if she doesn't get over this?"

She came over and patted his shoulder and looked sad for him. "I don't know, buddy," she said. "Sometimes it doesn't work. Sometimes it just doesn't."

He nodded.

"Go rest," she said.

It was a tremendous labor, just moving himself up the stairs. He closed the door to his room and took off his jeans, but he couldn't face getting the shirt off. So he lay on the bed half dressed. Two minutes later, he was asleep. He had strange dreams, deep ones that twisted inside of him and made him want to pull free.

Pulling on him. On his arm. He knew it and jerked his arm away.

"*Cody.*"

He groaned and gasped and tried to awake. The room was dark. Morning? He couldn't remember what day it was. And Sawyer was telling him something.

"*What?*" he asked. He was in bad shape. The pills had worn off.

"Elise is here," Sawyer said, maybe for the second time.

"Why's she—what time is it?" he asked, his voice coming from somewhere under the water. He shifted around, trying to relieve some of the pressure on his side. "What?"

"I don't know. It's around seven. Mom has your dinner when you want it. It's just that Elise is here, or we wouldn't have made you get up. Mom thought you'd better."

Cody groaned again and pulled himself up, pressing his hand to his side. "Would you get my jeans?" he asked muddily. "No. The sweat pants. I can't—"

"Here," Sawyer said, and the pants slapped Cody in the shoulder.

"Thanks," Cody yawned. "Go tell her I'm coming, okay? Would you? Thanks."

Sawyer went out, closing the door behind him. Seven o'clock and dark as pitch. It was raining. Like another day altogether. His mind was slow. He pulled on the pants and tied them, felt around for his socks, but wasn't interested in shoes.

He stretched his back a little. And then he leaned his head against the bedpost. Elise was here. *And what does that mean?*

He hadn't expected her to be in the front hall. He heard the voices as he stood at the top of the stairs, and he wondered if he was lucid enough to go through with the rest of it. Her voice. Erin's voice. No others. Not her parents.

Cody started down the steps. He took them slowly, heavy

headed and stupid as he was. "Here he is," he heard Erin say, and then his uncle disappeared into the office, leaving the door just ajar.

And there was Elise, standing by the front door with her coat still on. Nervous. Shifting her weight.

He sat down heavily on the bottom step.

She wouldn't meet his eyes.

And so he said nothing. And neither did she.

"Did you come to tell me—" he started. "Are you here to say good-bye to me?"

Her lips tightened, and she shrugged. Her face was strained. Her eyes were too dark.

"Whatever you want, Elise," he said. He was too, too tired for this. No hope just now. Too weary, too late for that. "Whatever you want me to tell you, I'll tell you. I know you've read the records. I know what they say. It's like my whole soul's been taken apart and examined by everybody in the world."

He put his head against the newel post. "Some of those things were true. Maybe the things about my mother were true."

She folded her arms and moved over by the wall.

"Why did you come?" he asked.

She looked at him, then away. She shrugged. She took a little gulp of air. He looked at her wistfully, offering her comfort with all his heart.

She took a deep, ragged breath.

"It says—" she stopped. "It says you might have killed somebody." She looked at him, and her eyes tore his heart out.

He considered his answer. "I never did," he said at last.

She blinked and put her head back against the wall. "You fight with knives," she said, and then she bit her lip.

He sighed. "Not every place is like your place," he said gently. "What's right and simple here might not be so simple somewhere else."

She sighed and looked down at her shoes—anywhere but at him.

"Let me show you something," he said. He took hold of the waist of his sweatshirt, set himself, and then pulled it up and off, gasping at the last.

She was watching now. There was the little silver medal hanging over his heart, and the big white bandage wrapped all around his middle.

"What's that?" she asked.

"Cracked ribs," he said.

"Oh," she said faintly.

"Can you see this?" he asked, tracing the six inches of scar that ran just over his left breast and down below the bandage. She nodded. He touched the sweat pants. "I'd have to take these off to show you where it ends. It's real old. Down here—" he touched a place over his stomach—"It gets to be about an inch wide."

She blinked at him, but she didn't turn away.

"When I was about twelve, one night I stayed at the store kind of late. Mr. Guicci had the flu, and the inventory had to be done. So I stayed to do it. It was like midnight when I finally locked up. I took about two steps away from the door, and this guy, he just came out of nowhere, and he pinned me against the building. I could smell the whiskey on him—and he said he was going to kill me. He said I better leave his sister alone. I kept trying to tell him, I was only a kid—" he sighed, and swallowed. He hadn't ever told anybody this story.

"He had a knife. And he cut me wide open with it. I had Mr. Guicci's big coat on, and I guess maybe that saved me. They told me it did. I don't know what happened after that. I guess he was after some guy who'd been after his sister. I think it was his sister who found us. Anyway, I woke up at Guicci's. With this."

He gave her an apologetic look; she'd gone a little white. "So I bought a knife of my own. I'd always been good at staying out of the way, you know? And I'd been a little street brawler since I could crawl—I had to be. We all were. But that . . . after that . . ."

He shrugged. "I got the knife. And I learned to use it, which means, I learned how to fight with it. And I must have used it a hundred times. Out at night. On the street. And people got to know my face. And they left me alone."

He sighed. "Elise," he said. "I never just went out and hurt somebody with it. I never robbed anybody. I never even started anything. I don't—"

He lifted his hands and dropped them.

"If you—" he started softly, shivering without the shirt. "It's all right. If you need—" He laughed, sadly, not finding the words. "If you don't want me, I'll understand. It was very good, you and me. I really loved it. But—"

She turned around and put her head against the wall and cried.

He groaned inside himself.

"Come here," he said, cajoling. "Please? If you're not going to go."

She turned around again, took a tremendous breath, and closed her eyes.

"Lise?"

Her eyes went to him. He put one hand out. She shook her head, her eyes streaming. But then she came to him anyway. He gathered her in close beside him on the stair, and she cried, and she cried, and he kissed her hair.

"I'm sorry," he said. But that didn't seem much comfort.

"Hey," he said, after a few minutes, bouncing her a little, "Hey. Hello?"

"Don't," she said, because he was trying to make her look up.

"I'm not going to kiss you," he said.

"My nose is running," she said.

"Uncle Erin," Cody said, not even raising his voice. "Do you have a Kleenex?"

There was a rustling behind Erin's office door, and then it opened and Erin came out with a box of tissue, looking a bit on the sheepish side.

"Sorry," he said.

But now Elise was laughing.

"What did you hear? Who else is in there?" Cody asked him.

"Nobody," Erin said, looking a little offended. "I just — I have some work to do," he said, and he went back into his office. This time the door went shut.

Elise sighed and put her head against Cody's chest. He was still shivering.

"Do you think we're friends?" he asked her.

She nodded.

"Do you think we're more than friends?" he asked.

Another nod. Slow.

"Maybe we just need to stay in the daylight awhile, huh? So you won't worry. So your mother won't worry." He ran his hand down her hair and patted her shoulder. "That's okay. Just that bit of you is more than I hoped I'd ever have."

She pinched his leg tightly.

"Ow," he said. "What was that?"

"You make everything so hard," she said.

"I told you. It's the way I was brought up." And then he made her look up, and he smiled at her, one of his honest ones — they were coming much easier these days.

She touched his cheek gently, one finger. "Don't lie to me," she said. "Don't hurt me." Her eyes begged him. "You were right. I'm naive. I don't want anything to be hard. I don't want anybody being hurt, or hungry, or scared."

He put his cheek down against her hair.

"It's always hard," he said. "In some ways. All the time, someplace or other." He paused. "I'm not a bad person, Elise. I think you could tell if I was. I think you could feel that. I know I'm not easy. But I'm worth it. Or I'm going to be. Listen to your heart. Listen to your God. Whatever you want from me, I promise you, if I can give it to you, I will. I'll even talk religion with you, if that's so important. And the offer includes leaving you alone. If that's what you want."

She sighed. He yawned. "You know," he said very reluctantly—his head was throbbing.

The door to the den opened.

"You should probably go on home." He gave her hair another tug.

She sat up.

"You still here?" Charlotte asked. "Everything okay?"

"Fine," he said. Elise nodded.

"There's a good old movie on," Charlotte said. "It hasn't started yet, if you want to come on in. Up to bed," she said over her shoulder to somebody in the den.

Elise brightened up. "You want to?" she asked. "I'll let you put your head in my lap."

"Oh, yeah?"

"You take your pills?" Charlotte asked him.

"Come on," Elise said. "I'll call my mom and tell her I'm staying. It'll make me feel better."

"Okay," he said.

Sawyer stalked out of the den and scowled at them. He stumped up the stairs, and when he got up to the bedroom, he slammed the door.

"Come see this movie," Charlotte said, opening Erin's door. He said something back to her, and she disappeared into the office.

Elise started off down the hall.

"Lise?" Cody said. She stopped and came back, put a hand on the banister, looking at him. He put out a hand. She came around and leaned over and kissed him—gently.

"Thank you for not giving up on me," he whispered.

She patted his cheek. "Put your shirt back on," she whispered back to him, and then she went off down the hall to call her mother.

28

"What is it," Cody asked, sitting next to Erin, out on the front stoop one warm October afternoon, "that makes people—who supposedly love goodness—so interested in things that aren't good?"

"Hmm," Erin said.

The trees in the yard had started to change, the maple by the east den window more than hinting at scarlet, and the birch by the driveway shimmering a perfect, clear lemon yellow.

"Specifics?" Erin asked.

Cody frowned, trying to decide how to explain. "I dunno. I just seem to be a lot more interesting now than I was a month ago—before all this happened."

"You think it might be because more people know who you are, now?"

"No," Cody said. "It's more than that. It's not just being recognized. I mean, people knew who I was when I was the new kid. It's more like one day last week—you know, you wear those mirrored shades, and it's amazing what kind of stuff you can see because people don't know you're looking at them—and these girls . . . I walk down the hall, and they just, like—*stare* at me."

"And that's bad?"

"It's weird. They do it all the time. One day, Elise and I were walking down the hall, and there was this bunch of junior girls standing around. I just happened to smile at one of them. And she drops her books all over the floor."

"*Really*," Erin said.

"Well, yeah."

"Flattering," Erin said.

"Stupid," Cody said.

"So, what did you do?"

"I helped her pick them up. And then I told her maybe she should hold on to them a little better, you know? And then, Elise and I were walking away, and they're all like giggling back there. Little screams and stuff. It was really embarrassing."

"What did Elise think about it?"

Cody grinned. "She didn't like it."

"And you think this is because of that whole mess—"

"That kind of thing never happened here before then. But it was like that in New York. These middle-class girls at school, they thought I was something. Like sushi, you know? Exotic. Not *me*, you understand. It was the image, or something. It was the trouble. It's like they thought that was romantic."

Erin nodded. "Women like a man they can reclaim," he said, smiling to himself.

"Is that it?"

"That's part of it, I think." Erin stretched his legs out. "You know—why is it that people will spend a heck of a lot more money to see *Jaws* or *Friday the Thirteenth* or something like that than they will *The Black Stallion?* You know, if you're in the film business you don't want to make a G-rated movie because it'll die at the box office. Personally, I think people generally have a love affair going with death. Not that it's a conscious thing. I think it's the only way we feel like we have any control over anything at all—to come right up to the wall, and then pull back, and cheat it out."

He blinked, squinting out over the lawn. "But you're right. Danger seems to be a lot more romantic than peace. Sad, I think."

He smiled at Cody. "Well, it sounds like you're doing all right, anyway. You look better."

"I feel a lot better."

"Your face looks a lot better. When did you get the stitches out?"

"A while ago."

"You move a lot easier. School okay?"

"It's good. I'm pulling some *A*'s. English. World History. Math. I'm passing physics."

"Passing?"

"Not an *A.*"

"You have an *A* in photography."

"Well," Cody said, grinning. He leaned over and picked up a stick. "Yeah. But they won't let me shoot the games anymore."

"You blow it?"

Cody squinted up at the sun. "Depends on your point of view. The pictures were great. I did some nice lens flare things."

"But they didn't like it."

"Oh, they liked the effects. They just thought I should've shot more of the actual game."

"I thought that's what you were supposed to be shooting."

"Well, it was. But you know, all those guys out there, mashing each other . . . it's not like there're any *faces*, you know."

"So, what did you shoot?"

"Oh, some crowd stuff. And some other things."

"Like what?"

"Like—I don't know."

"Like cheerleaders, maybe?"

"Yeah," Cody said, poking at his foot with the stick.

"Like—maybe *one* cheerleader?"

"I got some of the others."

"Did you shoot the game at all?"

"Yes, actually. I got one really good shot of this guy going up for the ball. It was great. It was really a good action shot."

"Wrong team," Erin said.

"Well, yeah—but should that matter? I mean, this is art," Cody was grinning.

"Journalists can be so narrow minded," Erin agreed.

"That's what I thought."

Erin yawned.

"We've got to start dinner. She's going to be home—" he checked his watch. "Aw, we've got another five minutes."

"Charlotte was *mad* at me last night," Cody said, breaking the stick into two pieces.

"When?"

"When you were at that meeting."

"What did you do?"

"I was helping Sawyer with that model. I mean, that was nice on my part, don't you think? That I'd be helping her little son do something creative."

"What did you do?"

"We forgot to put down newspaper, and we got glue on the table."

Erin grimaced.

"Yeah. She was kind of upset about it."

"Did you get it off?"

"Kind of. Except it took some of the finish off."

Erin screwed his eyes shut.

"She'll get over it, won't she?"

"I don't know. She still remembers stuff I did twelve years ago."

Cody blew out a breath and put his elbows on his knees and his chin in his hands.

"I'll help you fix it," Erin said. He was looking up at the big sycamore. "You know," he said, "Eventually, somebody's going to have to rake up all these leaves. I'm getting too old for that."

Cody laughed. "That's what I'm here for," he said. "To take care of you in your old age."

"Hullo, there," Cody said. "Waiting for somebody?"

Chris pushed herself away from the wall she'd been leaning against. She had both arms around her books, and she had, in fact, been waiting for somebody. The hall was the usual bedlam, loud with slamming lockers, kids laughing. Cody was on his way to photography lab.

She fell in beside him, looking a little grim.

He looked at her curiously.

"I've got to talk to you," she said, stopping where their two halls diverged.

"Okay," he said, but he was getting the feeling that this was not something he was going to enjoy.

She made an impatient little sound and glared at the lockers across the hall. Eventually, she turned that glare on him.

"What is it?" he asked, himself impatient.

"You know," she said, "sometimes you're really a jerk."

"Oh, thanks."

"No problem," she said.

"Okay, obviously, I've done something. Obviously, I don't know what it is."

"Everybody's been so concerned about Cody lately: Isn't Cody brave? Isn't it wonderful what Cody's doing? Isn't it sad about Cody's childhood? What can we do for Cody? Isn't Cody smart? Isn't he a wonderful photographer? Let's go shoot pictures. Let's go help Cody learn to drive. Let's make sure Cody gets an *A* in English.

"And okay, we know you think stuff like cheerleading is superficial. And okay, we know you think all the *social* stuff is bourgeois. We understand that. Okay, you have your rights. You can think what you want about those things. But did you ever happen to think that Elise might *like* football games? That she might really *like* dances?

"You're not the only intelligent person in the world, Cody. And some intelligent people actually *enjoy* social activities. As in, *being* with people.

"Has it ever crossed your mind that Elise is *always* doing what *you* want to do? Never mind what she wants—all she thinks about is what *you* want. Did you think she just *happens* to like all the same things *you* like? Well, she doesn't. She does a lot of stuff just because she knows you care about it. Because she cares about you.

"And who cares about *her*? You don't even care about what she likes, do you? And the few things you know about, you make fun of. You're so self-centered, you can't even be *neutral* about it. You don't care about what she likes, and you won't even allow her to *like* those things without making her feel like a jerk if she does. You don't even tell her she does a good job. You don't even go to the games to watch her. Did you ever think it would mean a lot to her if you let her know you were *proud* of her, instead of just tolerating what she's doing? But no—you're too busy taking care of yourself.

"Real nice, Cody. Well, Elise is a person, too. And she's been more than nice to you. I would think the least you could do was think about *her* a little bit. I'm late for class."

She stalked off and left him standing there with his mouth open. The hall had emptied out. "Really," he said. He was deeply offended. Also deeply guilty. Also embarrassed.

Later, contrite.

After that, concerned. And repentant. And a little scared.

But Elise wasn't angry when she came over to study with him. Not a hint that anything was wrong. And later, when he walked her home, there were still no hints.

They walked through the little park, and he gently backed her up into one of the big sycamores that grew just outside the street light, trying to be careful that he wasn't asking too much. When he slipped his arms around her, hers came around him, and he thought that maybe this was one of the things they both liked.

And then he told her how beautiful he thought she was, all the things he saw in her face, in her eyes. And he thanked her for being so sweet to him, for being so patient and so tolerant. And he told her other things, about how he loved to watch her with her family, about how smart she was.

Then he told her he had the homecoming game assignment, and he asked her to go to the dance with him afterwards.

He felt a little guilty after that, because the words hadn't cost him anything except a little thought, but the return on his investment had been so sweet to him, he'd had to cut it short and take her home before there should be a total run on the bank.

Even so, he lingered with her on the porch. And by the time she went in, he was so intoxicated with her and her rules, he was light headed and stupid. His heart slammed along inside him all the long, chilly, lonely way home. The park caught at him as he passed it, teasing his imagination—the strange beauty of the bright yellow trees, underlit with street light . . . wild seeming, the stuff of his dreams. He thought about her again as he passed into the shadow, and he didn't know how he could bear it.

"There's another one of those big letters for you," Sawyer said, bouncing down the front steps past Cody the next afternoon after school. "On the kitchen table." And, on second thought, "I'll show you."

"I know where the kitchen is," Cody said. But Sawyer trailed along behind him anyway.

"That came for you today," Charlotte said, pointing towards the table with the knife she was using to slice the potatoes.

"With cheese?" Cody asked, eyeing the potatoes.

"Don't ask me that," Charlotte said. "You know I hate talking about dinner before dinner."

Cody dropped his books on the table and pulled off his jacket, all the time his eyes full of that manilla envelope.

"Is it from John?" Charlotte asked.

"It's from New York," Cody said. He sat down, put his hands down on it, and took a deep breath.

"Will you open it?" Sawyer said, hanging over Cody's shoulder.

"What do *you* care?" Cody asked him happily.

"I just want to see if he drew all over your stuff again," Sawyer said, bouncing a little, impatient. "I'm supposed to be at Russ's. I was supposed to be over there fifteen minutes ago."

Cody shook his head and opened the envelope—but slowly, slowly. John's last letter hadn't been that long; this was something that had to be savored.

Sawyer made a sound of pure exasperation. Charlotte laughed.

Cody finally pulled the flap all the way open and reached inside. There was a lot of stuff in there. He pulled it out slowly, carefully—his pictures, all the ones he'd sent John. And then another—one of John's this time. *Kentucky*—John had written on the back of it—*In the family circle.*

It was a picture of a child, in the middle of the front room of a house. There were older people, sitting around the room—part of the picture, but not part. The child was dressed in what was obviously her special clothes, a ribbon in her hair, sitting primly but with a gentle look on her face, something like a smile but different—you couldn't name it, but when you *looked* at it you had to feel something peculiar and strong inside.

Some of the older people were sitting back, looking satisfied; some were preoccupied. A boy at the very edge of the picture, wearing a suit slightly too short at the ankles, sat at the end of the couch, legs dangling; he was just slipping his fingers quietly into a fish bowl that was sitting on the end table next to him.

The whole room had a feeling of age to it, as though it might have been new once, but it had been used a lot, and the edges were all smooth. The people were just people, but the way John had used the light—it was just the light coming through the window, filtered through the fine lace curtains—the faces had a transparency to them that made you feel almost otherworldly, as if something had just happened to lift them out of time into a sort of holy quiet. And Cody found himself wondering what the story was—it could have been the girl's birthday—a special one, somehow—or a baptism or confirmation, or you weren't even sure if she hadn't died and this was the very moment before she passed into the hands of God.

"It's beautiful," Charlotte said, coming away from her work, wiping her hands.

"It's weird," Sawyer said. "And he did it again. Did you see your pictures? He drew all over them again. He didn't draw all over *his,* you'll notice."

"Would you get out of here?" Cody said. He put one finger against Sawyer's nose and pushed him back off the chair with it. "Russell is expecting you."

"Fine," Sawyer said, miffed. He stuck his offended member in the air and slammed his way out of the back door.

Charlotte gritted her teeth, rolled her eyes, and shook her head.

"I'm sure you were just like that when you were little," Cody said.

"I'm sure I wasn't," she said, and she sat down next to him to look at John's photograph. "He's really good, isn't he?" she said quietly. "It makes you feel sad, somehow. It makes me remember a poem one of my professor's, Ed Geary, gave us in class one time: *'So much depends on a red wheelbarrow and white chickens,'* or something. I didn't understand it then."

But Cody understood. Something to do with how life had gone on after John had taken this shot—the faces had changed; the little girl had run out and put on other clothes; the boy undoubtedly would find himself in some trouble over the fish. The moment gone, and maybe no one would have known it, no one ever noticed. A succession of moments. And life, made out of them, quietly gone, except for this photograph which said everything, and nothing at all, about it.

Cody watched Charlotte as she studied the picture.

"I love you," he said. And then he flushed seriously and covered his face with one hand.

She didn't move for a moment.

"I love you too, Cody," she said. She got up, kissed the top of his head, and went quietly back to her work, leaving palpable evidence of that moment in the air behind her as she went.

He put the photograph down on the table and closed his eyes. He could see Charlotte's kitchen in his mind, the leaf-stained light coming down through the window, the bricks, the color on the wall. It was imprinted on his heart now, but in quiet grays that said more than color. He felt more complete in that moment than he'd ever felt in his life—knowing Charlotte was behind him, and Erin working away in his office. Knowing the children would be home soon enough, and all of them eating dinner together. A keen little pain; almost too much to be held.

He sighed and picked up the stack of his own pictures. John had drawn all over them, just as Sawyer had said. Cody studied them. "Tell me what he says," Charlotte asked, and he did, and he showed her what John had marked.

Then came the letter.

So it's nice to see more than one face in these. I sent along one of my own because I think we were both trying to do the same things with these shots—you told me a lot more about your life with your photographs of the family than you ever could have done if you'd tried to do it in words.

I told you once, you have a good eye. I was right about that.

I like the way you responded to my last little round of instruction. Your blacks are crisp, and your highlights work now: Your photographs are starting to take on a real quality.

285

Now, we need to work on exposure and chemistry so that the grain doesn't get in the way unless you want it to. I've taken the liberty of marking some composition things, and I'm going to give you some technical secrets here which will eliminate some of the unevenness in your grays.

I'll be out of the country until after Thanksgiving. Save your best stuff till then. In late spring—around the end of May I've got an assignment I'm going to have to shoot in Paris. —I'll be looking for an assistant. So far, I'm only taking one application—I think I've found my man. If you're interested.

"Ahh . . ." Cody breathed.

"What is it?" Charlotte asked him.

He read it to her, that last part. Read it with a sort of holy awe.

"That's wonderful!" Charlotte said. "That's *wonderful!*"

"You'll let me go?" he asked.

"*Let* you go?" Charlotte said. "Honey, I don't think that's at issue here. Are you going to go?"

He laughed, a bit of unbelief. "I guess I am," he whispered. But looking down deep into his soul, he couldn't really see it happening.

29

"Okay," Coach said, slapping his hands together and giving them a good brisk rub. "So much for theory. Let's get on the *mat*." He waved a hand at them. "Come on, sit all around here —yeah. We're going to do a little exhibition. Reidhead. Lindhal. Get out there."

All the guys crowded around the edge of the wrestling mats, jeering at Reidhead and Lindhal, who were standing there looking embarrassed, skinny legs, skinny arms sticking out of the gray gym clothes.

"How're the ribs?" Coach asked, poking Cody with his foot.

"Okay," Cody said. "Fine."

"Good," Coach said, then moved away and blew his whistle. "Knock it off, you guys."

Coach had never liked McClellan much; not in the beginning, anyway. *Not a team player.* He liked him better once he found out the kid was a street fighter. Cody didn't understand that. Marty explained, "Coach understands you now."

Reidhead and Lindhal went into a semicrouch, rolling their eyes at the coach. "Get tough," Coach said.

"*Right*," Lindhal said. "Get tough, Reidhead."

Coach blew the whistle again. "Go," he said. Then he started walking around the outside. "Okay, you guys—you're the officials. Keep your eyes open. What are the rules? Where are the points?"

Reidhead and Lindhal were sort of halfheartedly pawing at each other.

"Come on, guys. Let's see a little grappling here."

"*Right*," Lindhal said again. He straightened up. "No way am I grabbing *him*."

Reidhead lunged, caught Lindhal around the middle, and they both went over onto the mat, Lindhal's feet sticking straight up in the air. A great shout went up. "*Reidhead!*" the guys shouted. "*All right!*" Very funny. Everybody was dying.

"Great form, guys," Coach said wryly. "Okay, maybe we need a little more passion here, eh? McClellan, you're a passionate sorta guy. Get up here. And let's see . . . uuhhhhhh . . ."

A little thrill of delight went around the mat. They knew exactly what he was going for, and so did Cody.

"Ohhhh—hey—why not? Tour*quey*."

Pandemonium.

"Let's move it, guys."

Turk took a quick, ugly look at the coach as he got up, then glared at Cody, who was already standing easily at the other end of the mat. "Not my idea," Cody said, hands out. But he was pleased. Too many stories out. Too much brag. Put Tourquey down on the mat, everybody could forget the thing. Everybody but Tourquey.

"Keep your eyes open," Coach warned. "We're watching for technique here—we're looking for points." The whistle sounded, and Cody and Tourquey dropped into a crouch.

Yelling. Screaming. Some on one side, some on the other. Coach was crouching, too, following the wrestlers as they circled around each other. Cody was grinning. Legalized violence—it was a tremendous relief.

Tourquey was taking the thing a little more seriously, watching Cody, breathing hard.

"Are you guys going to do something?" Coach shouted. They could hardly hear him over the rest of the noise. It didn't ruffle Cody at all; he was in no rush. But it made Tourquey nervous, and he jumped in wrong, off balance. There was nothing to it, sidestep, grab, pull, turn—a little leverage and down with a knee on the chest. Tourquey never knew what happened.

The whistle blew and Cody got off him. Tourquey's face was dark. He got up slowly.

"McClellan's match," Coach was shouting over the bedlam. Cody's cheering section was bigger now.

"You shook me," Tourquey yelled at the coach. "I never got set."

Cat calls now. Jeering.

"I *wasn't*," Turk shouted at them.

"Okay, then," Coach said, turning to the rest of the guys. "Two out of three falls?"

Wonderful. Delirium. Two out of three—okay. *Do five out of nine. We don't mind.*

"You heard 'em," Coach said, pointing at Cody and Turk. "Let's go another one."

Cody leaned over for a minute, getting his breath, hand to his ribs; then he took his place and settled himself. He wasn't quite as mended as he'd thought. He looked into Turk's face and saw what he expected—the same crazy, ugly hatred as before, out on the street. Not so cocky, now—and maybe more dangerous for that. Maybe not. Add the humiliation. The guy was out of control.

Whistle.

No grinning this time. Cody went carefully, looking for surprises, keeping his balance solid. Circling. Turk came in on the first move again, not so stupid this time, still not good. Cody took him down, but not like before—they hit the mat and grappled. Cody slipped a hand between Turk's legs, two inches from a pin, and at that moment, Turk brought his knee up sharply into Cody's hurt side.

Cody lost his hold, gasping, and Turk jerked his arm out from under him, coming down on top. *Rules,* Cody shouted at himself, short of pulling Turk's eyes out. And he gathered himself up, shouldered Tourquey off, flipped him over, and pinned him. Same as before. But with meaning.

The room had gone quiet.

"Your knee's a little high there, McClellan," Coach pointed out quietly. At Turk's throat. A little high, yes.

"Sorry," Cody said, and pulled himself off. Stood up, breathing very hard. Pressed his hand into his side, gasping now.

Still quiet.

"Except for that last bit," Coach said, "McClellan kept his head. You keep the rules, and you have the advantage; you keep the rules, and you keep your mind clear." Tourquey was sitting up. "And I'll tell you what," Coach finished, "you may not win the match. But if you play fair, you win morally. You build character. No win is worth losing that. You got it?"

They had it.

"I want to hear it."

They had it.

"Okay. Hit the showers. You okay, McClellan?"

Still bent over, Cody nodded.

Marty waited. Cody straightened up and looked down at Turk. "Sorry, man," he panted.

Turk murmured something Cody just caught, something foul. Cody shrugged. "If that's how you want it," he said. And then he followed Marty into the locker room where, all of a sudden, he had a lot of friends.

"What are you *doing?*" Jeannie asked. She was watching as Cody stood over the developer cradling a limp, wet print in his hands.

"You trying to warm it up?"

He was breathing on one little area, the way you do when you're trying to warm up your hands on a cold morning.

"Yes, as a matter of fact," Cody said.

Thayne wandered over, curious. "Why?" he asked, and then a light went on in his face. "You heat the chemical up, so it reacts faster on that localized area—and that brings the area up faster. Clever. Very clever. How'd you come up with that?"

"A friend of mine taught me."

"What friend?" Jeannie asked.

"Like I don't have friends?" Cody said.

"I don't see any in here," Jeannie snapped, moving her print down a tray. He dropped his print back into the developer, just to even it off.

"His name's John Hanks," Cody said. "I met him on the way out here from the East."

289

"John Hanks?" Thayne said, blinking at Cody.

"Yeah," Cody said, draining his print.

"You mean, like—John *Hanks*?"

Cody looked at him. "Yeah? Is that significant to you?"

"Is that *significant*? Are you *kidding*? You know John *Hanks*?"

Jeannie rolled her eyes. "You're so weird, Thayne."

"You know," Thayne said, untouched by the irreverence, "I have an entire scrapbook of just John Hanks. By himself. Just the magazine stuff. Like, my parents hide the *National Geographics* from me now. Is that the John Hanks you're talking about?"

"I think so," Cody said, glancing up at Thayne. Even under the safelights, Thayne was looking a little pale.

"You know somebody famous?" Jeannie asked, dripping skepticism. "I thought you were brought up in a ghetto or something."

"A neighborhood," Cody said, scowling at her. "Where do you think people *go* when they want grass roots humanity?"

"Shut up, Jeannie," Thayne said. "Does he ever come out here?"

"No. Maybe. Probably. *I* don't know," Cody said. "If he had a reason."

"I thought you knew him," Jeannie said.

"I know him from New York. We correspond."

"Corre*spond*,"Jeannie said, one shoulder up, batting her eyes.

"He writes to you. He *writes* to you. Does he *write* to you?"

"Yeah."

Thayne moaned. "Oh, what would it be *like*?"

Jeannie made a sound of pure disgust and went back to her enlarger.

"I'll tell you what, Thayne. Next time I write to him, which won't be for a while because he's on assignment right now—"

"*On assignment,*" Thayne murmured.

"I'll tell him about you. Okay? And I promise, if he ever comes out here, I *promise* I'll make sure you get to meet him. Okay? You can come over and see what he sent me." He went back over to his enlarger and picked up another proof sheet. "He might be out here in May," he said thoughtfully. "If he's going to pick me up. But he probably won't. I'll probably just have to meet him in New York. Or maybe Charlotte'll want to meet him first."

"You're going to have to explain all that," Jeannie said out of the darkness, "if you don't want Thayne to die of apoplexy."

"It's just . . . he's going to take me with him, maybe. On an assignment he has in the spring."

"You?" Thayne asked. "Cody, you've got to be straight with me now. Is this the truth? I mean, there's a lot of weird stuff about you. You're not just like—is this true? Because if it's truly true, then I'm going to have to change my mind about something that's very important to me."

"Which is?" Cody asked, grinning. He pulled a negative out of its sleeve.

"Which is," Thayne said, straightening up and going back to his own enlarger, "that good things actually do happen. I never really believed it. Till now. If you—" he pointed his negative carriage at Cody, "—a simple child from the ghetto—"

"It was a *neigh*borhood," Cody said. "Not even ethnic."

"—with *no* advantages, *no* connections, *no* money, *no* education—"

"Would you stop, please?" Cody said.

"If an obscure person like you can actually *know* somebody like John Hanks, can actually *go* with him. On *assignment*—"

"He still could be lying," Jeannie pointed out.

"That's true," Cody said to Thayne. "I could be."

"Are you?" Jeannie asked him.

"No," Cody told her.

"—if such things can *be*, then eventually, and perhaps, even in my lifetime, I *could* get the cover of *Life*. Or *Geo*. Or *Photography*. Or *National Geographic*. Or *Foodhandler's Quarterly*—"

"You see what you've done?" Jeannie said sourly. She was draped over the rim of the trough, dangling the edge of her print in the developer. "You've made a Pollyanna out of him. Now he'll never be any good for anything except human interest stories."

Cody smirked, dropping his print in beside hers.

"Next thing you know," she complained, "you'll have me believing I could get a date to homecoming."

He looked up at her. "Stranger things have happened," he said.

She scowled, letting her print slide the rest of the way in. "Not really," she said.

30

Homecoming. And nobody could argue that he hadn't covered the assignment. By a fortunate error—born totally of boredom—while he was trying out the magnificent long lens Mr. Allen had let him use, Cody had managed to shoot the very instant of the winning touchdown. He couldn't have brought them anything better than that.

And it wasn't as if he was going to come back with fifteen rolls of one cheerleader, either—he'd shot the whole squad, using no more than maybe half a roll on Elise. He'd shot their little gymnastics, and their fancy formations, his eye full of pure femininity, thinking that shooting an afternoon's worth of very short skirts wasn't such a bad job.

For himself he'd done some nice crowd character studies, wandering around looking for interesting faces and good light.

He'd enjoyed himself. Well, almost. Well, pretty much.

At halftime, they'd announced the homecoming royalty. The principal had done it, standing in the middle of the field, the marching band behind him, using a stand-up mike hooked into the PA system.

Surprise, Cody had thought, leaning against the side of the stands with his arms folded: one of the cheerleaders made queen. Bored out of his mind with it, he pushed himself up and went to take her picture. They made Steven the king. It got better for Cody after that—Steven had to come out on the field in his uniform to get crowned, and he didn't look particularly comfortable about it. Cody had done very good pictures of that, taking a slightly irreverent perspective.

A surprise *did* come when he finished with Steven and turned around to find Elise. She and Chris were sitting very close together on the bench, and Chris had Elise's hand in hers, as if she was lending her comfort. About what? About *this*? Sweet, sad, brave face. Because she didn't get to be queen? Over such a stupid thing. And he hadn't known—hadn't even guessed that she cared about it. And then he wondered what nasty little things he'd probably said about homecoming queens the last couple of weeks.

He went around to the back of the bench and came up behind her, tucked the camera case down beneath the bench, and put his hands on her shoulders. She looked up, not expecting it to be him, and then leaned back against him.

"Sorry, baby," he whispered, leaning over close to her ear. He kissed her hair, patted her shoulder, all the time wondering why an intelligent person would waste passion on something so meaningless.

Later he sneaked some pictures of her, trying to catch that face so that he could look at it later and try to understand.

Then he was in the lab, processing the film all by himself with time to think. He stood in the black room, wondering as he did every time he shut himself in there how he could stand it.

And wondering how much more there was in the world that was so completely, utterly out of his understanding—as Elise could be. He didn't understand how there could be so much meaning—how it could change from person to person, what was important, what was worth desiring.

He suspected that his perspective wasn't the only sensible one in the universe, but he couldn't understand how he could change it and still be rational. But Elise was rational. Most of the time. Maybe all of the time. Rational, but different. As if they could both be rational at the same time, but feeling differently. Like the spectrum—only so much visible, but all of it real, visible or not. It was like trying to understand the end of the sky. Or like coming over that hill and seeing the world for the first time—no limits. Or like trying to imagine God.

He finished the negatives and clipped them to the hangers, taking them out again, reel by reel, to check them out against the safelights. Satisfied, he shut down the lab, locked up, shouldered the case, and went out to the car. It had been tiring work, but not wearying.

He got home just in time to have supper, shower, and get dressed.

"Where're you off to?" Charlotte asked him when he didn't linger at the table.

"Got a dance," he said. Then he went upstairs and tried to figure out what you wore to a homecoming dance.

He packed himself into the car and drove down to Elise's, his heart light and his mind resolved; he was a stupid, narrowminded, unaware idiot, but that could change.

He pulled up in front of Elise's house, hauled the case out of the car—it still had Mr. Allen's lens in it—and trotted through the lowering evening up her front walk and up the porch steps. He knocked on the door, and then went over to lean against the porch rail, amazed by the incredible autumnal paradise the neighborhood had become.

The front door opened. He turned around. His eyes widened and his mouth dropped open. Elise was framed in the doorway, wearing a dress out of a fairy tale—wine colored, dripping with lace, tucked-up waist, skirt sweeping all the way to the floor— simple and smooth and *very* soft about the shoulders. She had her hair done up a little, with flowers in it. His heart went wild. She was the prettiest, most ornamental thing he'd ever seen— except that her expression was not a whole lot unlike his own.

"I thought we were going to the dance," she said.

"We are," he said.

"We are?"

"Aren't we?" He blinked.

"Dressed like *that?*"

"Dressed like—you mean *me?*" He was nonplussed.

Her eyes traveled down his legs, and must have hit the camera case, because she said, with great menace to him, "You're going to shoot the dance, aren't you?"

He didn't understand the little flickers of anger he was seeing in her eyes.

"Sure," he said.

"I thought you were *taking* me to this dance. I didn't know I was going along on a *shoot.*"

"Elise, what's the difference?"

"You—" She made an exasperated noise and threw herself back against the door frame. "*Cody.*"

He felt so helpless. And he couldn't take his eyes off the places where the dress came down around her shoulders.

"What are *you* staring at?" she inquired stiffly.

"You," he said. "You look . . . you . . ." He gave up and shook his head, still staring.

"Well, thank you—I think," she said dryly.

"Elise, I . . ." He took a hesitant step forward. "I think maybe I don't know what I've done wrong."

She made a terrible face at him. Definitely out of place over that dress. Her mother said something from inside the house. "It's just *Cody,*" Elise said back to her. Not complimentary.

"Cody," she said. "It's *homecoming!*"

Blank face.

"Some guys hire *limousines* to pick up their dates."

Still blank. "Isn't it just at the school?"

"Yes, it's at the school. But it's *formal.*"

He looked down at himself. "Would you mind coming out?" he asked, because she was still standing inside the door. "Would you mind doing a little, like, cultural enlightenment? Because I've never seen anybody — " she came out and the door shut behind her — "in a dress like that. Not really." He put a hand out, but then thought better about it, considering the fire in her eyes. "What was it I was supposed to have done?"

She laced her fingers together and looked at him as if he was the lostest of lost causes. "You make me feel like such a fool," she said, and she went over and sat down on the porch swing, the long skirt of the dress flowing around her like smoke as she moved. His hands were itching to touch that dress.

"Please remember I'm culturally deprived," he said to her back. She sat.

"Come on," she said, resignedly. So he went over, and she twitched the skirt aside so he could sit down next to her. He sneaked a little stroke of the dress. It was very soft.

"You were *supposed* to show up here: A, in a tux — "

"A *what?*"

"B, with a corsage. C, without the camera."

"I was?"

"Yes. You were. You know how much this dress cost?"

He shook his head.

"Well, neither do I actually," she said. "But I'm sure it was too much because I'll probably never wear it again." She glared at him. "I *hate* when you do this."

"Do what?"

"Steven would have just come and looked wonderful and taken me to this stupid dance, and I could have enjoyed it and felt beautiful. Maybe later I'd look back and think how silly it was, but I would've *done* it at least. Just a little romance. Just something a little special . . ."

He was stung about the Steven part.

"But you always *have* to be different. You can't just . . ." She heaved a tremendous sigh.

"You could've gone with Steven," he said. But she looked at him reproachfully.

"Lise, I didn't mean to ruin this for you. I wasn't trying to pass any judgments. I just didn't *know.*"

"You could've asked somebody."

"Ask them what? I didn't know there was anything to *ask.*"

She turned around and slugged him hard on the arm.

"My grace, Elise," he said. "It's not like we can't *go.*"

"I'm not going with you if you're going to be shooting it."

"Why not?"

"Because this is *supposed* to be a date. This is *supposed* to be romantic. If you shoot it, it's *work*." And then she got cute and soft on him. "And then you're not there for me. You're there for the pictures."

He would have been willing to dump the whole camera case over the side of the porch just then. Except he couldn't. And he knew he couldn't. And she knew he couldn't.

"I should've known," she said. "I should've called your aunt just to make sure." Then she sighed again.

"Let's go," he said, cajoling. "I'll go get my suit on. It'll be fun. I don't want to ruin this for you."

She started to laugh.

"I *don't*."

"You *have*."

"Come on. I'll read you a little Hopkins after: *"Earth, sweet Earth, sweet landscape, with leaves throng . . ."*He got the kiss he wanted, and wanted another. But she pushed him away.

"Okay," she said. "But you're a jerk."

"I'll smell good," he offered.

"*That*'ll be a plus," she said. And he stood up and offered her his hand. She took it, looking a little surprised at the gallantry.

"I'm not *totally* a jerk," he said.

She looked him up and down. "We'll see," she said.

By the time they got to the dance, Cody was totally decked out in his dark, three-piece suit. He'd picked the last of Charlotte's mums for Elise, he'd borrowed Erin's car, and there was a *very* nice restaurant in town with a late dinner reservation under the name of Cody McClellan. It wasn't exactly what she'd been hoping for, but she seemed happy, and that made him happy.

They walked into the gym, Elise on his arm, and he was immediately uncomfortable. The place was dark and crowded, hung with all kinds of shadowy, drapey decorations. The band was loud, and the slap-back cross-reflections made the room sound like the inside of a giant boom-box.

Too much confusion. Too many shadows. Too easy to get hurt, and no way to see it coming.

But Elise was very comfortable. She looked up at him with joy on her face, even though he was nearly the only kid there without a tux. They walked around the outside of the room, checking the place out. Elise must have known everybody there. Her glory faded a little there, slightly upstaged by the fact that every girl there had on some kind of fantastic, unreasonable dress. But she didn't seem to mind that, either.

He had a whole list of specific people the yearbook staff wanted pictures of, and a whole list of shots for the newspaper staff. He found a relatively quiet corner, put the bag down, and took out the lists, looking them over. It was not going to be a fun assignment.

He worked at it doggedly, trying to be as low profile and pleasant as possible, circling the gym with camera in hand and bag on shoulder. He kept having to ask Elise, Where's this person? Where's that one? She finally sat down behind him on a folding chair as he worked with the lenses, her hands in her lap. Every time he remembered to look back at her—which wasn't often, what with the changing of lenses and trying to figure out the strobe Mr. Allen had checked out to him—she looked less and less as if she was having a good time.

About an hour and a half into the dance, when he was about to throw the inscrutable strobe across the gym, tear up the yearbook list, and murder Thayne, she came up softly behind him and put her hand on his shoulder.

"Couldn't we dance?" she asked. "Just once?"

"Elise," he said, drawing his temper in best he could. "After I *finish* this, we can do anything you *want*. I can't leave this equipment." He was getting a headache.

She didn't go away. She stood there, right next to him, and he had to keep brushing her skirt out of the way to find what he needed in his case.

He glanced up at her. She was gazing off into the room, looking slightly wistful.

"There's Steven," she murmured. "He's all alone. I can't believe he didn't bring anybody. Did he? He's just standing there all by himself. With Tony? Except—no, see. Tony's with Chris. Nope. Steven must have come by himself." She sounded satisfied.

"Cody," she said, taking hold of his shoulder again. "Would you mind if I went over there a second? He looks so lonely. I'll only be a second."

She stepped away from him, and his life was immediately easier to bear, not having to deal with that skirt.

"Elise," he said. "I'm going to take about three more shots. This list—" He scowled at it, crumpled it up in disgust and shoved it into one of his pockets. He picked up the camera and started rooting around in the case for some lens tissue. "Just be a little bit more patient. I know you want to talk to Steven. Just give me a second, and we'll both go over there—"

He looked up at her, but she was gone. He stood up straight, turned on his heel, looking, but she wasn't anywhere around. He finally saw her about halfway around the room, gliding over Steven's way.

"*Swell,*" he said. "Just . . . *swell.*"

He had five frames left on the roll. He shot them off with the long lens, looking for people who were *not* yearbook material. And when he finished, he jammed the jammable equipment back into the case—that included the strobe—and packed his camera away, releasing Mr. Allen's lens very, very carefully.

And then there was another skirt in his way, a dark green one. He finished wrapping the lens in its foam before he looked up. And then he did a double take.

Angela. Sultry, luxuriant Angela. He buckled the case, shouldered it, and stood up. She smiled at him. If Elise's shoulders had been soft, Angela's were unquestionably hospitable. It nearly took his breath away.

"Lost your girlfriend," she said. He looked across the room and saw Steven leading Elise out onto the dance floor.

"Evidently," he said, shifting the strap of the case.

"So?" she said. "What are you going to do now?" She came a little closer. He closed his eyes and willed himself not to look down.

"I don't know," he said.

"We could dance," she said.

"I can't leave the equipment," he said, a little breathless.

"Doesn't bother me," she said. "Keep it where it is."

"I don't dance," he said.

"Is that a statement of religious conviction?" she asked, dimpling.

"It's a statement of ignorance," he said, trying to smile at her without really having to *look.*

"Well," she said. "We can't have *ignorance* now, can we?" She took his arm and drew it around her waist. "That's the beginning," she said. He began to think Elise had been right in the first place; he was out of his league here. She took the other hand and held it so that it was tucked up in the hollow of her shoulder. He was beginning to sweat. Whatever was in her eyes when she looked up at him, it didn't seem to have much to do with dancing.

"That's all there is to it," she said, "for a slow dance." She was moving slightly, swaying—it was only mildly related to what he could hear of the music.

There was a guy standing a couple of yards away, two paper cups in his hands, watching them unhappily.

"Your date's back," Cody said with what was left of his voice.

He recognized the guy. One of Turk's friends. One of the four. And there was Turk behind him, his arm around a little red-haired girl. Cody thought he recognized her, but he couldn't think from where.

Angela drew herself in a little closer; her one hand—the one at her shoulder—came a little closer in too.

"I was bored with him, anyway," she said. And then she pulled away slightly—"You know, I was thinking, it's so loud in here—" Cody went weak at the knees—"You could come home with me. My parents are gone for the weekend. It's very quiet."

"Really," he said. And it suddenly sounded like a terrifyingly pleasant idea. He looked out across the room. Steven and Elise, still together, were dancing close. He saw Elise smiling; Steven said something to her, and they both laughed. He looked down at Angela. It had been a very long time for him.

"Come on," she said, and she had his hand.

"What about your date?" he asked.

"What about him?"

"What about him?" he agreed. No guilt there.

Somebody bumped him from behind, and the strap on his shoulder slipped. He caught the case, jerking his hand out of hers to do it. And suddenly, everything came a little clearer.

"Angela," he said, not without regret. "I appreciate the offer. But I can't go home with you. I have to go to Mr. Allen's."

"You could go to Mr. Allen's later," she said, and she took his hand again.

He freed himself gently. "I have something of his," he said. "I told him I'd have it back to him when I finished. I've got to get it back to him."

"Are you sure?" she asked, coming a little closer, making it very hard.

"I can't go home with you," he said, his voice gone husky. "It wouldn't be right."

"Ahh," she said, and she flashed him a look he had a hard time reading.

"I'm sorry," he said. Meaning it.

299

She cocked her head to the side, one wistful last chance. He didn't take it. She drifted away from him, a regretful look, leaving him to drown in the traces of her perfume. She rejoined her sullen date—who was undoubtedly in for a far more pleasant evening than Cody could imagine for himself.

He breathed again. And then he looked for Elise. Still dancing.

"I must be out of my mind," he murmured.

He wanted to filet Steven.

He threaded his way through the crowd around the gate, nearly tripping over Danielle on the way out.

"Where are *you* going?" she asked him.

"Home," he said, hiking up the strap and looking for an opening he could get through. He thought he caught a glimpse of somebody he knew.

"Where's Elise? I thought you were together."

"She found a friend," he said, trying to get around her.

The crowd parted. And there was Thayne. In a tux. With a girl. His first thought was to strangle Thayne for not having told him about the tux in the first place.

"You're leaving without her?" Danielle asked.

"*Danny*," he said. "She's going home with Steven. All right?" He sidestepped her. Jeannie. Thayne was with Jeannie. *I hope you have better luck than I do, my friend.* He didn't really want to leave Elise; his heart was hurting him about it.

"There they are," Danielle said. Cody turned around. He had a clear view of the floor, and of Steven and Elise, dancing slow, looking very comfortable together.

"See you," he said.

"Co-dy," Danielle said, making a reproachful little song out of it.

"Da-nny," Cody said, and struck out for the door.

He made it through. "Where's Elise?" somebody else asked. He didn't even turn around; it'd been Chris's voice, and that was one meeting he couldn't afford at the moment. Out of the door and into the relatively empty hallway. A couple of girls came out of the ladies' room. He headed down the corridor towards the far door.

His ears were ringing. He shook his head, trying to get rid of it. He was nervous all the way down the hall—at this point, he didn't want anybody interfering with him. And then he was outside. He stopped just outside the light and got his breath, digging for the car keys. And then he remembered where he'd seen that little red-headed girl. Marty's dream girl. *Sad. Very sad.*

He looked all over for the car; then he remembered he'd driven Erin's.

He finally found it, unlocked the door, shoved the camera case over on the seat, climbed in, and locked himself into the car. He hated what he was doing, but he couldn't see any way out of it.

As he pulled out into the main aisle of the lot, he looked back once more. Elise was just coming out of the door. She ran out onto the sidewalk, looking for him, maybe. That's what she was doing, because she saw the car right away and took a step off the curb, as though she wanted to catch him.

Steven came shooting out of the door after her. Cody almost ran into somebody's blue Camaro, watching them. Steven put a hand on Elise's arm, and Elise turned around, jerking away. Steven threw his arms up, and it looked as if he was yelling. They were having a little fight of their own. So, all was not so great in paradise. Cody wasn't grieving about that.

He had a terrible fight with himself on the way out to the street. There was a part of him hanging back, a part that couldn't bear leaving her like this, that wanted to go back and get down on his knees so he could stay with her.

But there were other parts—one that had been battered just too much, one that didn't take chances, wouldn't put anything more on the line; one that didn't know anything about love, and didn't believe in it; the ones that had been working for a long time, making it certain he'd never get anything he wanted— they were strong. And his pride. Those things together—not the gentle parts, but the very deep ones. They pushed the car forward, out into the street, and away from the school.

By the time he got to Mr. Allen's, he knew he'd done utterly the wrong thing. By then it was too late. It was always too late.

He got out of the car and went up the walk.

"Well, Cody," Mr. Allen said, answering the door, a skinny man in a rectangle of warm, yellow light. "Already?" He looked down at his watch. "It's not even nine-thirty." He leaned back into the house, peering around the door. "Well, I'm about five minutes slow. You want to come in?"

"No, sir, thank you," Cody said, and he opened the case.

"Come on in," Mr. Allen said. "Peggy'd like to see you."

So Cody had to go in. He followed Mr. Allen into a room at

the back of the house where there was a little fire going on the hearth and a nice-looking oriental woman, who turned out to be Peggy Allen, sitting on the couch with a book.

Introductions were made, Cody all the time feeling sick to his stomach.

"Sit down," Peggy said. So Cody had to do that, too.

"You get everything done?" Mr. Allen asked.

"No, sir," Cody said, digging around in the case for the lens. He came up with the crumpled list and threw it to Mr. Allen. "This list—" Cody started.

"It's a pain, I know," Mr. Allen said. He looked younger at home. And Peggy looked young.

"I don't know any of these people," Cody said. "I got as many as I could."

"If they don't like it, they don't like it," Mr. Allen said. "The world won't end."

"Are you all right?" Peggy asked. "I don't mean to invade your privacy, but . . ."

Cody couldn't answer. He closed the case and rested his elbow on it, fist against his mouth. "Yeah," he said, because what *else* was he going to say?

"Like fun you are," Mr. Allen said.

"I had a fight with my date. Kind of," Cody said.

And Peggy looked so sympathetic, and they were so friendly about it, he ended up telling them the whole stupid story. Peggy kept biting her lip all the way through it.

"You really left her," she said.

"She was with Steven. She was all right."

Peggy looked at him dolefully.

"Stupid move, huh?" he said.

"Well, she can't expect you to sit around all night while she dances with somebody else," Mr. Allen said.

"Well, he can't expect her to sit around all night while he's taking pictures," his wife retorted, giving her husband a very pointedly hot eye.

"He did have an assignment," Mr. Allen pointed out.

"He does have a life to lead," his wife answered.

"Everywhere I go," Cody mourned, "people start fighting."

The Allens looked at each other. Then at him. He shrugged unhappily.

"The question is," Mr. Allen said, "how's he going to get out of this?"

"I don't know," Peggy said. Not much hope there.

"It'll blow over," Mr. Allen said.

302

"I don't know," Peggy said, again. She got up. "You could start by having some cake," she said. She smiled at Cody.

"I don't know," he said, not feeling so well.

Peggy's smile widened. "You need it," she said. "A little sugar. And while you eat it, I'll give you a little womanly advice."

"You've had it, now," Mr. Allen told him.

"It can't get any worse than it is," Cody said.

"Oh, never say that, Cody," Mr. Allen said, rapping on the coffee table with his knuckles. "*Never* say that."

31

"I'm home," Cody said, leaning in through the doorway of the den. The family'd been playing at "movies" tonight, and they were still up, watching a video with all the lights out and eating popcorn.

He gave them a little wave and retreated, hoping to make the stairs without further discussion. He wouldn't have called any attention to himself at all if there hadn't been rules about his checking in with them at night.

"Hold it," Charlotte said, coming out of the den. The light from the television flickered weirdly behind her. Cody stopped on the stairs and watched as she came and took hold of a banister post, peering up at him. "Isn't this awfully early?" she asked.

"It's not that early," he said. "Those kids should be in bed."

"I thought you were going to dinner," she said.

For a moment, he wasn't sure how to answer that, not without having to talk about it more than he wanted to.

"It didn't work out," he said.

But she wasn't taking short answers tonight, any better than she usually did.

"What's wrong?" she asked.

He sat down on the steps, looking at her through the posts. "Everything," he said. "But it's all right. I'm just in a major depression, that's all. But I'll get over it, okay? It was just a terrible night, and I'll tell you about it tomorrow. But I just want to go to sleep, now. Okay? I'll tell you about it. I really will. But not now."

"Are you okay?"

He laughed. "No. But not to worry. It's no big deal. Honest."

She stood there a moment, weighing it all—the words and his tone of voice, probably. Trying to decide whether to trust him.

"Okay," she said doubtfully.

"Thanks," he said, pulled himself up, and went up to his room.

He went to ground in the dark of the bedroom, taking his clothes off and hanging them up, all without the light. And then he sat on the bed. His heart was aching inside of him. He only half understood that he was unhappy in some deep, untouchable way.

Why do I have to be so stupid? Why do I always have to make things so hard? He felt like he'd shrunk inside, and there was nothing left to take up the space but the cold.

He lay back on the bed and must have fallen asleep right off, because the next thing he knew somebody was shaking him gently, whispering, "*Cody, Cody, wake up.*"

He thought it was Mickey.

"You'd better come downstairs," she said. "*Now.*"

She straightened up when he started to move. "Could you make it out of the house through that window?" she asked.

"What?"

He got his eyes open, but she was gone. The bedroom door was open and the hall light was on. He groaned, turning over on his side, deeply disoriented. He rolled himself out of the bed, checked on Sawyer, but Sawyer wasn't there. It scared him, not knowing whether it was early or late, wondering what could be the urgency, what was wrong.

He felt around for his jeans and went to the drawer for a sweatshirt, not really awake, feeling that sick apprehension he always had when weird things happened in the middle of the night. His hands were shaking with the sleep, and he couldn't figure out the shirt at first. Nightmare quality to it all . . .

He went out in the hall, blinking and blinded by the light. Feeling for the stairs, thick headed and slow, rubbing his eyes, he made his way down the stairs.

"Cody," Charlotte said, her voice odd.

He looked up, chilling. There were two uniformed policemen standing in the doorway.

All of a sudden, none of it was real—there was no blood in his body, only fire, panic. Without thinking, he turned around and bolted down the hall towards the kitchen. But someone came up behind him and slammed him chest first into the wall, wrenched his arm up behind him so hard that he cried out in the pain of it and went up on his toes to relieve the pressure.

There was a lot of noise then, a lot of voices, confusion. They had weight against him, pressing him into the wall, and he couldn't breathe. Now he was awake. Now he understood that everything was real.

"Okay," he said, shouted, maybe. "Okay, okay—I'm not going to run. I'm not going anywhere—" He was half sobbing, "Okay? Okay?"

But they were reading him his rights, and he stopped believing he was awake.

"I want to know what's going on," Charlotte kept asking, angry voiced, scared.

"Tell her," Erin finally said. "You don't come in here like this without saying something."

So they did. One of them. Somebody had set fire to one of the dumpsters near the shop building at the school, just where the flames could get the roof of the building. Fire—some damage.

"When?" Erin asked them. "What time?"

Around nine forty-five. And there was an eyewitness.

"I didn't do this," Cody was saying into the wall, over and over, his brain shortwired. They were going to put cuffs on him.

"Don't do it behind," he pled with them, shouting. "Please. I'm not going anywhere. I swear it. Please." And he put his face against the wall as he heard Charlotte telling them—"He's claustrophobic. Don't do anything you don't have to. Please."

"I didn't do this," he began again.

"You want to tell us why you took off the minute you saw us, then?" the voice behind him said.

Cody tapped his forehead against the wall, grabbing for breath, and they turned him around to put the handcuffs on. He looked down at what they were doing, and it was as if his hands were miles away. "If you had a nightmare all your life," he panted, "and suddenly it was true, what do you think you'd do?"

One officer, an older one, stood back watching quietly.

"I don't believe he did this," Charlotte said. "I don't care if you think you've got a witness. If you treat him like a criminal before you're sure he is one, you're going to hear from me." She sounded furious, a little crazy. Erin had his hand on her shoulder.

"It'll be all right," Erin was saying. "Cody. We'll take care of it."

Now, Cody thought. *Now, before they stick me in one of their filthy little cages.* But nobody could stop it now.

"This is a good kid," Charlotte was saying, tears on her face. The kids were huddled down the hall, watching with huge eyes. Cody's wrists were locked together now, and he was terrified of knowing how short the chain between them actually was. "If you put him in a cell with anybody — *anybody* — who does him any harm, I mean *any* kind of harm — "

"Ma'am," the older officer said, his voice quiet. "Cody. My son knows Cody from school."

"Marty's dad?" Cody asked, breathing very hard, half dizzy because of it, keeping his wrists carefully, carefully together.

"I'll take care of him," Marty's father said. "Nobody's going to hurt him. But there was an eyewitness."

"If you put him in a cell, there'll be damage done. I've seen what happens to him when he's closed in."

But there was nothing anybody could do about that.

"We'll be down," Erin said to him. "We've got some things to take care of, but we'll be down there. Charlotte — can she ride with you? He's a juvenile."

"We'll have to ascertain that," the younger officer said, taking hold of Cody's arm and moving towards the door.

"Come when you can," Marty's dad told them.

"We'll be there, Cody," Charlotte said. "Hold on."

And they took him out of the house, one on either side, holding his arms hard, so he wouldn't run, wouldn't fall on his face, and it made him absolutely crazy inside that somebody could do this to him, that he couldn't do a thing about it, that after everything — this should be happening to him for something he hadn't even done.

A car was pulling up behind the police car. It's doors opened as they took him across the sidewalk, and the officers opened the back doors of the squad car. The air was very cold, biting, and him with no coat. Leaves rustling overhead.

Elise and Steven got out of the car, stood there while the officers put him, locked him, in the squad car. Cody sat against the far corner, his wrists pressed together, trying not to be sick.

She came up the sidewalk, Steven behind her; he could see them out of the corners of his eyes, coming right up to the window. But he closed his eyes hard, grasping at control, and the car moved away from the curb, smooth as glass, gliding out into the night.

32

Charlotte felt every moment that passed after that—every second it took, settling the children and getting somebody down there to stay with them—half listening to Erin on the phone, doing what he could.

She'd left the house on the run; she'd walked into the station almost before they'd shut Cody in his cell.

The older officer—she'd watched him be good about it, sympathetic, almost gentle. He'd done what he could, given Cody an empty cell—and that was better than she'd hoped for.

And they'd let her stay there by him, outside his bars, doing her best to keep him from coming apart, waiting for Erin, trying to keep Cody in touch with her, with reality. It was eternity before Erin finally made it there.

By the time Erin found them, by the time they'd let him through that heavy metal door—rivets as big as mushrooms in it, she'd always remember—by the time she heard his step echoing in the cold, dimly lit hall, Charlotte was herself closer to the edge than she'd ever been, tired to the bone, close to desperate with not knowing what to do.

"He won't tell me what happened," she said to Erin, "and he's not going to hold out much longer." She pointed to where Cody was, sitting cross-legged in the very middle of the cold cement cell floor, his eyes screwed shut, his face shiny with sweat, murmuring to himself.

Erin pressed his face to the bars, trying to hear him.

"This is all there is, this is all there is," like a mantra, the breathing all wrong, too quick, too shallow—but as if he was trying to force himself to slow down, trying to remember a rhythm.

"For a long time," Charlotte whispered, "he wasn't saying anything. For a long time, he just sat there. He had his eyes shut like that all the way in here, before they even put him in. I've been trying to talk to him, to explain what we're trying to do. I thought, if he couldn't understand me, maybe just the sound of my voice would help; but then he started this, almost like he's trying to shut me out."

"Cody," Erin said. He said it aloud, and his voice cut like a clear, silver light through the dimness. Cody jumped. There was a stirring of protest in the next cell and down. Charlotte looked at Erin, seeing he'd heard those noises. He looked perplexed.

Cody didn't answer him. Just sat still as death, eyes shut, whispering to himself.

"*Cody*," Erin whispered, directing the sound sharply across the space between them.

And Cody stopped whispering. He stopped breathing, too, for a moment. And then the breathing started again, cautiously, his head up slightly, but his eyes still shut.

"It's going to be all right," Erin said.

Cody was silent for another moment, the light reflecting off the sheen of sweat on his face.

"Don't tell me that," he said finally, his voice hoarse. She imagined how dry his throat must be and wondered if anybody had even thought to offer the child a drink before they'd put him in here.

"It's going to be all right," Erin said again, keeping his voice soft, level, making it a caress. He could do that well; she'd heard him calm the other children with it enough.

"No, it's not," Cody said. "It's over."

"It's not over," Erin said.

"It's justice," Cody said, sharply, cutting him off.

Erin looked disturbed. "Why is this justice?" he asked. "Did you do this thing? Did you set that fire?"

"*No*," Cody hissed. His hair, wet now with the work he was doing, was dark, curling and wisping away from his face. Her throat burned; looking at him, he seemed so young.

"Then it's not justice, is it?" Erin said.

"Long time coming," Cody said. "For a lot of things."

308

"For what?" Erin asked him. "Justice for what?"

"Everything. Broken windows, spray paint, knives—everything I am. For my mother. For *attitudes.* They wanted me a long time. Ironic." He swallowed. "Don't you think this is ironic? They can finally prove it on me, but in the end, it's something I *didn't* do. That's funny." He sobbed once, and then he pulled himself in.

She pressed her face against the bars.

The breathing began to speed up.

"Cody," Erin said, picking up on the change in the rhythm, warning Cody—*hold on, just hold on.*

"I'm working on it," Cody said, whispering between breaths, then slowing down, finally the effort showing between his eyes, breathing with his mouth slightly open.

He's going to hyperventilate, she was thinking. *Maybe that's good. Maybe it wouldn't be so bad if he could just pass out for a while—just till we can get this going. He's going to end up hurting himself if he doesn't.* She was blinking back the sweat in her own eyes.

"The thing is," he started again—and she wished he wouldn't, that he'd just shut up and stop making himself crazier —"it was just a matter of time. It's like coming home, in the end. Finally here. Maybe it's the only place I ever belonged."

"Not true," Erin said. And Charlotte heard herself saying, "Sawyer and Tyler and Matty and even Mickey; your grandparents and that man, that Parker, and your friend, the photographer, John; and Erin and *me,* Cody; and Marty and Elise—"

"Better off without me," he said, and if it was self-pity, it was dark enough that she knew it was tapped into something else, something that made a deep fear inside her, listening to it.

"That's not true. I don't think Elise thinks she's better off just now, Cody," she said, pulling a little discipline into her voice, instinctively throwing him something he could hang on to, someone with familiar authority.

Cody laughed, a dry, unhappy sound. "Elise would have been better off if I'd stayed where I was in the first place." The talk was quick and shallow, all run together, as though he couldn't stop it. "I never should have come here. It was stupid. I don't know what I thought I was doing. I should have stayed where I was, where I belonged, and Elise should have stayed with her Steven, because that's what works for her. They fit— you don't know him. He's got everything—the broad shoulders, the letter sweater, and, oh, heavens, the money. He's so squeaky clean, you could use his face for a mirror. Money all his life—he'll never get his hands dirty. He'll be a doctor or something, go to college, and do anything he wants because of the money and because he doesn't make mistakes. Not like this. He wouldn't know how."

"Elise loves you," Charlotte said. "We all love you."

He dropped his head back, and then brought himself upright again. "You all love broken things," he said, and he wiped at the corner of his mouth, still blind, with the heel of his hand.

"That's not why," she said.

"He takes care of her. She can have all the broken things she wants because he's behind her all the time, waiting, just in case. He's not broken—not even when she hurts him, he's still there. He's still perfect. Never makes mistakes; doesn't get mad. Just waits, quiet—and then this happens—" his breathing went off again—"and he can just step in. That's why they fit. They just fit." And then he pulled his face in tight and whispered through his teeth, a sound like pain. "I hate that guy."

He drew a deep, ragged breath. And then he rubbed at his eyes jerkily with his hands, elbows on knees.

"Cody," Erin said. "Listen. Did anybody see you tonight? Did you go anywhere? Did you come straight home from the dance? Did anybody see you leave?"

No answer.

"Look," Erin said. "We're going to take care of this. We're going to get it over with right now, tonight. We know a judge—I did a house for him last year. Sneeds. You've seen the plans. It took a long time, and we got to know them pretty well. He owes me. And I got him down here. He can take care of this tonight, but you gotta talk to me."

Cody shook his head, slowly. "Won't help," he said.

"Cody, he's coming in, and he's going to run an informal hearing. He understands about this. We're not going to leave you in here. And you're not going to have to come back. We're going to *finish* it. Where did you go? After the dance. Did you come home?"

Charlotte grabbed Erin's arm. "He had that lens. He told me he was going to have to take it back tonight. Cody? Did you take it back?"

Breathing got quiet.

"Did you?"

"Yes."

"Where? Allens'?"

"Don't do this," Cody said. "It's too late." Grief. "I'll never get out of here. This is the way my mother told me it was going to be. Just a matter of time. She knew it. She said, you're that kind of kid, and she knew what she was talking about."

"She was wrong."

"She called it right," he said. "She called it right from the beginning."

"Your mother was *wrong*," Erin said.

"I'm *here*," Cody pointed out.

"Could you shut up?" a voice growled out of the dark to the side.

"She knew me. She knew from the ground up. She was my mother. She was smart. She knew what I was made of."

"She was your mother," Erin said, angry now, "and she was a selfish, self-interested, compassionless, nasty human being. She was *wrong*, Cody. She said that to *hurt* you. You think she could let you grow up any happier than she was herself?"

"She was my *mother*," Cody cried.

"She was a *fool*," Erin said, in exasperation. "And she always has been."

The words had taken Cody by surprise. His eyes opened, and he stared at Erin.

"She was ridiculous, and she was *mean*," Erin said. "Selfish to the bone. And she was wrong about you. If I'd known what kind of kid you were, I would've gone out there and gotten you years ago. God forgive me for not doing it in the first place."

Cody's stare broke. And then his eyes began to flick from barred wall to ceiling to wall again, around and around the room, eyes fixed wide in his face, his shoulders beginning to heave.

Someone was unlocking the heavy door at the end of the hall.

"We've got to get him out of there," Charlotte said, shoving Erin towards the door. "Call Mr. Allen. I don't know his first name. *Call* him."

Cody was wiping his mouth again on the back of his wrist, his breathing gone completely wild. "Oh," he was panting, his eyes darting all around, glancing off the bars and going hollow. With a muffled cry for help, he finally scrambled to his feet, standing there, wild, in the middle of the cell.

She put her hand through the bars, reaching for him.

Marty's father came down the hall at a run, key out. And then the door was open, swinging to the side. Charlotte caught

311

the door. Marty's father stepped through, cautious now, his eyes on Cody's face—there was nothing rational left in it. Charlotte came through after him, but stayed back, stayed clear.

Cody's eyes weren't focused on anything. Not until Marty's father got close enough, and then he saw the uniform. Charlotte saw it when Cody's face slammed shut. His body tensed, half crouched, absolute aggression on him now, his eyes fixed on Marty's father but without sanity, without rational thought. Cody took a step back.

Marty's father put his hands up, showing them empty. "Okay, Cody," he said, his voice smooth, practiced—*He's not stupid,* Charlotte wanted to yell. *He'll hear the institution in your voice if I can.*

But the words went on, and the man was making a music out of them, a gentleness, a kindness. "It's all right," he said, over and over. "We're going to get you out of here now."

A face pressed against the bars to the side of the cell. "He's crazy," it said, watching from the shadows.

She was shocked at the grace in Cody's movements, at the control in every line of his body, and at the strange fixing of his face—like some kind of nighttime predator. He was poised and there was no question he was dangerous, but he kept moving back, back away from Marty's father, who was just as poised, just as dangerous.

"It's just fight-or-flight, Cody," Marty's father was saying. "You've got a little bit of trauma going here, and it's feeding you the wrong signals. Fight-or-flight. Listen to me. You're a smart boy, Cody, don't let it fool you like this. You're going to be all right. Hear me, now—" all soft, continual.

And then, "*Cody,*" he said sharply.

Cody blinked at the man.

"You hear me?" Marty's father asked.

Cody came up hard against the cinder-block wall at the back of the cell. Charlotte winced. He stayed that way for a moment, plastered back against it, still staring at Marty's father. But the wildness had passed. He slid down the wall till he was sitting on his heels, he buried his face in his hands. Marty's father stood up straight and took a slow breath. Charlotte came forward a step.

Marty's father hunkered down on his heels. He put out his hand.

"Look at my hand, Cody," he said.

For a moment, Cody didn't move. And then he looked up, focusing on the hand, drawing wet breath.

"Take it," the man said.

Cody didn't move.

"Take it," he said again, gently.

Cody reached out slowly. Their hands linked.

Marty's father breathed again, relieved. He patted Cody's hand with his other one. "Okay?" he asked.

Cody looked up at him for a moment, blinking. And then he nodded. "I need . . ." he said, looking at the man and trying to be rational. "I need to leave here."

"I know. That's what we're working on," Marty's father said. "We're going to go and talk to the judge about it. He's a good judge. He likes kids. He's going to be fair. Okay? We'll explain it to him, okay?"

Cody nodded wearily.

"Let's get you out of here," the man said. He pulled Cody upright and held on to him, walking him out of the cell. Charlotte stood aside as they passed, staying behind. She wanted to be alone in the cell for a moment, wanted to try to understand what Cody had seen, what he'd felt. She looked around, and she realized she would never understand. Then she shuddered and followed them out.

The chambers weren't as large as she'd expected. They were panelled with honey-colored wood and were full of chairs and tables, all arranged to face the judge's bench.

There were quite a few people in the room already, an amazing number considering the lateness of the hour. Erin had stayed out in the hall, trying to make sure that everybody who needed to be there had gotten there.

They sat Cody down behind one of the tables, and Charlotte went over to sit next to him as guardian. She was watching him closely. He had no color, and he was shaking badly, chilling. She stood up again and put her jacket around his shoulders. He sat there quietly, and then he put an elbow on the table and leaned his forehead in that hand.

"Are you all right?" she asked softly as she sat down again, touching his knee.

He sighed, and then he raised his head and blinked. He glanced at her and pulled a short, tight smile. "My head hurts," he said. He had very little voice left. Hollow eyed he looked around the room. She tensed; there were no windows in there.

She wasn't sure what would set him off again. Evidently, this room didn't bother him too much. He stared down at the table top a moment later, and some of that old hardness came back into his face. She was almost relieved, seeing it—thinking he was getting himself in hand. Then it struck her—what she'd been seeing and taking as strength might all along have been fear and denial of hope.

The judge came in, his hair wispy and disordered, curling out around his face, his eyes slightly bleary. The bailiff called the room to rise, but the judge waved him silent, yawning. He climbed up behind his bench, fastening on his robe, and sat down, folding his hands in front of him on the polished wood. He spent a moment in silence, looking over the faces in the room.

Cody hadn't stirred, still staring at the table with his hands folded in his lap.

"All right," the judge said. He was a large man with a fine moustache, grayed, the same color as his hair. *Like Mark Twain*, Charlotte thought. *A judicial Mark Twain.*

"So. We're here to ascertain whether or not Cody McClellan needs to spend any time with us after tonight. Will you read the charges, please?"

Cody flinched, and he moved one hand up over his stomach. Charlotte was keeping a careful eye on him.

The charges were read. It was more than malicious burning. The roof of the school had caught. It was arson.

This is a nightmare, Charlotte thought.

"There's an eyewitness?" the judge asked.

"There are still a few people missing," the bailiff told him.

"I see that," the judge said, looking over a paper he had in front of him. "The state informs me that they will be here, however. So . . ." he looked out over the room.

"We really appreciate your doing this," Erin said. He'd just slipped in through the door and taken a place back against the wall. He was waiting for the Allens.

"Thank Mr. Meyer here. He's representing the state. And our recorder here. Above and beyond the call, don't you think, Mr. Meyer? Let's just make sure this doesn't become a precedent." The judge was being fairly cheery about the whole thing. Charlotte was no little amazed; *Out of bed at one-thirty in the morning, just for Erin's sake. What kind of man did I marry?* She found that she was studying her husband's face.

Cody was looking at Erin now too.

"Well," the judge said. "Why don't we ask someone to tell us what they remember about tonight's events? I'd like to keep this rather informal, if we can sustain order—nobody minds, do they? At this time of the morning, nobody should mind. All right." He surveyed the paper again.

"Miss McCall," the judge said. "Would you mind telling us about your evening? Start as early as you can, and tell us everything you can remember in connection with Mr. McClellan here. Just sit right where you are. Speak up."

She did it. It was a long story, and she did well with it. Charlotte had always been impressed with Elise. The fact that she was an intelligent girl was no surprise.

The more Elise told, the deeper the unhappiness Charlotte could see in Cody's face. He'd had a hard night. *Major depression,* he'd said earlier. Two fights with Elise. Cody finally storming out of the dance like an idiot, angry and hot headed.

Looking at him now, Charlotte could see that Cody was embarrassed. His dirty laundry always seemed to get aired in public. She wondered—he'd been angry and embarrassed when he set the first fire. He'd certainly been angry, hurt, and embarrassed tonight.

"Did you see him anywhere near the shop building when you came out?" the judge was asking.

"No, sir," Elise said. "He was already in his car when I got out there, and his car was parked a way away from the building."

"And what time was that?" the judge asked.

"I don't remember," she said.

"All right." The judge put his glasses on, perching them on the middle of his nose and peering down through them at the paper. Cody was massaging the palms of his hands, sweating again, and his breathing had gone quick again.

Charlotte put a hand on Cody's arm, meaning to be a comfort, hoping she wasn't making things worse with the gesture. He swallowed and put his hands palms down on his thighs.

"It was around twenty after nine," somebody said. Charlotte turned around. It was the boy from McCall's barbecue who'd spoken, sitting back there next to Elise. The notorious Steven, of course.

"Thank you," the judge said. "What happened after that, Miss McCall? After you saw Mr. McClellan drive away."

"Steven and I—we had a—we stood there and yelled at each other. He wanted to take me home, and I didn't want him to, because I thought Cody might come back. Steven said he wouldn't. Among other things."

"Wouldn't what?"

"He wouldn't come back."

"Did he come back?"

"Not while I was there," she said.

"Go on."

"That was it. I went back inside."

"Did you see anybody else out there? Anyone near the shop building?"

"No, sir," Elise said. "There were just the two of us."

"And you'd had a fight. So you both were angry. And you went inside. So your friend was the only one left outside the building?"

So there'd been more than one mad kid in that parking lot. *It could have been Steven,* Charlotte thought. *Jealous and angry and hurt. Heaven knows he's had enough reason to want to get Cody out of the way. It could have been Steven.*

She looked at Cody. There was something dark in his face, and he'd moved his hands onto the edge of the table. He made as if to look back over his shoulder, but then he didn't do it. Something was working in his face, some severe distress.

And then, suddenly, he was standing up, leaning forward against the table as if he had no strength to his legs, and his hands were shaking as if he had a deep fever in them.

"Excuse me," he said, his voice thin and stretched. The judge raised an eyebrow.

"Mr. McClellan," the judge said, acknowledging him.

Cody's face was completely bloodless now. She waited—along with everybody else in the room—wondering what on earth was going on inside of him.

He took a few ragged breaths and looked up at the bench, swallowing with some difficulty. He closed his eyes, "I set that fire. I'm guilty of it. That's all. You don't have to go any further."

The room was silent.

Erin's face had gone white. They were all staring at Cody.

And then, a voice from behind. "McClellan." Steven's voice. And there was in it something between amusement and disgust. "It wasn't me, if that's what you're thinking. I'm not worried about it. You don't have to worry about it."

316

Erin frowned, studying Cody from the side. And then, as if he'd finally understood something, the color came back into his face and he looked absolutely transported. Of course it would be Erin who understood it first. She looked up at her nephew, still standing there, looking surprised and a little foolish, and she realized what he'd been trying to do; for all it would cost him, giving himself in Steven's place. Protecting *Steven.*

The judge cleared his throat. "Would you like to reconsider your statement?" he asked Cody.

Cody muttered something under his breath, looking even more embarrassed than before. "Yes sir," he said.

"Then sit down," the judge said, and Cody did. Charlotte took his hand and held it tight. Cody put his head down on the desk and sighed.

"And you are?" the judge asked, looking over Cody's head.

"Steven Hewlette."

"And how long were you outside after Miss McCall left you?"

"I don't know. About ten minutes."

"And did you see Mr. McClellan come back into the parking lot?"

"No sir, I didn't. And he didn't set any fires before we went out, either. He wouldn't have had time."

"Thank you. And did you see anyone else?"

"When I went back into the building," Steven said, "some guys passed me, just going out."

"Some guys?"

"Three kids. And I think they were probably the ones who did it. They knew about what was happening with Elise and Cody because they were saying something about it before they saw me." He paused; someone in the back was asking him something. "It was Turk," he said, answering. Then to the judge, "These guys have a grudge against McClellan. They ganged up on him and beat him up about a month ago. I didn't see them set the fire, but that's who I'd be talking to about it."

"You would," the judge said, face sober but eyes amused.

"Yes sir, I would," Steven said. "They were out there at about that time. And at least one of them would like to get McClellan."

There was a general sigh in the room. The doors opened, and a tired-looking woman came in, followed by a red-haired, red-eyed, red-nosed girl, a man behind her with his hands on her shoulders. The Allens followed them in.

317

"And *you* are?" the judge said, looking at Mr. Allen.

"Alvin Allen," Mr. Allen said. There was some soft laughter from the back of the room. Mr. Allen looked around, hitching up his pants, and scowling good-naturedly. He had his pajama tops on under his jacket, his hair was standing all on end, and he looked like a very sleepy man.

"All right, Mr. Allen," the judge said, smiling to himself. "And you saw Mr. McClellan tonight?"

"He was at my house for a while tonight, yes," Mr. Allen said.

"And what time would that have been?" the judge asked.

"From nine-thirty to about ten-fifteen," Mr. Allen said.

"You're sure of the time?"

"I checked the clock when I saw him. I'm sure."

"You'd be willing to testify to that in court?"

"Yes sir, I would," Mr. Allen said. "It's the truth. Anyway, this is a responsible kid. He's not going to go around setting fires to things that don't belong to him."

"Thank you," the judge said. "And now, we have one last detail." He looked up, peering down his nose through the glasses. "Miss Debrower. You, it seems, are our *eye*witness." He stretched his back, and then he settled with his arms resting on the bench in front of him.

"Did you, in fact, see Mr. McClellan set this fire? Consider well before you answer."

Charlotte turned in her chair, following the judge's eyes. The red-haired girl. Looking miserable.

"No," the girl said.

The room began to buzz.

Charlotte connected with Erin, grinning relief. She looked to Cody for some clue about this girl—who she was, and why she'd have lied about him. He had nothing to tell her; he looked as puzzled as she felt.

"But you told the policemen who were there at the scene that you, yourself, had seen Cody McClellan set that fire," the judge said, sitting up straight with a sudden, sober dignity.

"Yes sir," the girl said, sounding very scared, very small.

"But it wasn't true?"

"She was under some pressure," the man behind her said. "The boy who was with her told her that *he* had seen it, but that no one would believe him if he said anything, because he'd had problems with this other boy before. And then he made it more

318

or less a matter of blackmail, which is something I don't believe we need to get into here. Suffice it to say, she was scared."

The judge sat silent for a moment. He gave the girl a long, grave look. "Do you realize," he said quietly, "what you put this boy through tonight? What might have happened? Because you were scared, you did something that very well could have scarred another human being for the rest of his life."

The room was very quiet.

"I know," she sobbed. "I'm sorry."

The judge took his glasses off and rubbed his eyes. "Well," he said, "Mr. McClellan, I think it's abundantly clear that you're innocent of these charges. We have no case here." He picked up his gavel and made a halfhearted strike at its pad. "So, go home. Just please, *please*, if you ever get into trouble again, do it during the day."

And it was over, just like that. Charlotte felt as if she'd passed through the fire and out again. She was exhilarated.

Cody was sitting there as though he hadn't quite understood. And then he put his face down on the table in front of him and wept like a child. She put her hand on his shoulder, patting him, trying to rub some comfort in.

She felt as if she'd been reborn.

33

Whatever it had been—the surface tension, the nightmare, the frigid rim of ice—whatever had kept him alone and insulated all these years suddenly was broken.

Everyone in the room was reaching through it, touching him, holding on to him. He was embarrassed, crying in front of them all, but he couldn't stop it. He was too exhausted.

When he finally sat up, sheepishly rubbing the tears off his face, the people were there, close around him. It should have made him short of breath, having so many so close. But it didn't.

A lot of people had left. The girl was gone, and the judge. The Allens patted him on the back, Mr. Allen winking and yawning, privately pointing at Elise and making a sly OK sign. Then they left too.

Charlotte was still beside him, and he understood that she wouldn't move until she was sure he didn't need her. Guardian angels. It made him scared he'd cry again.

Then Steven was there, smiling down at him—with the usual half-disgust. And Elise leaned over and kissed Cody on the forehead, sweat notwithstanding.

"I'm going to take Elise to get something to eat," Steven was telling him. "We thought you might want to come along."

Cody felt a stab of guilt and chagrin that he had been so utterly naked in front of them in the last hour, that Steven should be moving into his place the way he had tonight. And the thought of tagging along with them now filled him with instant pique.

But then he looked at Elise—at that sweet face of hers—and the resentment turned to shame. Why had they come here tonight? No one could look at that face and see anything but genuine concern there. And he began to understand what she had been trying to tell him all along.

It wasn't a lover he really wanted. And it wasn't territory, not just a place he could hold for his own. What he needed was to be loved—in spite of himself. *Because* of himself. And suddenly, he was seeing with incredible clarity: this crowd of people that had been here tonight, out of their beds at a terribly inconvenient hour—they had been here for him. *For* him. These were people who had already forgiven him for what he had been, for being the kind of kid who could get himself in this kind of mess; that was old news with them.

He pushed back a little, trying to look at everybody, *seeing* them, these people who had somehow taken the place of his old, colder walls—who had moved in to protect him, ringing him about, a new kind of living wall that shifted and breathed, and they let the good air come in to him, sweetly scented with the healthiness of their lives.

He ached for his camera, wanting to make a record of this, somehow—wanting to hold on to them. But it struck him that no picture he could take of them now would be whole, not unless he could be in it himself.

In that moment of understanding, something that had been stiff and tight and old inside of him was released.

He accepted Charlotte's close gifts, and Erin's broader ones. And he realized that what he wanted from Elise was her friendship; he wanted to be a quiet part of her, the way her old shoes were, something she knew too well to be able to live comfortably without.

And there was one last thing: he finally understood his yearning after Steven. That Steven should ever return any of the respect that had been nearly wrenching Cody out of his soul for the last few months, that Steven should be willing to laugh with Cody and spar with him, and maybe want to understand him — it was as consuming a desire in Cody's heart as the one he had for Elise or Charlotte or Erin. And the realization of it left Cody deeply embarrassed.

"Hello?" Charlotte said, patting his hand. Cody came back to himself to find everybody watching him.

"I'm okay," he said, assuming that was what they were wondering.

"So, you going to go?" Steven asked. "Because we're starving."

Cody looked up at his two friends and felt color come up in his cheeks.

"That's nice of you, Hewlette," he said. But it just didn't feel right. And then the devil stirred inside of Cody again. He cocked an eyebrow at Steven, knowing full well there was never going to be much sentiment in this relationship, and he finished sweetly " — wanting to buy me dinner."

"Wanting to—" Steven said, pleasantly incredulous. "*Excuse* me?"

"You *were* asking me out?" Cody said. "Me and Elise."

Steven's face flushed. Elise was grinning.

"*You* must feel better," Charlotte said to him, and she started to put on her jacket.

"Actually," Steven said, not to be outdone. "I was thinking, for the trouble you've put us to tonight—and considering you didn't end up having to spring for dinner at *Chez Marquis* after all, which omission should have left you with a sizeable bankroll—maybe *you* would be the one to buy."

Cody put his hands to his pockets, suddenly realizing he didn't have *anything* in them. Charlotte sighed when he looked

321

to her, very theatrically but with a great air of satisfaction, and started digging around in her purse.

But it was Erin who had the money in his hand, and he passed it to his wife, who passed it on to her nephew.

"However," she said, holding the bills just out of reach, "I want you to promise me that you will be home *soon*, and that you will *not* get into any more trouble for at least—" she looked at her watch, "twelve hours."

"Never make promises you can't keep," Elise advised him, grinning and tugging at his arm.

"I'll be home soon," Cody promised, and then, on an impulse, he leaned over and kissed his aunt on the cheek. "Thank you," he said. And he looked at Erin. "Thank you," he said again.

"Get out of here," Erin said cheerfully. "We're not waiting up."

Elise pulled Cody up out of his chair.

"Just one thing I don't understand," Cody said, looking at Steven. "If we're both taking her to dinner—well, I mean, if I pay, am I the one who gets to kiss her good night?"

"Not if I'm alive to prevent it," Steven told him, grinning.

"You're asking the wrong person," Elise said, poking Cody in the chest. "Come on, you guys." She slipped an arm through each of theirs and started tugging them towards the door. "Good night Mr. and Mrs. McClellan," she called over her shoulder, and Steven echoed her.

"I'm telling you," she said, snug between Cody and Steven and hugging their two arms close in an ecstasy of satisfaction. "You guys are *really* going to get to be friends."

Steven caught Cody's eye and rolled his own.

"You think so," Cody said, laughing down at her and feeling as if the sun had come up inside of him.

"I *know* so," she said, and from the look on her face, it was certain—this time, she was going to have things her own way.